Postcolonial Lesbian Identities in Singapore

Taking lesbians in Singapore as a case study, this book explores the possibility of a modern gay identity, in a postcolonial society, that is not dependent on Western queer norms. It looks at the core question of how this identity can be reconciled with local culture and how it relates to global modernities and dominant understandings of what it means to be queer. It engages with debates about globalisation, postcolonialism and sexuality, while emphasising the specificity, diversity and interconnectedness of local lesbian sexualities.

Shawna Tang is a Postdoctoral Fellow at Western Sydney University, Australia. Formerly a Lecturer at the Department of Sociology, National University of Singapore, Postdoctoral Fellow at the Asia Research Institute, National University of Singapore, and former Deputy Editor of *International Sociology*, she obtained her PhD at the Department of Sociology at the University of Sydney.

Routledge Research on Gender in Asia Series

3 Sex Trafficking in South Asia
Telling Maya's Story
Mary Crawford

4 Religion, Gender and Politics in Indonesia
Disputing the Muslim Body
Sonja van Wichelen

5 Gender and Family in East Asia
Edited by Siumi Maria Tam, Wai-ching Angela Wong and Danning Wang

6 Dalit Women's Education in Modern India
Double Discrimination
Shailaja Paik

7 New Modern Chinese Women and Gender Politics
Ya-chen Chen

8 Women and the Politics of Representation in Southeast Asia
Engendering Discourse in Singapore and Malaysia
Edited by Adeline Koh and Yu-Mei Balasingamchow

9 Women and Conflict in India
Sanghamitra Choudhury

10 Gender, Governance and Empowerment in India
Sreevidya Kalaramadam

11 Social Transformation in Post-conflict Nepal
A Gender Perspective
Punam Yadav

12 Motherhood and Work in Contemporary Japan
Junko Nishimura

13 Gender, Violence and the State in Asia
Edited by Amy Barrow and Joy L. Chia

14 Intimacy and Reproduction in Contemporary Japan
Genaro Castro-Vázquez

15 Postcolonial Lesbian Identities in Singapore
Re-thinking global sexualities
Shawna Tang

16 Unmarried Women in Japan
The drift into singlehood
Akiko Yoshida

Postcolonial Lesbian Identities in Singapore
Re-thinking global sexualities

Shawna Tang

LONDON AND NEW YORK

First published 2017
by Routledge
2 Park Square, Milton Park, Abingdon, Oxon OX14 4RN

and by Routledge
711 Third Avenue, New York, NY 10017

First issued in paperback 2018

Routledge is an imprint of the Taylor & Francis Group, an informa business

© 2017 Shawna Tang

The right of Shawna Tang to be identified as author of this work has been asserted by her in accordance with sections 77 and 78 of the Copyright, Designs and Patents Act 1988.

All rights reserved. No part of this book may be reprinted or reproduced or utilised in any form or by any electronic, mechanical, or other means, now known or hereafter invented, including photocopying and recording, or in any information storage or retrieval system, without permission in writing from the publishers.

Trademark notice: Product or corporate names may be trademarks or registered trademarks, and are used only for identification and explanation without intent to infringe.

British Library Cataloguing in Publication Data
A catalogue record for this book is available from the British Library

Library of Congress Cataloging in Publication Data
Names: Tang, Shawna, author.
Title: Postcolonial lesbian identities in Singapore : re-thinking global sexualities / by Shawna Tang.
Description: New York : Routledge, [2016] | Series: Routledge research on gender in Asia series ; 15 | Includes bibliographical references and index.
Identifiers: LCCN 2016019401| ISBN 9781138855175 (hardback) | ISBN 9781315720500 (ebook)
Subjects: LCSH: Lesbianism–Singapore. | Sexual orientation–Singapore. | Postcolonialism–Singapore. | Sex role and globalization–Singapore.
Classification: LCC HQ75.6.S55 T36 2016 | DDC 306.76095957–dc23
LC record available at https://lccn.loc.gov/2016019401

ISBN 13: 978-1-138-60468-1 (pbk)
ISBN 13: 978-1-138-85517-5 (hbk)

Typeset in Galliard
by Wearset Ltd, Boldon, Tyne and Wear

In loving memory of my beautiful mother,
Sally Tey Kwi Hong (1944–2013)

Contents

Acknowledgements   x

1 **Introduction**   1
   Women who love women in Singapore 1
   Queer-ed in an Anglo-American way: the globalisation of same-sex identities 3
   The queer Asia critique and specificities of Asian queer sexualities 7
   The arsenal of Asian 'lesbian' research, and the absence of Singapore 10
   Locating female non-normative sexualities in Singapore's modernity 12
   Subjects in question, central provocations and theoretical interventions 15
   Road map 18

2 **Conceptual underpinnings of global queering**   22
   SECTION ONE
   A genealogy of the global gay? 23
   Globalisation in the global gay domain, and Altman's antimony 26
   Specifying the 'other side': non-Western sexualities in the global gay domain 28
   Theoretical problematic and persistent logics: an elementary framework 34
   Searching for historical tradition *and specific* local *cultural experience 36*

   SECTION TWO
   Towards a postcolonial LGQ studies 38
   The postcolonial orientation of queer Asian scholarships 42

viii *Contents*

    Re-theorising hybridisation 44
    Turning to 'transnationality' 47
    Coda 50

3 Postcolonial Singapore: state, nationalism and sexuality   51
    Sexuality, state and nationalism in a postcolonial world 52
    Setting the conceptual context: 'state', 'nationalism' and 'sexuality' 54
    Specifying Singapore's postcolonial historical context 57
    State policing, portrayals and pronouncements of homosexuality in Singapore 62

4 Sexual politics in Singapore: sodomy law and lesbian resistance   76
    A parliamentary petition against Section 377A 78
    A leadership tussle over lesbianism 85
    Coda 89

5 Transnational politics of local queer activism and lesbian activists   91
    Fostering queer consciousness in fraught discursive tropes 93
    Queering Singapore: local to transnational spaces for lesbian and gay organising 99
    Pink Dot *102*
    The reverse implantation of Pink Dot *106*
    Reflections on the local queer movement 108
    Early lesbian agency in Singapore 112
    Transnational lesbian activism 116
    Politics of 'coming out' and 'gaining visibility' 118
    Political significance of hybridising, transnational sexualities 119

6 'Modern' lesbian lives in postcolonial Singapore   124
    Prelude 124
    Analysing Singaporean lesbian women's experiences 126
    Agency, subjects and structure 127
    Queer? No way! I am not weird: *labels and gendered lesbian lives 129*
    'Coming out' in the city-state 147
    A queer turn 159

7 Recollections, remarks and re-making the relations:
a postcolonial politics of difference 162
Poststructuralism, state-sexuality relations and local resistance 165
Final notes 168

Methodological appendix 170
References 179
Index 198

Acknowledgements

Coming out is inevitable with this book. I have carried it with me as an awkward adolescent coming to terms with my sexual orientation; as an undergraduate running away from confronting the real and imagined consequences of my sexuality; as I tentatively stepped in and out of the closet with friends and family; as I waltzed into, and wrestled with, my relationships; as I found myself sensitive towards, and subject to, cultural and institutional resistances of my sexual identity. These experiences shaped the book in profound ways. But the book is far from mine alone. It belongs to the women who generously allowed me into their worlds, entrusted me with their stories, and whose lives helped me make sense of what it means to grow up gay in Singapore.

It is impossible to acknowledge all who helped make the work. What follows is no more than a start. For fieldwork support, *Sayoni* has been crucial. For advice, comments and discussions of the thesis version of this work, my deepest thanks go to Associate Professor Fran Collyer and Professor Raewyn Connell. For professional and institutional support, Professor Chua Beng-Huat and the National University of Singapore's Asia Research Institute and Sociology department, Professor Kerry Robinson and the Sexualities and Genders Research group at the School of Social Science and Psychology, Western Sydney University. For mentorship and moral support, Dr Michelle Miller and Associate Professor Catriona Elder. For energy and emotional support, my wonderful family: mum, dad, Loong, Ko, Jin Ying, Bernice, Ethan and Emmanuel Tang. Finally, my best friend and faithful companion, Ling, who encouraged me to begin this, keep at it and made this all possible from start to finish.

1 Introduction

Women who love women in Singapore

I watched the lesbian documentary *Women Who Love Women: Conversations in Singapore* (2006) for the first time, ironically, when I had just arrived in Sydney from Singapore. By July 2008, the documentary had made its rounds locally through a number of screenings at privately-organised venues: the Singapore International Film Festival, pride events, niche cinemas, lesbian and gay bars, and a local LGBT support group. Played to local sell-out crowds and described as a 'quiet hit' (*Straits Times* 2008a), the documentary also travelled to queer film festivals in Hong Kong, Berlin, Bali and Jogjakarta. Eventually, it was uploaded onto the internet, and made available for open viewing where I tuned in from almost 4,000 miles away.

The documentary features three Singaporean women sharing openly about what it means to be lesbian. Directed in an interview format, the documentary captured the women lounging around in a large living room, seated in a designer home, leaning against closet doors, conversing casually about their 'coming out', their childhood, their relationships with family, friends and colleagues. In other words, the women do nothing but talk. The simple format was a deliberate strategy to convey 'the story of their lives as honestly as I could', explained director, Lim Mayling (quoted in the *Straits Times* 2008a). As it turns out, the simple approach proved to be the special appeal of the documentary. It received positive reviews for its 'honest' portrayal of lesbians in Singapore (see Tan 2008), and for preserving the 'authenticity' of the women's experiences (see Ortmann 2008; Wei 2008).

The film opens with each of the three women introducing themselves to the camera. The audience meets Swee Jean, 23 years old and 'recently graduated', Sabrina, a 38-year-old 'lesbian living in Singapore' and 22-year-old Amanda 'working in communications' (*Women Who Love Women*, henceforth *WWLW* 2006). All three are Chinese, college-educated and English-speaking, who spoke confidently and articulately. The opening scenes immediately reveal the women to be young, upwardly mobile, modern, cosmopolitan lesbians who are busy professionals, and 'out and proud' women who love travelling, photography and their pet cats. Thus, even though the film was meant to be 'one of the few documentaries ever made about lesbians in Singapore' providing 'a rare glimpse into lesbian lives in Singapore' (*WWLW* 2007), the immediate images of these lesbian women are those we already find familiar, if not stereotypical. The women spoke at length about acceptance and self-love, and how they self-consciously worked at presenting positive representations of themselves as lesbian women. This involved maintaining long-term relationships with their partners. It also involved, curiously, an assertion of their womanhood even though two of the three protagonists appear 'like a man' or have been called '*abang*'[1] as the women themselves disclosed. But 'no way in hell', said Swee Jean (*WWLW* 2006), 'would I want to give up my femaleness'. Equally familiar with the American 'lipstick lesbian' as they are with the Western butch-femme categories, the masculine women seem to eschew gendered roles in favour of more egalitarian same-sex relationships. By denouncing their obvious masculinity, the women consolidate around an idealised 'originary' model of Euro-American lesbianism, repeating the position associated with lesbian feminist thinking: that lesbianism means *women* loving *women* minus the compromise of heterosexist mimicry, thus perhaps the title of the documentary *Women Who Love Women*.

Despite its claims to novelty, reviewers found the film to be 'pretty normal after all' (Ortmann 2008), described the documentary as a 'nice old blanket – comfortable and familiar' (Peizhi 2007), wondered if 'we will remember them?' (Wei 2008), and wrote that the documentary will 'not have brought anything new to the table in terms of the issues and struggles that the gay community has dealt with hitherto' (Hsieh 2007). These responses to the documentary suggest that the women's narratives and experiences, while honest and compelling on a personal level, were perhaps, in another way, not so novel. The women in fact remind us of our taken-for-granted impressions of homosexuals around the world: educated, well-travelled, seemingly wealthy, socially mobile individuals whose sexual orientation is a visible and antecedent aspect of their identity.

Yet, the film is by no means regarded as unimportant. One common response is that the documentary provided not just a voice and a face for lesbian women (Peizhi 2007), but also 'positive examples for lesbians in Singapore' (Alicia 2007). This was certainly the intent of the protagonists who wanted to 'pave the way' (Amanda, quoted in an interview with *Fridae.com* 2007a) for other gay people to be 'assimilated and accepted by society at large' (Sabrina, quoted in *Fridae.com* 2007a). Implicit in these responses is the expectation for gay women to be honest and 'come out', put a voice and a face to their sexual leanings, overcome their struggles, and eventually triumph to become role models.

This certainly seems to be the call of the documentary-makers who are members and supporters of the local gay community. Deploying a particular film technique unflinchingly focused on the women's coming out stories, inserting inspirational quotes celebrating their decision to 'live authentically' (*WWLW* 2007), and reeling off spiels on the state's statutory discrimination against sexual minorities, the techniques of the documentary production reinforced the politicised message these lesbians brought to bear on the big screen. The pathway to the development of lesbian consciousness and liberation portrayed in the documentary is one clearly defined by a specific trajectory: coming to terms with one's lesbian sexuality, coming out publicly and then confronting entrenched patterns of legal and cultural oppression in an ascending movement. Thus, reviewers concluded that the documentary showcased a 'human portrayal of three women's *evolutionary* process' (Hsieh 2007, italics mine), and that the 'real revelation' of the documentary 'is in showing once more how *the* homosexual experience (*in coming out especially*) is a journey on a *path of liberation, self-discovery and universal character building*' (Ortmann 2008, italics mine). Conversely, a concealment of same-sex identity and desire implies self-alienation and inauthenticity (Seidman 2004). Overall, the tone and manner in which the documentary was produced and received was discernibly celebratory and self-congratulatory on the arrival of 'modern' lesbian identities in Singapore.

In an interview, the director Lim Mayling offered a vision for her documentary, that is, for it to 'serve as a platform for others to build upon' (quoted in an interview in *Fridae.com* 2007a). My work takes up this invitation in that it also focuses on the same sexual subjects: mainly middle-class lesbians who are in their twenties to forties, who are economically independent and educated, and who make up a visible part of the population of Singaporean women who love women. For this reason, the documentary is a useful prelude to 'modern' lesbian lives in Singapore. But this is not the reason I introduce the documentary. The cultural artefact of the documentary is for me both a starting point and also a point of departure for my study of female non-normative sexualities in postcolonial Singapore.

Queer-ed in an Anglo-American way: the globalisation of same-sex identities

Women Who Love Women: Conversations in Singapore (2006) foregrounds the ways in which 'coming out' and the liberationist telos articulated by the protagonists, directors and reviewers speak to a certain universalisation of gay identity. The view that lesbian and gay people – as they become visible everywhere around the world just as lesbians are now appearing onscreen in Singapore – are moving along a single 'evolutionary' path towards 'liberation', 'self-discovery' and 'universal' authenticity (see italicised quotes by Hsieh 2007 and Ortmann 2008 above) continues to be a taken-for-granted one, drawn from a hegemonic Anglo-American or Euro-American conception of same-sex identities caught up in a post-Stonewall narrative.

The Stonewall riots in Greenwich Village, New York, 1969, are widely regarded as the tipping point of grassroots lesbian and gay activism in America. In the watering hole of the Stonewall Inn some 40 years ago, a regular crew of dykes, drag queens, effeminate men, hustlers and street people, having endured years of targeted and routine police raids, finally reached the upper limits of restraint. Throwing punches, paving stones and parking meters at police forces, the community found the strength to fight back for the first time. It was an epiphanic moment that empowered a movement. Within weeks, sexual dissidents in the Village had organised themselves into activist groups protesting and resisting police brutality. The riots and resistance that erupted in the Stonewall Inn became the defining moment, marking not just the beginning of the gay liberation and gay rights movement in the United States (US), but also around the world. Outside the US, in places such as Nicaragua and India for instance, gay pride celebrations culminate around the June 28 anniversary of Stonewall.

What it means to be homosexual within this post-Stonewall narrative, as scholars have pointed out, stems from a developmentalist perspective beginning with a persecuted, 'unliberated, "pre-political" homosexual practice, and culminating in a liberated, "out", politicised, "modern", "gay" subjectivity' (Manalansan 1997: 487). Post-Stonewall culture, as Seidman (2004: 255) notes, 'fashioned a romantic narrative of the homosexual heroically struggling to be free of the oppression of the closet'. This struggle – to come out of the closet – became the rallying cry of gay liberationist politics in America in the 1970s (Humphreys 1972; Jay and Young 1992 [1972]). Moreover, 'coming out' continued to signify, not just *the* politics of the queer movement (Gross 1993; Signorile 1993, 1995), but an '*ethos* of lesbian and gay existence' (Blasius 2001: 143, italicised emphases mine). A 'politics of visibility or coming out of the closet has become the centre of the lesbian and gay movement' (Seidman 2004: 255). Propagated in post-war America in a sort of 'from-Stonewall-diffusion-fantasy' (Bacchetta 2002: 949), this politics and ethos of queer life continues to be integral to the discourses of contemporary queer communities, exemplifying what Manalansan (1997: 485) terms as being 'in the shadows of Stonewall'.

Media and popular consciousness have long assumed and taken for granted that the global proliferation of same-sex forms will converge around a modern global gay model privileging Western definitions of same-sex practices (see for example *The Economist* 1996). Academic and cultural analyses of the growing worldwide visibility of lesbian and gay communities have initially produced universalising analyses, suggesting cultural imperialism and a trend towards Westernisation or the Americanisation of gay identities. Consider the following remarks by Dennis Altman (1996a), a leading gay theorist and a key figure theorising the globalisation of gay identities:[2]

> The 'macho' gay man of the 1970s, the 'lipstick lesbian' of the 1990s ... One sees unmistakable signs of American lesbian/gay imagery and self-presentation in almost every part of the rich world ... American books, films, magazines and fashions continue to define contemporary gay and lesbian meanings for most of the world.

Apart from Altman, who initiated the debate on the 'apparent globalisation of postmodern, gay identities' (1996b: 77) and his claims that a new global gay would emerge from a certain homogenisation of queer identities around the world, there is also Ken Plummer (1992: 17) who pointed out that 'same-sex experiences have become increasingly fashioned through the interconnectedness of the world':

> Magazines circulate freely in the Western world ... sending out messages of what it is like to be gay and lesbian. Organisations grow, fostering international alliances. And the disco – that archetypal modernist institution of male gay desire – gets bigger and bigger as its sounds and lights flash from Brixton to Berlin to Boston.

Plummer (1992), however, warned against the suggestion that homosexual lifestyles would converge across the world. In subsequent analyses, Altman (2001) also paid more attention to the cultural specificities of same-sex communities. Nevertheless, as I attempt to show in this book, the conceptualisation of global gay identities in the work of these two pioneering and prominent theorists contributed to paradigmatic assumptions and consequently certain logics were 'locked in', leaving unchallenged the privileged positions of Northern discourses, understandings and perspectives on gay and lesbian identities and practices.

Following Altman and Plummer, who bring questions of globalisation to the fore in studies of same-sex sexualities, an avalanche of work on the globalisation of queer identities has been spawned (notable works include Cruz-Malavé and Manalansan 2002; Binnie 2004; Boellstorff 2005; Rofel 2007; Wieringa et al. 2007). In 2001, Plummer noted that 'although globalisation is well recognised and very much discussed, very few studies ever talk about the connections of this process to the intimate life' (2001: 249). By the mid-2000s, however, a sustained scholarship brought queer sexuality research to bear on globalisation studies. Within a span of about five years, a global queer perspective gained 'critical importance' (Blackwood and Wieringa 2007: 1) and the 'role that globalisation has played in the construction of sexual identities' became indispensable and 'the most popular theme' in the literature on queer sexualities, particularly in non-Western contexts (Corboz 2009: 1).

Apart from the early initiatives of sexuality theorists along the lines of Plummer and Altman, the growing interest in globalising queer identities also came from feminist sexuality scholars who, starting from the 1990s, gave considerable attention to the relationship between sexuality, globalisation and nationalism. Povinelli and Chauncey (1999) urged queer studies to 'reconsider the self-evident nature of the national, the local, and the intimate' (1999: 442) in light of transnational processes that transform the sexual politics and cultures of many nation-states. In modernity, Grewal and Kaplan (2001) argued that sexual identities are imbued with power relations as they circulate in a globalised domain of encounter and exchange. These power relations are 'connected to inequalities that result from earlier forms of globalisation, but they have also generated new asymmetries' (Grewal and Kaplan 2001: 663).

The theoretical directions provided by feminist sexuality scholars are eminently relevant to queer globalisation. Lesbian and gay cultures and communities certainly took very visible shape early in the 1970s and 1980s in the United States and Europe – ahead of elsewhere – and these events gained not just global media coverage but also substantial academic attention in Western scholarship (Seidman 2004; Duberman 1993; D'Emilio 1983; Weeks 1977, among others). The cultural and historical facts of these events continue to be constitutive of lesbian and gay knowledge, identification and organising around the world, as observed for instance, among Filipinos (Manalansan 2003), in the 'Arab World' (Massad 2002), in India (Bacchetta 2002), and Nicaragua (Babb 2003), among other non-Western contexts. The West, as Gunkel (2010: 11) noted in her work on female sexualities in South Africa, is also continually mobilised as 'the reference point of modernity/development' in sexuality studies. The Western dominance of lesbian and gay cultural life and lesbian and gay studies, Binnie (2004: 5) noted, is one sustained by the social mobility and privileges of the 'authorship and autobiography' of white researchers studying global gay culture. Well aware of these implications, Manderson and Jolly (1997: 22) reflexively wrote in the preface of their edited volume on Asia-Pacific sexualities that:

> As researchers and theorists of sexuality, we often not only occupy the site of the West but take it as our point of view as the normative measure of sameness and difference. We thereby presume our global centrality and deny our global connections.

As queer cultural production and queer identity politics around the world continue to fall 'in the shadow of capital' (Lowe and Lloyd 1997: 1) and under the institutional hegemony of queer movements and academic centres in Europe and America, these interrelations of cultural, economic, intellectual and political spheres in globalising processes over-determine the asymmetries of global gay relations in what I call the 'global gay domain'.

In this global gay domain, I argue that lesbian and gay identities around the world have been overwhelmingly queered in Anglo-American ways, stretching from popular culture through to dominant theorising. The cultural artefact of the documentary, the response towards it, the books, films, magazines, 'lifestyles and appearances' that Plummer (1992) and Altman (1996a) write about, in journalistic accounts, academic writing, activist discourse and everyday life, a hegemonic Anglo-American 'global gay' (Altman 1997) has wittingly and unwittingly been conceived as a figuration of what it means to be gay. Supported by a panoply of cultural forms ranging from magazines to popular images, Western academic centres and queer institutions, the figure of the global gay stands at the pinnacle of a pathway of gay liberation and modernity while non-Western sexualities are situated at the far end, rising inevitably and eagerly toward a single eventuality.

The question thus arises: how do we understand the specificity of non-Western homosexual identities in this universalising turn? Among Singaporean lesbians whose sexual identities have been assumed, taken for granted and queered in an Anglo-American way, the question becomes more pressing and pertinent. By all appearances, evident in the documentary, Singaporean lesbian subjects seem to provide yet another exemplification of the global gay identity.

How then do we conceptualise the specificity of local non-normative female sexualities? My aim is to resist the theoretical impulse to refer to Anglo-American antecedents when thinking about Singaporean queer subjectivities and beyond.

The queer Asia critique and specificities of Asian queer sexualities

Some will assert that this enterprise is no longer novel. Over the last decade, the figure of the global gay has been beaten down many times over with the phenomenal rise of scholarships focusing on the 'heteroglossia' – to borrow Chu and Martin's (2007: 483) term – of non-Western queer sexualities in 'other' societies. Organised in terms of region, the two areas with the widest spread of non-Western queer scholarships are Latin America and Southeast Asia (Boellstorff 2007a). There is also an emergent critical South African literature (see for example Tamale's 2011 edited volume). In Asia, the rise of queer Sinophone studies (Chiang and Heinrich 2014) has placed East Asia firmly on the map, expanding the area of Asian sexualities and gender studies occupied mainly, though not exclusively, by Southeast Asian queer localities (Sinnott 2010). I ask after the location of Singapore within this intellectual field by charting some of the contours of this regionwide scholarship.

The surge of academic work in Asia began around the turn of the twenty-first century. Configured variously as 'critical regionalities', 'queer regionalism', 'Asian queer studies', 'queer Asianism' or 'Asian queer cultural studies' (Johnson et al. 2000; Sinnott 2010; Kong 2010; Chu and Martin 2007; Welker and Kam 2006; Wilson 2006 among others), the field offers a range of approaches emphasising the specificity of globalising Asian sexualities with an explicit mandate to 'challenge and correct' (Wilson 2006) the Western dominance of queer studies. As Wilson (2006) proposed, 'a focus on the region (understood in a post-Orientalist and transnational way) provides an overlooked counterweight to Eurocentric, Western hegemonic frames for gay, lesbian, transgender or queer worlds in Asia'. I will simplify the many names given to the scholarship by using the 'queer Asia critique' to capture how it is always positioned in response to, or as a critique of, Western sexual hegemony.

A key source of the fecundity of work in the region is the AsiaPacifiQueer network (APQ). Based in Australia and the Office of Human Rights Studies at Mahidol University in Bangkok, APQ was set up in 2000 to bring together 'academics and research students in a collective attempt to inscribe queer studies within Asian studies and, equally importantly, to locate Asia, and the non-West, within queer studies'. The mission of APQ is twofold: one, to intervene in an Asian studies the APQ felt was devoid of queer research; and two, to intervene in queer studies, which APQ critiqued as dominated by an overriding interest in Western queer cultures. In 2005, APQ organised the First International Conference of Asian Queer Studies in Bangkok, and published a collection of essays in *AsiaPacifiQueer: Rethinking Genders and Sexualities* (Martin et al. 2008).

8 *Introduction*

In 2008, the Hong Kong University Press established a Queer Asia series sharing similar aims and involving founding members of the APQ. Printed in each of its publications is an introduction stating that the Queer Asia series is 'focused on non-normative sexuality and gender cultures, identities and practices in Asia' with the aim to 'challenge ... and correct' the dominance of queer studies and queer theory by 'North American and European academic circles'. By 2011, a total of five titles had been published as part of the series: three monographs with fieldsites in Hong Kong (Tang 2011), Taiwan (Huang 2011) and China (Kang 2009), two edited volumes focused on China (Yau 2010) and Bangkok (Jackson 2011), and counting. In addition, the Queer Asia series has included three other titles for which Hong Kong University Press holds distribution rights. These studied queer cultures in Hong Kong (Leung 2008), the Philippines (Garcia 2008) and Indonesia (Blackwood 2010). According to *Asia-PacifiQueer* editors, Fran Martin, Peter Jackson, Mark McLelland and Audrey Yue, the regionwide intellectual must begin by 'first placing side-by-side the largely separate histories of queer studies in each Asian country' (2008: 9).

What are some of the key proposals in this broad intellectual project to provincialise the West? First, it takes a 'world areas' perspective wherein 'Asia' is invoked as distinct and separate, providing 'a vantage point from which to problematise naïve and uncritical writing on ... the "globalisation" of gender and sexual identities' (Johnson *et al.* 2000: 361). Marked out in terms of geographical regions, this involves 'invoking' (Wilson 2006: para 10) or a 'recuperation' (Johnson *et al.* 2000: 366) of area studies despite its risks. Second, the focus is on intra-regionality, that is, the 'conditions and flows *within* the geopolitically constructed region of Asia' (Wilson 2006: para 1 accessed online, italics original) where overlapping histories and the intersection of people, information, ideas and identities across intra-regional borders shape the formation of genders and sexualities in Asia. These regional processes are delineated from Western-centric globalisation processes, establishing versions of the 'global' in Asia (Johnson *et al.* 2000). Third, the delimited 'world area' of Asia with its intercultural comings and goings encompasses a pre-colonial and colonial historicity. Sexualities, genders and queerness are therefore generated and constituted under symbolic and material processes. Fourth, it involves a commitment to the development of 'situated knowledge(s)' (Johnson *et al.* 2000: 361), that is, a methodological and theoretical partisanship towards 'localised, "customised" theoretical discourses' (Chu and Martin 2007: 484) to produce and interpret in-region case studies of sexuality. 'Situated knowledges' is positioned against the metropole's treatment of local queer 'phenomena' as data to be processed through a Euro-American theoretical lens with no effort to engage local critical efforts which, even if inadequate, are 'opportunely effective' given their enunciative contexts (Chu and Martin 2007: 484). Fifth, an insistence that a critical regional perspective, or what Johnson *et al.* called 'critical regionalities (2000), is productive for identifying 'recognisable patterns ... and similarities ... historically conditioned by the expectation of being in and of the same region' despite the recognition that a sense of an intrinsically Asian order of things is being produced. The assumption of 'Asia' is 'a theoretically and politically necessary fiction' (Johnson *et al.* 2000: 361), casting a 'different centre of gravity' (Wilson 2006: para 12) to foster the provincialisation of the West.

The productivity of work is remarkable as is the apparent, if cautious, strategic essentialism the queer Asia critique employs. Even as the literature is filled with caveats of a porous, open-bordered Asia and speaks of regionalisation as a process elucidating the transnational flow of genders and sexualities, I argue that an intentional project that delineates itself in terms of a specific 'world area' and unquestioningly assumes that Asian queer sexualities are rooted to a 'traditional' pre-colonial historicity (presumably untouched by Western modernity) lends itself to a number of problematical theoretical manoeuvres to specify queer Asian sexualities vis-à-vis the West. First, the intellectual project runs the risk of producing self-Orientalising and essentialising accounts. Second, it risks interpreting sexualities within a limiting set of binaries of what is local versus global and 'traditional' versus 'modern' built on an entrenched master narrative of a Western sexual modernity, the mechanics of which will be discussed in this book as a central theoretical problematic. I am not suggesting that the queer Asia critique is ill-conceived. Certainly, the field has been replete with case studies of local genders and sexualities with a theoretical inclination towards undermining the thesis of global universalisation by emphasising cultural differences. However, in a project that hinges on an area studies perspective pitting Asia in a binary against the West, a growing compendium of regional sexual histories and empirical case studies does nothing more than create an enlarged essentialism resolved superficially through 'difference'. Ella Shohat's critique of area studies as well-intentioned but problematic is instructive. In global feminism, the legacy of area studies generated 'an "international" or "multicultural" lacunae' within a 'sponge/additive sponge approach' in which privileged perspectives and paradigms are extended onto the lives of 'others' whose diverse lives and practices are absorbed into an homogenising, over-arching master narrative (Shohat 2001: 1270):

> This kind of facile additive operation merely piles up newly incorporated groups of women from various regions and ethnicities – all of whom are presumed to form a separate and coherent entity, easily demarcated as 'difference'.

This form of internationalism could well undergird queer regionalism. An insistence on the 'productivity' of Asia with its many queer cultures and multiplicity of regional processes does nothing to 'fundamentally' interrogate the asymmetric relationality between the West and the non-West in the globalisation of queer identities. The valorisation of Asian regionalism as a counter against 'the global', where the global gay domain continues to be underwritten by hegemonic scripts provided by Anglo-American queer activism and academic institutions, leaves the primacy of the West intact. We remain stuck, then, with the question of how to upend the hegemonic West in this intellectual project. In the absence of a critical interrogation of the power asymmetries in the global gay domain, the production of ever-increasing numbers of case studies on queer Asian sexualities does not serve to provincialise the West if these studies continue to be interpreted within the entrenched paradigm of a Western sexual modernity. Given the force of the West, persistent Eurocentric frameworks might then be reflexively extended onto queer regionalism's conceptualisations of Asian globalities and processes, and continue to condition how we think about global queer identities. If this were indeed so, rather than being decentred, the dominant West is duplicated in this scholarship, critical of Western hegemony.

What is needed, I argue, is an analysis that troubles the Asia-West binary, addressing and re-orienting the axes of asymmetry between them. To this end, this book offers a broad postcolonial perspective, which helps to explain and understand the situation of Singaporean queers caught between diverse contexts of reception in a globalised nation without recourse to essentialising notions of pre-modern Asian traditions or local cultural difference to establish their specificity. The tendency towards this search for historical origins and essential differences is perhaps, I suggest, why the case of Singapore has been missing from, and cannot be located in, the queer Asia critique.

The arsenal of Asian 'lesbian' research, and the absence of Singapore

A growing subset of research on female non-normative sexualities in Asia has made significant empirical contributions to the queer Asian literature focused on disrupting Western queer dominance in the globalisation of gay identities. This body of research strongly objects to approaches which dismiss the experiences of non-Western homosexuals as not 'original' or as exemplifying the Western global gay. The research on female non-normative sexualities also extends the conversations on global queer identities in important ways by addressing the specificity of lesbian women's experiences in the patriarchal regimes of Asian societies largely subsumed under the category 'queer'. Ethnographic monographs on female non-normative sexual identities and practices have appeared across Asia in Japan, India, Indonesia, Hong Kong, Thailand and Taiwan (see for example Chalmers 2002; Bacchetta 2002; Bhaskaran 2004; Blackwood 1999, 2005; Sinnott 2004; Chao 2000). Further exemplary research work focusing on lesbians in Asian contexts can be found in Wieringa et al.'s (2007) collection, as well as Khor and Kamano's (2006) edited volume. These studies represent salient proposals aimed at 'decolonising global queer studies' (Wieringa et al. 2007: 4) by paying attention to local gender and sexuality regimes in Asia.

If it has been suggested in queer regionalism that the difference between Asian sexual life and that of the West is the 'exegesis of specific categories of sex/gender identification' (Wilson 2006: para 16) or 'the language variations of English queer terms' (Wilson 2006: para 17), then female non-normative sexualities in Asia provide much fodder. For example, *T-Po* pairings in Taiwan, the *Tom-Dees* in Thailand, and the *T-Bird* in the Southern Philippines offer evidences of gendered couplehood, while the English term 'tomboy' has variant terms in the form of *T* in Taiwan or *tomboi* in Indonesia and the Thai category *tom* in the region. The women's gendered erotic identities and their linguistic particularities highlight their particular cultural appropriations and inter-cultural parallels within the region, arguably enabling new critical perspectives on Asian queer sexualities to emerge and challenge the centrality of Western understandings. Ethnographic studies of female same-sex sexualities have thus appeared across Asia, complicating and contributing to these core debates in the globalisation of gay identities, but Singapore has been missing from this literature.

This anomaly is particularly evident in *AsiaPacifiQueer* (Martin *et al.* 2008). Inside this collection, Singapore featured briefly in the introduction as an emerging site of queer intellectualism, and singled out as the 'queer Mecca of Asia' (Martin *et al.* 2008: 13). Yet Singapore did not appear as a case study even though Japan, Thailand and Taiwan – the other three Asian contexts featured alongside Singapore in the book's introduction – made interesting research contributions to the collection. Several of these studies paid critical attention to the experiences of lesbians in Taiwan (Silvio 2008), the *toms* and *dees* in Thailand (Sinnott 2004) and the tomboys in Hong Kong (Kam 2008; Tong 2008). If these collections (Wieringa *et al.* 2007; Khor and Kamano 2006; and Martin *et al.* 2008) exemplify scholarly interventions into the Western-dominated gendered universe of queer studies, then Singapore's absence within this scholarship needs to be explained. Why has Singapore been disengaged from this academic arsenal challenging Anglo-American colonisations of same-sex sexuality?

Returning to queer regionalism's two-pronged measure of 'establishing the difference of Asian sexual life from the West' (Wilson 2006: paras 16 and 17), the exclusion of Singapore is perhaps understandable given that the linguistic practices and political strategies of the local lesbian and gay community correspond to the progressive narratives of a universal Western model. Lesbians in Singapore seem to possess exactly those sorts of investments that lead to the assumption of a global gay identity. Linguistically, there are no indigenised terms to refer to lesbians in Singapore. In Taiwan, lesbian identities are coined in terms of *T* and *Po* (Chao 2000); in Japan the term *rezubian* is commonly used in place of 'lesbian' (Wieringa 2007; Chalmers 2002); in Indonesia, there are the *tombois* and *lesbi* (Blackwood 1999; Boellstorff 2005); and in Thailand *ying rak ying* refers to same-sex love between women whose sexual identities are characterised chiefly by the categories *toms* and *dees* (Sinnott 2004). Some of these terms reveal obvious forms of borrowing from the English language, but do not share 'the same meanings and resonances as their English counterparts' (Blackwood 2005: 223), capturing instead forms of cultural appropriation which inform their particular contexts. In Singapore, however, women who desire women themselves identify with the terms 'lesbian' or 'queer'. Where gendered roles figure in local lesbian relationships, 'butch' and 'femme' are common labels. These terms are developed from Anglo-American contexts, and imbued with historical and cultural meanings specific to the West (Blackwood, 2002; Wieringa *et al.* 2007). In employing these identifications, might lesbian women in Singapore be seen as relying on Western ideas to define their sexuality and desires? If so perceived, Singapore then becomes complicit with the universalising global gay thesis and inevitably rendered ineffective as material for the Asian queer critique.

Furthermore, unlike parts of Asia where local and culturally-specific meanings about transgressive female bodies, sexualities and genders could be invoked from historical evidences of indigenous ritualised forms of transgendered practices, such cultural blueprints appear lacking in Singapore. For example, in Indonesia, the androgynous priestly figures of the female *bissu* and *bailan* recorded from the 1500s provide culturally-specific artefacts of female gender transgressions, even if scant, distant and disconnected from contemporary subjectivities (Blackwood 2005). In Japan between the twelfth and fourteenth centuries, images of the traditional *shirabyoshi*, female dancers who 'dressed in men's *suikan* overshirts and high caps, and wore daggers with silver-decorated hilts and scabbards' (Wieringa 2007: 38, citing Leupp 1995) provide some semblance of cultural legitimacy and authenticity to transgressive female behaviour.

In Singapore, however, women who form a visible element of the local community and adopt non-normative gender roles, such as butch lesbians, lack a similar recourse to a regime of pre-colonial tolerance uninfluenced by Western infiltration and definitions. In the absence of indigenous terms and a temporal trajectory connecting female non-normative sexualities with historical forms, contemporary lesbian identities in Singapore appear as irredeemable Western derivatives, converging on a unitary global conception of homosexuality. Same-sex love has most certainly existed in Singapore for a long time, but the formation of lesbian identities and subjectivities in Singapore took visible shape around the arrival of the internet at about the same time as information technology gave rise to 'modern' queer cultures around East Asia (Berry *et al.* 2003). As one informant quite earnestly reminded this researcher, 'You must remember nothing happened before the internet!' The birth of female non-normative identities and forms of selfhood in Singapore must be viewed as one delivered through the city-state's umbilical connection to the global system.

Locating female non-normative sexualities in Singapore's modernity

I wish to place at the outset the female same-sex-desiring subjects of my study in the material and cultural context of Singapore, and take as foundational their transnational linkages as an integral part of the women's sexual selfhoods. Unlike homosexuals in other parts of Asia whose gendered and sexual subjectivities could be traced and connected to archetypical indigenous forms, religious legacies or evidences of historical homoeroticisms (see for example Garcia 1996; Jackson 1999, 2001, 2003; Blackwood 2005; Wieringa 2007, among others), the Singaporean same-sex-desiring subjects in this study appear stereotypical of the 'modern' homosexual, with no claims to similar cultural blueprints, produced as they are in the particular modernity of Singapore.

Singapore has always been a modern city, and Singaporeans, *avant la lettre*, have never been strangers to processes of modernisation and globalisation. Fortuitously located at the crossroads of the East and West, Singapore was conceived and designed as a free port by the British East India Company, deeply engaged in mercantile capitalism since the nineteenth century. Its early beginning was one of steamships and vessels sliding by between Europe and Asia, of warehouses and go-downs bursting with material goods from all over the world, of immigrants arriving from South and Southeast Asia and the Far East, and merchants from the metropolitan centres of Europe all converging on the trading port for economic opportunities. Singapore is in these senses a product of a European legacy inextricably tied to global capitalism. As a bustling centre of global trade and commerce, Singapore, as Chua (2005: 19) wrote, 'could not have been narrowly defined as a "traditional" nation' and was 'never a third world location, culturally and economically isolated on the periphery'. There is no pre-colonial nostalgia, 'traditional' culture or a tribal regime to speak off. A Western colonial construct, the nation's existence is a thoroughly Western occasion. The construction of its 'Asian-ness' can never be defined externally to the West. By all appearances, Singapore does not fit the Orientalist image of the non-Western 'Other'. Unlike the intricate indigenous symbols associated with Indonesian and Japanese culture, for instance, Singapore's historical association is that of its 'modern' Western parentage. The British colonialist, Sir Stamford Raffles of the British East India Company, is routinely commemorated as the 'founder of modern Singapore' in school history textbooks. His life-size statue now occupies the centre of Singapore's central business district. Historically embedded in global capitalism, then sped through fast-paced development, the modern nation state has enjoyed decades of economic growth since independence, producing a hyper-capitalist middle-class society. Rapid and sustained economic success in the city-state has transformed every aspect of Singaporean life.

Women who love women in Singapore inhabit a thoroughly modern and globalised space. High employment and education levels in a successful economy have provided Singaporean lesbians with varying levels of economic, social and cultural capital, which the women wield as queer cosmopolitans. 'Queer cosmopolitanism', borrowing Binnie's (2004: 127–128) explication, constitutes not just individuals from the professional elite class, but also the lesser-privileged or 'working-class cosmopolitans' (Werbner 1999) bound into an 'imagined cosmopolitanism' (Schein 1999) by their shared desire and longing to be a part of global consumer culture (Binnie 2004). Although Singaporean lesbians come from varied socioeconomic and ethnic backgrounds, they engage in global consumption through various means: via the internet, on television, through reading, and in occasional and regular travel for work and leisure. On overseas trips, some would organise ahead on the internet to meet lesbians in foreign cities. Like the women who love women in the documentary, the Singaporean lesbians in this study all self-identify as same-sex-desiring subjects, even if not exclusively; they understand and identify with the categories of 'lesbian' and 'queer', even if not completely; and consume global queer circulations of contemporary LGBT film, magazines, art and politics with much savvy. Unlike same-sex-desiring women in other parts of the region, such as the *toms* and *dees* in Thailand (Sinnott 2004) or the *lesbi* and *tombois* in Padang, Indonesia (Blackwood 2010) who mainly speak their native language and rarely travel outside their respective countries, the Singaporean lesbian subjects in this study all read and speak English, are socially mobile and proficient in internet technology. Inevitably then, Western tropes such as 'coming out' and 'gaining visibility' permeate the self-understandings of local lesbian and gay Singaporeans, as we saw of the lesbian subjects in the documentary *Women Who Love Women* (2006). Whether talking about forms of selfhood or forms of sexual citizenship, the women can be easily imagined as queer cosmopolitans and regarded as significant in the construction, framing and reproduction of a global gay imaginary.

At the outset, Singaporean lesbians can appear so mundane in the context of more 'exotic' Asian queer cultures: English-speaking, cosmopolitan Singaporean lesbians are the types resembling 'many things that looked familiar' to Western scholars when, as Jackson (2001: 3) observed, they began looking at Asian gay and lesbian cultures in the 1990s. Lacking an indigenous 'tradition' or language, local lesbian subjectivities appear to be 'just like', and no different from, dominant images of LGBT persons around the world: ostensibly modern, educated, English-speaking elites who access and appropriate global circuits of Anglo-American-inflected queer discourse, and cannot be understood outside of dominant understandings of Western homosexuality. By appearing to possess all the sorts of investments fundamental to the production of a global queer elite, the expectation is for these women to express a self-consciousness or awareness of their sexual identity that do not trouble a Western global gay model.

However, rather than romanticise – as the actors, reviewers and producers of the Singaporean lesbian documentary did – that Singaporean same-sex-desiring subjects are on the trajectory of an 'evolutionary process' converging with a 'liberated' modern gay identity (Hsieh 2007 and Ortmann 2008), I wish to go against prevailing assumptions and seek an alternative interpretation and conceptualisation of 'modern' lesbian subjectivities in Singapore. Returning to the evidence presented in the documentary, women who love women in Singapore have been queered in a taken-for-granted Anglo-American way, appearing 'comfortable and familiar' (Peizhi 2007) and not bringing 'anything new to the table' (Hsieh 2007). So queered, local lesbian sexualities have become self-evident, and sidelined by non-Western scholarly interventions into the global queer domain.

Thus, taking the documentary as a point of departure, this book argues for a re-queering of lesbian women in postcolonial Singapore in such a way that local lesbian identities can be poised to interrogate, rather than merely imitate, the putative global gay. It will probe further the globalisation and circulation of queer identities and discourses beyond the theories of 'Western' cultural imperialism.

In other words, I wish to *re-queer* the lives and experiences of lesbians in Singapore to tell the story of a different sort of non-Western queer, which speaks in a transformative way to existing conceptualisations of the asymmetric relations in the global gay domain.

Subjects in question, central provocations and theoretical interventions

To address the question of 'modern' same-sex identities under the condition of globalisation, this study uses empirical data on Singaporean lesbians. Lesbians in Singapore are visible along two fronts. One, the mostly Chinese, college-educated activists who are closely connected to international LGBT organisations and circuits, and who operate in the public sphere engaging the state on questions of political and civil rights; two, the group of non-activist Singaporean lesbians who embody and assert their non-normative sexual selfhoods within the more private domains of their family and personal life. In this book, I address the specific question of how we might understand the sexual subjectivities of these female 'cosmopolitan queers', located as they are in a non-Western Asian context by nationalist rhetoric at the same time as in a 'modern', globalised 'world city'. Are English-speaking, educated, economically independent and well-travelled lesbians who make up a large, visible part of the queer community in Singapore inevitable products of a universal global gay discourse? How do we theorise the lived experiences and meanings these women give to their sexual subjectivities within the historical specificity of postcolonial Singapore?

In this study, I engage mainly with the topic on the globalising of gay identities, taking the premise that non-normative sexualities in Singapore cannot be analysed without taking into account the effects of global flows, and the role globalisation has played in the construction of local lesbian identities. Crucial to understanding lesbian subjectivities in Singapore is their access to, and reception of, international lesbian and gay symbols, discourses and practices. Therefore, I explore the women's life worlds and individual subjectivities by placing the object of local lesbian lives in the context of globalisation and global flows. I consider the ways in which the practices and politics of lesbians in Singapore inevitably draw from, and intersect with, globalised gay identity politics and cultural practices. But I am also interested in how local lesbian practices and subjectivities, located in the particular modernity and development of postcolonial Singapore, maintain their distinction by re-working hegemonic queer models of sexuality in the global domain. Thus I explore the following questions: How are dominant queer discourses circulating in the global domain taken up by lesbian women in the local-cultural context of postcolonial Singapore? How do the articulations of the cultural, political and economic domains shape the women's sexual subjectivities, making them always a part of global processes and yet not always partial to global discourses? Although Singaporean lesbian lives and subjectivities are examined in this book, it is more than the women's sexual stories or the tantalising tales of romance between them that this book wishes to tell.

16 *Introduction*

The book is mainly a theoretical inquiry aimed at grasping 'modern' forms of globalising non-normative sexualities outside of dominant understandings on what it means to be a global gay. How do we theorise the distinct subject positions of 'modern' Singaporean lesbians? How do we view the Singaporean lesbian who mimics the Westernised sexual subject without losing sight of her historicity and specificity? These are the central provocations of the research.

The study engages chiefly with the theoretical work on the globalisation of gay identities, which since the late 1990s has been continually concerned with 'the extent to which queer identities, everywhere, are becoming the same or different through global social, cultural and economic flows' (Corboz 2009: 2). I share the perspective that there is an 'enduring relevance of "globalisation" for understanding sexuality' (Boellstorff 2012: 171). My work builds on the domain of queer globalisation scholarship problematising the notion of a universalising, homogeneous global gay identity, albeit Singaporean queer sexualities could cynically be regarded as being too much the same as what they purport to challenge, and in this sense, not considerably useful counter evidence.

An aspect of Asian queer scholarship has undertaken narratives of difference to undermine the West in processes of queer globalisation. However, rather than attempting to prove the difference of Singaporean non-normative sexualities and providing yet more evidence showing how non-Western Singaporean lesbians are different from Western sexual subjects, I turn to postcolonial theory and feminist critical sexuality studies for conceptual tools to move beyond the impasse of sameness and difference, which is part of the edifice of problematic binaries such as global/local and modern/traditional underpinning persistent postulations of same-sex subjectivities as originating from, and oriented towards, the West.

This is my point of intervention in the global queer discourse. While objections to universalising Western assumptions in the literature have been rife – such as those posed by the queer Asia critique discussed earlier – it is my contention that the West is still seen as the universal signifier of 'modern' homosexuality in Asia and around the world. The stubborn orientations towards the West may be explained by how existing understandings of global gay identities continue to be conditioned by certain dominant logics which do very little to de-centre hegemonic Western understandings. Consequently, as Western-defined gayness is unquestioningly reproduced by these logics, the asymmetric relations in the globalisation of queer identities get a prolonged lease of life as they 'generate new asymmetries' (Grewal and Kaplan 2001: 663). Conceptualisations of global gay identities, as Grewal and Kaplan (2001) point out, must therefore 'fundamentally' address these unequal power relations and 'the contentious relationship between Western and non-Western same-sex sexual identities and practices' (Oswin 2006: 777).

It is these entrenched power relations, orientations and logics that this work attempts to disentangle and dismantle, for despite several counter conceptions of the specificity of non-Western sexualities, the centrality of a Western queer model remains intact. I propose an elementary framework capturing these deeper rubrics and their attendant binaries, and it is this framework that forms the theoretical backbone of this research. Moving beyond images of the out-of-the-closet, liberated elite queer, constructed, commoditised and conveyed globally through the multiple spheres of the economy, popular culture, and the academy as pointed out earlier, I focus on the intellectual domain and attend to the *developmentalist* and *cartographic* logics that, in my opinion, continue to dominate conceptualisations of global change and how we think about the globalisation of lesbian and gay identities. What are these deeper logics and binaries that lock in the assumption of an Anglo-American model as the crux and centre of what it means to be gay?

What is at stake, as I shall elaborate, is the 'authenticity' and agency of the non-Western queer identity. 'An Anglo-American model of global gay imagery', as Provencher (2007: 5) writes, 'prompts demands for "authenticity"'. Privileging a hegemonic Western model as the crux of global same-sex identities, or the core from where they are spread, is to render the rest as an imitation, non-original, mimetic form, imported or 'forever in the place of deferred arrival' (Rofel 2007: 91). What this does is to deny the specificity and legitimacy of the complex reckonings of other same-sex subjectivities.

To the extent that scholarships on the globalisation of gay identities continue to grapple with issues of sameness or difference to the West, I argue that scholarly understandings have tended to operate within limiting logics and binaries. Studies within the domain of non-Western queer scholarship, including the queer Asia critique, have tried to assert their difference from the West by an insistence on recuperating what is 'traditional' about their same-sex practices, or an insistence on what is 'indigenous' of non-Western sexual identities in their cultural context. These efforts, however, reproduce the traditional/modern, local/global binaries which are static and do nothing to forward our understanding of the specificities of non-Western same-sex sexualities, except within the static logics of sameness and difference. They neither fundamentally address nor re-orient understandings of the relationship between the Western and non-Western queer.

Furthermore, if these developmentalist and cartographic logics, structured by the binaries of traditional/modernity and global/local respectively, were to be applied to Singapore, which, as previously mentioned, was born out of 'modern' capitalism lacking in pre-colonial 'tradition' or indigenous culture, then it would be seen as the one nearing the pinnacle or the one mimicking the Western 'original'. Is this why it has been left out of an emerging Asian queer scholarship countering the hegemony of the Western model? How then do we think about the specificity of Singaporean lesbian identities? How do we respond to this vexed question of non-Western, modern, same-sex identities?

My recourse is to a broad theory of postcolonialism. I use the conceptual tools of 'hybridisation' from postcolonial theory and 'transnational sexualities', a subset of postcolonial theory advanced within critical feminist studies, to capture the specificity of 'modern' Singaporean lesbian sexualities. I view my work as belonging and contributing to what Boellstorff has identified as 'a category of scholarship that might be termed "postcolonial LGQ studies"' (1999: 478), a domain which challenges the ethnocentric assumptions of what constitutes identity, visibility, activism, politics and social movements in global queer studies. Certainly, theories of 'hybridisation' and 'transnational' processes in sexuality studies are not wholly new: they have been increasingly deployed in an expanding scholarship over the last decade (Boellstorff 1999; Tan 2001; Sinnott 2004 and Blackwood 2010 are notable examples among others). However, it is my view that there is room to return to these concepts as they are used within the extant queer Asia literature, for neither have been fully exhausted nor elaborated on. As a result, various problematic analytical moves have been perpetuated, leaving the dichotomous and developmentalist imaginations of Western queer models intact. The theoretical work in this book will show how 'hybridic' and 'transnational' sexualities, when developed further and considered together, comprehensively dismantle the temporal and spatial binaries that continue to condition existing scholarly thinking within the study of global queer sexualities. It is with the adoption of this postcolonial perspective, beyond dichotomous temporal and spatial imaginations of global queer studies, that we may articulate the specificity of Singaporean same-sex sexualities.

A re-conceptualisation of the power relations between the Western and non-Western queer is necessary for us to conceive of lesbian sexualities in Singapore as an important object of investigation. In attempting to conceptualise and make sense of Singaporean lesbian practices in particular, and non-Western sexualities in general, what is also entailed is the examination of Eurocentrism inherent in LGQ (Lesbian/Gay/Queer) studies. That is to say, pursuing this puzzle of 'modern' lesbian sexualities in Singapore provides, on one level, an opportune platform to re-orient studies of same-sex desires and practices outside the West in queer globalisation, and, on another level, a pathway towards a more engaged and much-needed critique of Western hegemony, biases and academic assumptions within global queer studies. This is the wider relevance the work hopes to achieve.

Road map

This book is, first and foremost, a theoretical inquiry aimed at grasping forms of globalising non-normative sexualities outside of dominant understandings on what it means to be a 'modern' global gay. Following this introduction, in Chapter 2, I re-stage the global gay debate identifying authoritative sources and central figures contending the relationship between Western and non-Western same-sex identities and practices. I suggest how pioneering work may have relied on, and locked in, developmentalist and cartographic rubrics in conceptualising global gay identities. Then I begin to unlock these logics by re-theorising the concepts of 'hybridisation' and 'transnational' sexualities, combining these in one framework to form the central theoretical scaffolding of this book. The challenge in engaging postcolonial discourse, and to a lesser extent feminist theory, is that concepts and language are often steep in these academic traditions and not readily understandable to a general readership. I have tried to write in a manner that is as accessible as possible, and have also developed diagrams and illustrations to present more straightforward and lucid interpretations of these theories. Chapter 2 provides the core analytical framework to help us think through how we might conceive the hitherto 'absent' case of Singapore and Singaporean lesbians.

In Chapter 3, the character and trajectory of the postcolonial development state in Singapore is outlined, showing how the government has been pervasive in many spheres of social and intimate life. When it comes to sexuality, what is acceptable, what is desirable, what is respectable, under what circumstances, and how sexuality can be channelled towards socially productive ends, are all key points of concern for the postcolonial state in Singapore. The historical analysis of the postcolonial nation state provides insights into the material conditions as well as the ideological discursive context from where homosexual identities, discourses and practices have emerged. Lesbians and gay men in Singapore are not only excluded from social policies unrelentingly predicated on heteronormativity, they are also the direct targets of negative state discourse, and, for gay men in particular, the direct objects of criminalisation. In this chapter, I trace the role of the postcolonial state in structuring and disciplining non-normative sexualities in three sites: one, through the maintenance of Section 377A of the Penal Code criminalising gay sex; two, through negative portrayals of homosexuals in the state-controlled media; and three, through official constructions of homosexuality as anti-nationalist in the rhetoric of its postcolonial elites. The empirical material is analytically contextualised via what I call a 'theoretical economy of state-sexuality relations' emphasising poststructuralist, queer and critical feminist sexuality approaches. Combining these approaches to understand state-sexuality relations provides a critical point of intervention against state power. In calling for a 'sexualising' or 'queering' of the state, these scholarships prompt sexuality scholars to unravel the monolithic categories of 'state' and 'nationalism', making conceptual room to view these sites as fraught and contested.

Then, in Chapter 4, extending queer and feminist sexuality re-theorisations, I argue that sexuality is not just a passive site of state discipline and control, but also the very site from where power unfolds and disperses in the form of a 'reverse discourse' (Foucault 1978). This chapter examines two local instances of a 'reverse discourse' in which a particular unravelling of state power was engendered through specific acts of resistance. The first is the local mobilisation against the male sodomy law. The second is the leadership tussle in the women's advocacy group, AWARE,[3] over lesbian issues. Through the unfolding of these events, we see how Singaporean gay and lesbian lives came into national consciousness and debate, creating widespread discursive contestations in the public sphere over the issue of homosexuality. As government officials grew anxious over what they perceived as culture wars between Christian conservative groups and progressive segments of society supporting the growing visibility of the local gay community, these events illustrate the disassembling of state power over the issue of sexuality and play out the complexity and disjunction of state-sexuality relations. Throughout the chapter, I argue that state-sexuality relations are deeply dialectic and cannot be seen as uni-directional. Such a conceptualisation usefully paves the way for us to understand the agency of same-sex-desiring subjects in postcolonial Singapore, to which the next chapter turns.

Chapter 5 begins with an analysis of queer activism in Singapore, in which lesbian activists played prominent roles. I discuss several early initiatives of local activism and its particular politics and trajectory. As queer activists and analysts in Singapore tended to rely on a progressive logic of Western gay liberation to assess the local queer community, I ask after the extent to which local queer activism has been interpellated into a hegemonic global gay ideology. Then I offer an analysis of Pink Dot, Singapore's largest annual pride demonstration, through a postcolonial lens. I demonstrate how the hybridising, transnational product of Pink Dot Singapore – one which found inspiration in Western queer politics but, in a postcolonial twist, re-territorialised Western queer understandings through the engendering of a Singaporean nationalist discourse – achieved a specificity that led to its very success and eventual export to Utah, New York and Alaska. Operating visibly in this context of queer activism are Singaporean lesbians. I explore the politics and subject positions of leading lesbian activists in Singapore who are themselves closely connected to transnational circuits of queer knowledge production. I share a 'public' encounter I had with an activist on Facebook, which revealed how her close alliance and uncritical acceptance of Western queer strategies such as 'coming out' and 'gaining visibility' led to an unintended political irony: in calling for queer women in Singapore to engage in a transparent politics of recognition and visibility, the activist had, in this episode, effectively erased the sexual subjectivities of the women she claims to represent. This chapter concludes by underscoring the political significance of theory and theorisation: the ways in which transnational processes of identification are conceptualised and imagined shape popular and activist discourses and the kinds of identities that are enabled or erased in queer politics.

Moving from an examination of the politics and sexual subjectivities of local lesbian activists, in Chapter 6, the lens is turned onto the subject positions and narratives of non-activist lesbian women. The two groups of lesbian women are differentiated by their political affiliations and distance to international gay discourses and its central tenet of 'coming out'. I examine the accounts of non-activist lesbian women, exploring the ways in which the women identify themselves, the labels they use, their gendered identities, their same-sex desires and practices, the pragmatic strategies they adopt to navigate 'in' and 'out' of the heteronormative family. The women's life stories and everyday practices reveal their sexual subjectivities to be complex, contradictory and contingent. I argue that these ways of being gay cannot be read as 'queer' in the manner of the West. Located in the postcolonial context of Singapore, the ways in which the women re-queer hegemonic concepts of homosexuality are, in my analysis, crucial moments of reconfiguration and transformation – not mere reception –

of what it means to be 'modern' global lesbians. This is the specification of Singaporean women who love women.

Then, in the concluding chapter, I draw together the theoretical insights and empirical concerns to make a final argument for the relevance and importance of a postcolonial study of global sexual identities. I underscore how, through postcolonial understandings, the case of Singaporean lesbians has been deployed in this book to offer a more productive way of challenging the hegemony of universalising Western assumptions premised not on static and unproductive binaries but in a dynamic, mutually-constituting relationality between the Western and non-Western queer. This approach contributes to a 'foundational' shift in our understanding of the asymmetric relationship between the Western and non-Western queer, and provides an important insight and contribution to the debate on the globalisation of gay identities. In the final analysis, I suggest that such that a postcolonial study of global sexual identities offers a way of challenging the global gay discourse based not just on oppositional identities and practices but on non-oppositional, mutually constituting positions created in the interplay of hybridising and transnational sexualities. The distinction of the postcolonial politics of difference, I suggest, is its notion of non-oppositional difference. I discuss the implications of this in relation to the Western notion of 'queer', which originated from US and Australian academic and activist circles as a form of oppositional politics against heteronormativity. I argue for the potential of queer to be more democratic and inclusive when it is thought of not in terms of oppositional difference so foundational to its politicised inception. To 're-queer' is to think of difference in non-oppositional terms – sometimes colluding, sometimes contingent and sometimes contradictory – but all the time legitimate, complex and 'not weird', to quote a respondent. This is how the book deploys the case of 'modern' Singapore and Singaporean lesbians to rethink what it means to be 'queer'.

Notes

1 'Abang' means 'brother' in Malay.
2 I select Altman's snapshot of this global queering because he continues to be widely acknowledged in the literature (Berry 1996; Rofel 1999; Morton 2001; Oswin 2006; Akiko 2008; Corboz 2009; Kong 2010) as one of the first to point to the 'internationalisation of a certain form of social and cultural identity based upon homosexuality' and 'the emergence of "the global gay"' (Altman 1996b: 77). A fuller picture of Altman's 'global queer' (1996a) will be sketched in a subsequent chapter, where I will also be arguing that Altman's 'global gay' preposition created a problematical precedent and contributed to a paradigmatic universalist assumption in the generation of a scholarship engaged with what I call 'the global gay debate'.
3 AWARE stands for the Association of Women for Action and Research, and is Singapore's most established women's advocacy group.

2 Conceptual underpinnings of global queering

In the Singaporean lesbian documentary (*WWLW* 2006), in popular opinion, in journalistic writing such as in *The Economist*, and in initial academic analyses, it is remarkably obvious how Western traits have been interpolated into the global space as the reified global queer. What requires attention in the global gay domain, therefore, are the asymmetric relations between the Western and non-Western queer. Although one-sided Western understandings of global sexual identities have been taken for granted as what being gay means – evident in the construction and commodification of idealised Western queer images circulating in the multiple spheres of the economy, queer politics and popular culture – my intervention is in the intellectual domain. I argue that re-conceptualising the relations of global sexual identities allows us to capture the specificity, authenticity and legitimacy of same-sex identities outside the West, including that of Singapore's. This is the theoretical task of this chapter. How do we think about global same-sex identities? Particularly, how do we think about the specificity of same-sex identities and practices in Singapore?

This chapter is divided into two sections dealing with the conceptualisation of global queering. In the first section, I explore the genealogy and contours of the global gay domain, which I have identified as being over-determinately queered in an Anglo-American way. The global gay domain is dominated by the assumption of a universalising global gay identity, produced most notably in Altman's (1996a, 1996b, 1997) influential writings. As it was Altman who arguably sparked intellectual interest and debate in the rise of a universal gay identity – embodied in an 'international gay/lesbian' (2001: 86) subject whom I refer to as the 'global gay' in this book – I trace the genealogy of the global gay in Altman's account. Then I turn to two pioneering works attempting to articulate the specificity and legitimacy of 'other' same-sex identities and communities in the face of this dominating global gay identity. These contestations form the contours of the global gay domain and constitute the first-generation studies of global queer identities.

Revisiting these contestations clears conceptual space for a deeper theoretical engagement. Through an analysis of these early scholarships, I propose an elementary framework capturing their *teleological* and *cartographic* logics and attendant binaries, which I argue are premised on the idea of sameness and difference to the West, and do very little to advance our understandings of the specificity of non-Western sexual identities and practices, including Singapore's. The task in this first section of the chapter is to elaborate on this theoretical problematic.

In the second section, I advance postcolonial theory as a means to overcome the entrenched logics and binaries within the global gay domain. I specify how a broad postcolonial approach will be applied in this study. I also argue that the extension of a postcolonial perspective into global sexuality studies re-orients existing analyses of global gay identities in a way that accounts for 'modern', non-Western same-sex subjectivities, including those of Singaporean lesbians. This chapter demonstrates that a postcolonial perspective is pivotal in grasping how modern queer subjects, such as lesbians in Singapore, are located and formed. Thus, in positing a postcolonial approach, I seek to turn the problematic of locating lesbian Singaporeans into a demonstration of how this enables us to rethink the asymmetric relationship of the non-Western queer and the Western global gay.

As mentioned before, I turn specifically to two related postcolonial conceptual processes, that of 'hybridisation', drawn from and already deployed in emergent 'postcolonial LGQ studies' (Boellstorff 1999: 478) and 'transnational' sexualities, drawn from the 'transnational turn' (Povinelli and Chauncey 1999: 439) in feminist queer studies. These constitute a second generation of scholarships more attuned to the inequities of globalising same-sex identities. Although global queer identities have already been theorised as 'hybrid' and 'transnational', certain misconceptions in the literature suggest that these concepts remain under-theorised and not fully understood. Thus in this chapter, I attend to the postcolonial processes of 'hybridisation' and 'transnationality', elaborating on, and incorporating in, these concepts a material dimension so that they capture the historical development of same-sex subjectivities in Singapore. I argue that combining these two conceptual processes in a revitalised postcolonial framework directly dismantles the particular temporal and cartographic binaries which have underpinned and hindered understandings of same-sex desires outside the West.

SECTION ONE

A genealogy of the global gay?

This book engages with a key debate in queer scholarship, that of the globalisation of homosexual identities, and the asymmetric relationship between Western and non-Western same-sex identities and practices within the global gay domain. A longstanding debate with a scholarly genealogy of over two decades of pitting the categories of 'Western' versus 'non-Western', the scholarship is built on entrenched assumptions of globalisation as a homogenising force or a neo-colonial movement of cultural forms and capital from the West to 'the rest'.

Global sexual identities are, in this frame, produced through linear relations of power emanating from an Anglo-American axis. This asymmetric conceptualisation of global gay relations is not just a matter of theoretical debate but reflects a social reality structured by Western capitalist development. As Spurlin (2001: 200) observes, 'Western cultures have had the capital means to circulate queerness as a commodity and the economic power to appropriate emergent forms of queer cultural production'. Western queer forms are, in this sense, continuously imbued with power, and what is generally at stake is the agency and specificity of the non-Western homosexual against her antithesis: the modern, Western homosexual hegemonic in the global gay discourse. On one side looms the imperialist figure of the White liberated lesbian. On the other, the subjugated figure of the indigenous sexual subject with same-sex desires. When McLelland (2000) began his study with the question, 'Is there a Japanese gay identity?' he reflected a certain preoccupation among scholars studying non-Western queer sexualities, that is, 'Who counts as gay?'

A pivotal moment in the pronouncement of the 'monumentalist gay identity' is the one made by Altman (Rofel 1999: 455). Arguably the one who inaugurated the debate on the 'apparent globalisation of gay identities' (Altman 1996b: 77), Altman's work continues to be taken by scholars as a point of entry into the global gay domain (Shimizu 2008 and Kong 2010). Following this scholarship, I take Altman's (1996a, 1996b, 1997) work as foundational, for the assumptions and logic underpinning his conceptualisation of global gay relations have provoked and pervaded subsequent scholarship, spawning a substantial literature on the global gay phenomenon.

In his essay, *On Global Queering* (1996a), published online in the *Australian Humanities Review*, Altman began with the observation that a 'major revolution has occurred in how we imagine homosexuality in the contemporary world'. The change in attitudes towards homosexuality, Altman argues, is captured in *The Economist*'s (1996) three-page spread with a cover story proclaiming, 'Let Them Wed'. In it, the journal suggests a rapid rise in, and global shift towards, new concepts of homosexual identity and acceptance:

> In effect, what McDonald's has done for food and Disney has done for entertainment, the global emergence of ordinary gayness is doing for sexual cultures.
>
> (Quote taken from Altman 1996a)

While Altman objects to the liberal optimism and overtones of *The Economist*'s (1996) article (which in his view glosses over the everyday and entrenched discrimination faced by homosexuals in most of the Western world), he does not indicate the content and shape of what this 'global emergence of ordinary gayness' might be. Instead, he quickly agrees that:

> *The Economist* was right in pointing to the rapidity of change both within and outside the Western world in the past decade.

Given that *The Economist*'s invocation of 'ordinary gayness' was made in relation to notions of McDonaldisation and Disney entertainment, the presumption is that this source of 'global emergence' is the United States, a point which Altman (1996a) does not refute but reiterates that 'it is sensible to begin a discussion of new sexual politics with the United States', for 'change in America influences the rest of the world in dramatic ways'. Although he attempts to differentiate between 'western Europe', 'Australasia' and America, he does this only to compare the progress of gay liberation movements in these places where one can 'claim roots' to the emergence of global gayness. Altman then reaches the conclusion that 'it is Stonewall which has become internationally known as the symbol of a new stage of gay self-affirmation ...' Ultimately, what Altman espouses and consolidates is a Western liberationist model in the global emergence of gay identities.

As Martin (1996) expressed in her online response to Altman, his model of global gayness is one colonised by 'Western-inflected "global gay/lesbian culture"' wherein the 'incursion of literature or imagery' originating in America, Australia and Europe flow unilinearly to the rest of the world such that:

> ... 'a very Western notion of how to be homosexual' is swallowed whole and easily digested by women and men in those other cultures who then begin to exhibit the symptoms of the 'global gay/ lesbian'.

Elsewhere in *Global gaze/Global gays*, Altman (1997) writes of an emerging universal gay identity among gay groups in Asia which is 'as much about being Western as about sexuality' (1997: 433). Furthermore, he states, 'there seems no reason why a Western-style gayness should not prove as attractive as other Western identities' (Altman 1997: 420). Here, the imagination of Western-style gayness is for Altman (1996b: 77–78) a vivid one:

> He – sometimes, though less often, she – is conceptualised in terms that are very much derived from recent American fashion and intellectual style: young, upwardly mobile, sexually adventurous, with an in-your-face attitude toward traditional restrictions and an interest in both activism and fashion.

This 'ordinary gayness' is transposed to the Asian context as:

> Images of young men in baseball caps and Reeboks on the streets of Budapest or Sao Paulo, of 'lipstick lesbians' flirting on portable telephones in Bangkok or demonstrating in the streets of Tokyo – none of which are fictitious – are part of the construction of a new category.

Beyond style and fashion, Altman, at other points (1996b: 80–84; 1997: 422–423), lists what he sees as 'new self-concepts' of what being gay means: it is a form of sexual transgression, no longer expressed or experienced as forms of gender inversion but as a desire for the same without the denial of one's femininity or masculinity; it centres on an emotional same-sex relationship, not homoerotic sex engaged on the side; it leads to the creation of a public gay community, visible in commercial, social and political spaces; and finally, it entails a willingness to adopt a gay political consciousness. These ways and characteristics of being gay have been worked out 'several decades ago' in the West for which Altman (1997: 422) now sees parallels 'in much of urban Asia'. To assert oneself with these new self-concepts, Altman states (1997: 423), 'is to adhere to a distinctly modern invention, namely the creation of an identity and a sense of community based on (homo)sexuality'. Elsewhere he has written about this new gay identity as 'more accurately the expansion of an existing Western category that is part of the rapid globalisation of lifestyle and identity politics' (Altman 1996b: 78). There are other examples, but the above accounts amply illustrate Altman's caricature of a universal global queer through Western same-sex desires, practices and images. It is, in my opinion, ironic that the Western queer has been appropriated within this global gay discourse as an over-determined signifier of the modern global gay when the Western queer has been conceived by widely-understood Foucauldian analytics emphasising the cultural genealogy and historical specificity of how it discursively came into being.[1]

Globalisation in the global gay domain, and Altman's antimony

Altman's original understanding of global gay relations is based on a basic interpretation of globalisation as a process of homogenisation: the idea of the world as converging through commercial, cultural and technological forces emanating from the West. It is also interpreted as a process wedded to modernity. This is to effectively equate globalisation with Westernisation and then Westernisation with modernity, a formula replicating all the problems of Eurocentrism which general social theory has been relentlessly contending over the last several decades (cf. Pieterse 1994; Connell 2007, 2011, among other globalisation analysts).

Nevertheless, theorising in the 1990s at a time when uni-directional understandings of globalisation processes were being thoroughly contested by authoritative sources outside the field of sexuality (Robertson 1992; Albrow 1996; Featherstone 1990, 1995, 1998, among others), Altman, in his accounts of globalising sexual identities, also cautioned against taking the:

> ... narcissistic transition narrative in 'diffusion', whereby the trajectory of the Third World has already been traversed by the First.
> (Connors 1995, quoted by Altman 1997: 432)

Hence, Altman's understanding of global queer identities also includes assessments and acknowledgements of cross-cultural conceptions of homosexuality.

In the conclusion of one analysis, Altman (1997) states that the new gay groups in Asia and other non-Western contexts will be interesting developments as they 'adapt ideas of universal discourse and Western identity politics to create something new and unpredictable' (1997: 433). Although Altman seems to show a subsequent concern for cultural specificity and sexual diversity, his conceptualisation of the global gay domain is substantially about the familiar picture of how:

> ... the images and rhetoric of a newly assertive gay world spread rapidly from the United States and other Western countries after 1969.
> (Altman 1996b: 86)

The year 1969 is significant for it marks the period of sexual revolution in postwar America. Implicit in this discourse is the reassurance that any fears over unilateralism or cultural imperialism from the West could be allayed with the liberatory promise of Western-style sexual politics.

Having caricatured and reified the new concept of the universal global gay with specific Western characteristics, while problematising the non-Western queer's easy correspondence with Western assumptions, Altman's antinomy is apparent. On the one hand, he sees the emergence of a universal gay identity, particularly among those groups espousing 'Western-style politicised homosexuality in Asia' (Altman 1997: 417). On the other hand, he perceives 'the problems of claiming a universality for an identity which developed out of certain historical specificities' (Altman 1997: 418). When addressing Altman's contradiction, scholars credit his recognition of sexual diversity whilst criticising his analysis as 'suspiciously evolutionist' (Shimizu 2008: 358) and as a 'narrowly conceived model of Americanisation' (Chao 2000: 383).

Indeed, Altman's (1996a) analysis of the global gay domain, as noted earlier, is mostly a one-sided account of 'Exporting the American dream' wherein 'American books, films, magazines and fashions continue to define contemporary gay and lesbian meanings for most of the world'. In other words, as Rofel (1999: 454) remarks, 'he merely reads globalisation as the spread of Western models of homosexuality'. Such an account of the globalisation of sexual identities, as Martin (1996) points out:

> ... assumes that it is always only the Western side that holds the power, and that the 'other side' will never return seriously to disrupt 'our' assumptions and forms.

Regarded within the scholarship, somewhat cynically, as the 'father-of-all-gay-knowledge' (Berry 1996: para 1), as 'an elder statesmen' within the academy of queer theorists (Morton 2001: 214), and for holding an authoritative 'position in gay politics' (Rofel 1999: 454), Altman's reified construct of the global gay has been a 'particularly productive instigator' (Oswin 2006: 780) of the global gay debate. Altman's antinomy, each aspect of his logic persuasive in itself, has drawn polemical responses from scholars seeking to explain gay identities within the global domain. The majority share Altman's call for sexual diversity and this has led to the creation of a significant body of empirical literature proposing ways to conceptualise the specificity, agency and authenticity of non-Western queer identities through various strategies and manoeuvres.

Specifying the 'other side': non-Western sexualities in the global gay domain

During the last two decades, an avalanche of scholarship has emerged offering alternative specifications of non-Western queer models in relation to the universal, Western-inflected global gay. Apart from Altman, the other distinctive voice is of the pioneering sexuality theorist, Ken Plummer. While Altman writes from the point of view of a 'privileged, White, Australian gay intellectual' (Altman 1997: 418), Plummer hails from the academic centres of the UK and the US from where he has contributed widely to lesbian and gay studies. As early as the late 1980s, Altman (1989) had begun asking the question of 'which homosexuality?' However, his articulations, discussed earlier, tended to 'subspeciate', to borrow Appadurai's (1996) term, into a form of Americanisation. By the early 1990s, Plummer had also joined the fray, offering ways to understand how 'homosexualities have become globalised' (1992: 17). Together, these men represent the first generation of theorists bringing queer sexualities to bear in globalisation studies. I examine each in turn, beginning first with Altman.

Altman's teleological conception of Asian same-sex identities

Along the facet of his logic, seeking sexual diversity and different homosexual forms, Altman situates global sexual identities within what might be seen as a developmental continuum marking 'traditional' sexualities and the 'modern' gay identity. This might have been glimpsed earlier in Altman's (1997: 422, 433) comparison of the:

> ... new ... urban gay groups in Asia ... adapting ideas of universal discourse and Western identity (which) parallels (from) several decades ago in the West.

Returning to the critique of Altman in the previous section (before we proceed to identify Altman's attempts to specify the cultural difference of non-Western or, more specifically, Asian gay identities), I would like to highlight how Altman's list of new self-concepts for the modern queer includes, among other things, an abandonment of gender inversion in the expression of same-sex desires. What this means is that modern gay men no longer need to put on forms of femininity or deny their masculinity in the expression of their homosexuality. For Altman (1996b: 82, italics mine), this is a modern 'evolution' achieved through the progress of the Western gay movement:

> ... the homosexual man who behaves like a woman ... is a *'traditional'* view. But for most Western homosexual men (gender subversion) *ended with the development* of the gay movement.

In this conception, one develops along a specific homosexual trajectory: from a 'traditional', illegitimate identification (mostly expressed as gender inversion) to a 'modern', liberated same-sex sexuality (legitimate, politicised and placed at the forefront of one's identity, neither tied to, nor masked by, gender-role expectations). By tracing the gay movement in the West as the endpoint of 'traditional' homosexual identifications, the Western experience is located at the apex of this schema. This is archetypical of a developmentalist logic at work within a framework of a Western sexual modernity.

This teleological conception is akin to, or based on, the modernisation thesis conjectured in the 1960s by US developmental specialists (Marshall 1994), where the notion of change and development is taken as a standard, linear movement from a pre-modern past to a modern future understood in terms of a Western experience. The theory has been subject to relentless criticism and objection, with scholars long critical of its inherent asymmetry. Where the West is taken as the first historical example of the paradigm of modernity, developing countries are treated as infant or deviant examples to the West. This means their 'development' is to be studied in terms of their approximation to Western experiences (Nettl 1967). The question of Eurocentrism thus becomes central, and remains an important point of contention (see for example, Bhambra 2007), for its vehicles (such as modernisation theory) surface ever so insidiously and unconsciously in contemporary social thought, including thinking on same-sex identities. Another relevant and insightful critique is Bernstein's (1971) view that the modernisation thesis sets up the tradition-modernity divide as an ideal-typical divide located within a linear, evolutionary pathway. This assumes:

> ... an 'original state' view of underdevelopment and development (where) what are in fact empirical generalisations or concepts of limited applicability ... have assumed the status of generalising ideal-types.
> (Bernstein 1971: 150)

Bearing these criticisms of modernisation theory in mind, it would appear that Altman has assumed and applied the teleological logic of modernisation theory to his understanding of global gay identities. In Altman's theorisation, the ideal-types of 'traditional' sexual identities and the 'modern' Western gay model mark the endpoints of the developmental continuum, as Altman (1996b: 91) states:

> Clearly what is at work is a complex compound of tradition and modernity, themselves better understood as ideal points on an academic continuum than as a descript of fixed realities.

The developmentalist logic, arguably, allows Altman to resolve his antimony. On the one hand, it allows Altman to claim that non-Western, Asian sexualities are changing and developing along a teleological pathway towards a modern Western form. On the other hand, to make the case for the specificity of non-Western sexual forms in the globalisation of gay identities, Altman, in Rofel's (1999: 454) astute observation, is able to resolve this within the same developmental, evolutionary frame by placing the various sex and gender orders in Asia 'on a continuum from tradition to modernity'. Rofel writes:

> While acknowledging their coexistence, he denies their coevalness, placing the forms that are culturally marked for him into the category of the traditional and the ones that approach what he conceives of as 'Western-style' into the category of the modern.

According to Rofel (1999: 454), 'Altman then concludes that in Asia "self-identified homosexuals" view themselves as part of a "global community" whose commonalities override cultural differences.' Building on this critique, I observe that within this same teleological frame, Altman attempts to articulate the specificity of non-Western sexualities and mitigate the inevitability of a universal gay identity by positing the problem as 'one of finding the right balance between tradition and modernity' (Altman 1996b: 79).

For Altman, the conceptual task of specifying Asian gay identities becomes one of holding 'in balance the impact of universalising rhetoric and styles with the continuing existence of cultural and social traditions' (Altman 1997: 420). Implicit in this interpretation is the idea that in order to 'count as gay' and assert authenticity in the global gay domain, non-Western or Asian homosexualities must exhibit their cultural difference in terms of an ideal-type 'tradition' to hold in balance and tension the homogenising 'modern' global gay form. Altman urges (1996b: 89) that:

> ... a discussion of new or modern homosexualities needs to incorporate a sense of the continuing importance of pre-modern forms of sexual organisation.

What Altman seems to be saying is that non-Western homosexualities are 'authentic' only insofar as they can trace a history or 'origin' to the 'traditional' ideal-type. The argument for the specificity of Asian same-sex identities is thus advanced on a developmentalist logic, stipulating the Western global queer as the acme of a modern gay identity. In such an articulation of the specificity of Asian same-sex identities, what is reproduced and reinforced are the binaries of 'tradition' versus 'modernity', the then and now, and the imitation against the ideal. In the end, Altman's argument for the 'authenticity' and agency of non-Western sexualities continues to be 'fundamentally' woven around issues of sameness or difference with respect to a privileged Western model. Boellstorff (1999: 478) makes the interesting observation that interpretations of non-Western lesbian and gay subjectivities within a developmentalist paradigm or 'pathway' often fall into two reductionisms in LGQ studies: first, as 'just like' lesbian and gay subjectivities in the West, 'characterised by a supposed essential sameness that has been there all along, hidden under a veneer of exotic cultural difference'; or second, as 'traitors' to their traditional subjectivities because they have an 'essential difference, hidden under the veneer of the terms *lesbian* and *gay*' (Boellstorff 1999: 478–479). Either way, non-Western same-sex subjectivities occupy one point on this continuum, locked in a temporal fix and maintaining Western homosexuality as the ideal-type pinnacle of modern homosexuality.

Given Altman's influence in the scholarship concerned with the globalisation of sexualities, the persistence of a developmentalist perspective might have been sown here, and the conception of global queer identities as becoming more similar or different to a Western model becomes paradigmatic. Boellstorff, for instance, refers to the 'vexed binarism of sameness versus difference that permeate most discussions of LGQ identities outside the West' (1999: 480). Propped, as it were, by the binaries of tradition/modernity and sameness/difference, a developmentalist perspective underpinning the conceptualisation of non-Western same-sex identities neither troubles nor topples the West but in fact entrenches its dominance. The fault lines of power between the Western and non-Western queer are reinforced in this teleological specification of non-Western, and, in Altman's case, Asian, same-sex sexualities.

Plummer's cartographic configuration of multiple sexual modernities

Ken Plummer (1992) points out that the unitary phenomenon of the modern homosexual has been challenged by the multiple, polymorphous appearance of non-normative sexualities everywhere. Modern gay identities are, in Plummer's understanding, part of the '(post)modernisation of homosexualities' (1992: 13):

> The search for the truth of a unitary phenomenon designated 'homosexual' is discredited precisely because there is no such unitary phenomenon ... What we have are a multiplicity of feelings, genders, behaviours, identities, relationships, locales ... and so forth, that have been appropriated by a few rough categories like 'homosexual', 'lesbian', 'gay'.
>
> (Plummer 1992: 14)

While Plummer (1992: 17) spoke of same-sex experiences as 'increasingly fashioned through the interconnectedness of the world', he disagrees with Altman's 'Americanisation of homosexuality' (Plummer 1992: 16) interpretation of lesbian and gay culture and politics around the world. Deploying his postmodernist thesis, Plummer's (1992) analysis of the global development of same-sex experiences points to the multiplicities of sexual meanings, behaviours, identities, cultures and politics – what he refers to as a 'global sexual melange'

(Plummer 2010: xiv; Bech 1992). Plummer positions his postmodernist understanding of global same-sex identities against the developmentalist perspective based on the modernisation thesis. He states:

> Rather than seeing homosexuality as a tribal and universal group, or seeing it as evolving to a more advanced state of being gay, same-sex experience moves in fits and starts along diverse paths to disparate becomings.
>
> (Plummer 1992: 16)

In contrast to Altman's suggestion that new globalised queer identities would ultimately replace older indigenous identities, Plummer's proposal of 'disparate becomings' is a recognition of the diversity and difference marking the lives of people in same-sex relations.

While Plummer veered his understanding of global gay identities towards the theoretical sophistication of postmodern complexity, his response to how homosexualities have become globalised appears to be conditioned by the dichotomous imagination of the 'localisation/globalisation of homosexualities' (Plummer 1992: 15–18). Against what Plummer (1992: 17) observes as the superficial appearance of a mass homogenisation of gay cultural products in the global domain, one in which 'gay and lesbian identities, politics, cultures, markets, intellectual programmes which nowadays quite simply know no national boundaries', he suggests that:

> ... the globalisation case must never be overstated. It would be dangerous to suggest a convergence in homosexual lifestyles across the world – into one true universal gayness ... each national and local culture brings its own richness, its own political strategies and its own uniqueness. Along with *globalisation* comes an *intensification of the local*. With the process of globalisation comes a tendency towards *tribalism*: a fundamentalism winning over difference, a politics that separates rather than unites.
>
> (Plummer 1992, italics mine)

Plummer's (1992) suggestion of 'uniqueness' and an 'intensification of the local', and his forebodings of 'tribalism' and 'fundamentalism' as ways to specify global same-sex identities, appear to fall into an ethnocartographic 'area studies' framework seeking essential traits within supposed indigenous cultural areas. Ironically, even though Plummer (1992: 13–18) claims a postmodernist position, his reading of global gay relations is one based on the notion of bounded societies and national categories – territories that are themselves long-disputed in sociological debates on postmodernity. Perhaps, as Gupta and Ferguson (1992) suggest, it is because we live in a world where identities are increasingly coming to be deterritorialised, and actual places and localities ever more blurred and indeterminate, that ideas of culturally and ethnically distinct places are even more salient. It is precisely in a postmodern condition when more and more of us find ourselves in what Said (1979: 18) has called a 'generalised condition of homelessness' that it becomes more urgent for imagined communities (Anderson 1983) to be attached to imagined places.

In a late modern world when an interconnected global sexual domain of identities, politics, cultures and markets circulate with no national boundaries, what is needed to counter universalist views, Plummer (1992: 18) argues, is an approach 'sensitive to the self-determination' of local and national lesbian and gay cultures. When it comes to questions of identity politics, it is important to 'think globally', but the strategy for self-determination is also to 'act locally'. Lesbian and gay scholarship, Plummer (1992: 18) states, 'needs to be clear about this international connectedness yet local uniqueness'.

For Plummer, the conceptual task of accounting for sexual specificities and cultural difference in the global domain is the local. The 'local' functions as a site to disrupt the universalist assumptions of the 'global'. Implicit in this interpretation is the idea that in order to 'count as gay' and assert agency and 'authenticity' in the universalising global gay domain, homosexual cultures and identities around the world must express their cultural difference by locating a supposed local indigenous culture as a bulwark against the global. In other words, sexual identities, as they are increasingly caught up in an international interconnectedness, must at the same time assert the cultural purity of their native same-sex desires.

When the local and the global meet, the range of transgressive sexualities emerging from this amalgamation of local and global forces is explained as a process of globalisation and glocalisation in Plummer's (2010) analysis. This results in what he sees as a 'global sexual melange' (2010: xiv). However, recalling Connell's (2007: 374) instructive remarks in a separate analysis of globalisation in sociological theory, 'To speak of "glocalisation" is to resolve nothing. It is to assert both terms of a static polarity at once'. Indeed, to speak of the 'local' and 'global' sets up yet another imaginary binary indexed to the 'us and them' and reiterates the same issues of similarity and difference while risking the problem of essentialism. Plummer's (1992, 2010: xiv) conception is seductive because it endeavours to capture the multiplicity of same-sex identities and cultures around the world in terms such as the 'global sexual melange'. It is advanced on a cartographic conception that casts global flows along spatial pathways creating 'disparate becomings' – to quote Plummer (1992: 16) again – instead of universalising temporal flows along a developmentalist pathway.

The cartographic conception is in this sense an attempt to challenge the developmentalist logic. Despite its attempts to override the Eurocentric bias of a temporal pathway, the cartographic casting of global flows – through theorisations of multiple localities, multiple identities and multiple modernities – is, however, built on a global/local dichotomy that does not 'fundamentally' challenge the Western hegemonic core signifying global queerness. 'Though now having multiple sources', as Oswin (2006: 784) maps in global queer geography, 'a uni-directionality of flow persists'. While multiple sexualities and modernities have emerged in this cartographic conception, the West is still believed to be the point of origin from where global flows are dispersed in an 'import/export calculus' (Wilson 2006) to the non-West. Therefore, the multiple modernities paradigm, as it has come under intense scrutiny in sociological theorisations of modernity and globalisation, is insufficient in that it fails to re-orient global flows and processes in any meaningful way. It is anti-teleological but still Western-centred. Specifically, what remains amiss in a cartographic conception is a re-theorisation of the actual unevenness, asymmetry and inequality in global gay relations. Consequently, the assumption remains that global flows occur from a Western-inflected centre to the peripheries.

Just as in Altman's developmentalist conception, where the lesbian and gay subject is trapped in a temporal fix moving along a continuum of sameness and difference to the West, so the homosexual subject fashioned in Plummer's cartographic conception is frozen in a spatial fix where the only movement is a unilinear one from the global to local as gay identities globalise. Global flows in the global gay domain are thus re-oriented from a developmentalist, temporal pathway to a cartographic, spatial trajectory, but the West is not de-centred.

The developmentalist and cartographic logics underpinning Altman's and Plummer's conceptions of global same-sex identities rely 'foundationally' on dichotomies. These binaries leave the symbolic power of the Western queer intact and lock the non-Western homosexual into temporal and static spatialities, leaving unchallenged the privileging of Western queer dominance in our discourses, perspectives and understanding of lesbian and gay identities and practices around the world.

Theoretical problematic and persistent logics: an elementary framework

What I have tried to excavate in this section are the deeper rubrics and assumptions conditioning the conceptualisations of global gay identities. The operation of developmentalist and cartographic logics in understanding non-Western sexualities in a universalising global gay domain, I argue, do very little to advance our understanding of the specificities of non-Western same-sex identities. Built on a traditional/modernity binary, the *developmentalist logic* operates on the assumption that the Western global gay model is the pinnacle and end point of a pathway towards which all non-Western sexual identities will inevitably flow and converge (see left side of Figure 2.1 for an elementary illustration). Built on a local/global dichotomy casting global flows with similar effect but in a different direction, the *cartographic logic* assumes the West as the centre from where ideas about what it means to be gay are diffused into the peripheries, and all 'others' will eventually start to mimic the centre (see right side of Figure 2.1). Convergence, homogenisation and universality are the inevitable outcomes of these two entrenched logics.

Grasping this theoretical problematic, I suggest, provides an elementary framework for scholarships proposing different ways to conceptualise the agency and 'authenticity' of the non-Western queer. This is what is at stake. First, understanding same-sex practices and politics in terms of a developmentalist

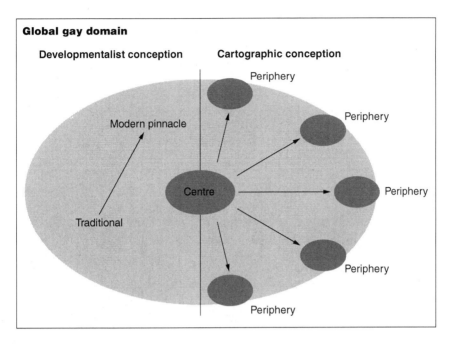

Figure 2.1 An elementary framework of persistent logics in the global gay domain.

teleology privileging Western definitions is to situate all other non-Western forms in a static past to the West, moving in only a very small way along a continuum of sameness or difference to the ontological West, thus denying these non-Western sexual forms of more complex, alternative reckonings and agency. Second, taking for granted the hegemony of Western images of what it means to be gay is to banish to the periphery and marginalise the non-Western queer as the 'inauthentic', non-original 'Other' always in need of education to become fully assimilated and liberated (Grewal and Kaplan 2001).

Having identified this elementary theoretical problematic and excavated its deeper binaries and assumptions, I argue that studies attempting to counter the hegemony of the Western queer and its universalising assumptions must dismantle the teleological and cartographic frames that continue to condition how we think about global same-sex identities. In the absence of a theoretical framework countering these logics and their attendant binaries, counter conceptions of non-Western same-sex identities in global queer studies tend to leave the crux and core of a dominant Western queer model intact. To what extent have these logics fed into Asian queer scholarships and contributed to paradigmatic assumptions?

Searching for historical *tradition* and specific *local* cultural experience

Reflecting on his anthropological explorations of Indonesian same-sex identities, Boellstorff (2007b: 189) makes the observation that:

> The historical analysis of non-normative sexualities and genders in Southeast Asia has been dogged by the temptation to seek origins for these sexualities and genders in terms of 'tradition' or 'indigenous' culture.

Within the Asian queer literature, seeking for 'tradition' involves the search for historical forms of sexual and gender transgressors. To draw from an example cited earlier, the androgynous *bissu* and *bailan* female figures from sixteenth century Indonesia might, for instance, serve as symbols of the 'origin' and 'authenticity' of modernised non-normative sexual identities and practices in contemporary Indonesia. In excavating these evidences, however, Blackwood (2005: 850) makes the qualification that she was 'not tracing the "history" of transgendered females, nor ... suggesting the existence of a transgendered identity that transcends time and place, appearing in different guises'. Nevertheless, Blackwood (2005) found in her review of the literature that 'Western scholars' who initiated studies of non-Western sexualities starting from the 1990s:

> ... assumed that an underlying homosexual 'nature' connected these different practices across the centuries. Their assumption reflects a Western view of transvestism or transgenderism (called 'inversion' in nineteenth- and early twentieth-century Western science) as an outlet for homosexuality.
> (Blackwood 2005: 850)

Perhaps conditioned by a developmentalist logic and its tradition/modernity binary, these scholars first sought to understand non-Western sexualities based on an essential historical form. As Blackwood's (2005) account suggests, the scholars turned to 'tradition' to articulate the specificity of the non-Western sexual forms they discovered. Then they proceeded to replicate and apply a Eurocentric linear theory to construct and make sense of what they found in these non-Western field sites.

Perhaps conditioned also by the local/global dichotomy, scholar after scholar has ventured into various non-Western sites and returned with evidence of the local heteroglossia of homosexual subjectivities to counter the singular global gay. Referring to research on Asian sexualities, Jolly and Manderson (1995: 5) note that 'variation' became a 'chronic refrain' in the literature. Local knowledge is what is needed if we want to try to understand what is happening in areas different from, and outside of, the West. Thus, in Thailand, Morris (1994) and Jackson (1995, 1997a, 1997b), for instance, tried to prove that new forms of sexual identity in Thailand are based on pre-existing cultural patterns. The 2001 issue of the *Journal of Homosexuality*, as Wong (2007) observed, was an outgrowth of the initiative to return to the local. Drawing also from an example used earlier, the indigenised variation of the term 'lesbian', such as Thailand's *ying rak ying* or Indonesia's *tombois* and *lesbi*, even as these are Western-inflected, were deployed as useful places to establish the particularity of the local when it meets the global. Theorists thus often preface their deliberate use of these indigenised terms as a means of delineating the local subjects they study from Western global gay subjectivities. Many forms of local difference, as Weeks (2007: 219) observes, are 'helping to dissolve the idea of a single universal lesbian or gay identity'.

Jackson (2001: 10) also made the observation that scholars sometimes connect their discovery of local indigenous difference to a past, local history:

> ... when a gender/sex category in an Asian society happens to be labelled with an indigenous term, such as the *kathoey* in Thailand, then Western analysts are often prepared to grant that category a local history.

When this happens, the cartographic logic of specifying the 'local' experience of non-Western sexualities as a source of resistance and cultural identity to the universalising 'global' West, is combined with the teleological logic of the 'traditional' opposing a Western-influenced, commodified 'modern' queer identity sexuality. Indeed, excavating forms of local cultural difference and their pre-modern traditions as oppositional sites to Western queer culture has been the particular strategy of Asian global queer studies, undertaken – as Blackwood (2005) and Jackson (2001) have indicated – mainly by Western scholars.

Rather than offer these strategies as effective counter conceptions to disrupt and dissolve the idea and symbol of the universal global gay, I argue that the focus on the 'traditional' as a resistance to the inevitable 'modern', or the 'local' as an opposing site to the seeming homogenising force of the 'global', may not always be fruitful when the 'traditional' and the 'modern', the 'local' and the 'global' are placed within static teleological and cartographic logics as binary opposites rather than as processes and constructs that permeate and define one another. In all of these attempts to re-articulate Asian queer sexualities and decolonise global queerness, the Western queer's position at the top of the evolutionary pathway or as the origin of queer globalisation is reinforced. 'There is no reason', as Oswin states, 'to presume that flows from these models are anything but "downward" or "out there" in the West flowing to the non-West' (2006: 784). In short, such conceptualisations fail to interrogate the transcendence of the West and the law of origin.

Furthermore, the failure to interrogate these logics is made more problematic by the construction of Asian queer cultures as different and 'other' within the categories of knowledge of the West. This compulsion of 'othering' and 'otherness' from positions of power has long been problematised by Said's (1978) well-known Orientalism arguments.

What I have argued as a central conundrum in global queer studies is the question that Blackwood (2005) raised in her observation of Asian queer sexualities: how do researchers make sense of the complex relationship between cultural locatedness and global connectedness without re-creating the hierarchical dichotomies of traditional/modern and indigenous/international practices? Or, put another way, how to re-queer the global gay domain such that it no longer relies on these phantasmal fixings?

Crucially, for the purpose of this study, I argue that we can only properly capture and articulate the specificity of lesbian identities in Singapore outside of these static logics and binaries. For the Singaporean lesbian subject with faint historical blueprints, whose sexual subjectivity emerged out of an umbilical connection to the global system through Singapore's particular cultural location, who recognises herself as 'lesbian' or 'queer' unmitigated by an indigenous language, who, in other words, is the perfect mimicry of the Westernised sexual subject, can only be seen within developmentalist and cartographic logics as the ultimate sell-out: the one close to the pinnacle or the one mimicking the Western-inflected centre. What then of the specificity of the Singapore sexual subject who, as I argued earlier, has been missing – not coincidentally – in the queer Asia critique? Predictably, if lesbian subjectivities in Singapore were to be comprehended through the simplistic invocations of 'sameness versus difference', she would be seen as 'just like' the transcendental global gay subject, a thoroughly globalised or McDonaldised version alienated from her indigenous region.

We cannot speak for very long, or with any exactness, or even at all, about an 'indigenous' Singaporean lesbian experience, identity or history without acknowledging the global disjunctiveness of their same-sex identifications, which constitute the 'uniqueness' of a Singaporean cultural location. It is opportune, after examining the global queer literature, to return to the central research question of this book: how do we recuperate the specificity or 'uniqueness' of 'modern', non-Western queer identities such as the Singaporean lesbian subject who mimics the global gay immaculately? I develop my answer to this via a postcolonial perspective.

SECTION TWO

Towards a postcolonial LGQ studies

The term 'postcolonial' entered the academic lexicon of literary and cultural studies from the early 1980s, and quickly gained wide currency and circulation within the social sciences in fields as diverse as subaltern studies, women's studies, cultural studies and lesbian and gay studies. Given the scope of its usage and the range of intellectual positions associated with the 'postcolonial', its conceptual employment in any one domain must necessarily be explained. However, any attempt to define a term with as much breadth as the 'postcolonial' will also necessarily fall short, and this one is no exception. As Dirlik (1994: 332) observes, 'even at its most concrete, the significance of *postcolonial* is not transparent because each of its meanings is overdetermined by others'. For its deployment in queer globalisation centred on this case study of Singapore, I unpack 'postcolonialism' into what I identify as its three relevant dimensions – political, historical and theoretical – and apply these to a re-conceptualisation of global gay relations.

First, 'postcoloniality' can be used to denote an oppositional political praxis, what Homi Bhabha (1994: 277) calls a 'contesting, antagonistic agency', deployed to repudiate Eurocentric master discourses within sexuality studies and the assumptions of what constitutes activism, social movements, visibility and identity in non-Western contexts. Taking Gandhi's (1989: 12) assertion that the 'postcolonial' can be seen as 'a theoretical resistance to the mystifying amnesia of the colonial aftermath', this work follows the insistence of postcolonial theorists who, in the likes of Homi Bhabha, Partha Chatterjee and Stuart Hall, maintain that questions of agency, identity, belonging and citizenship in contemporary non-metropolitan worlds cannot be analysed when abstracted from the forces of globalisation and neo-colonialism. Chatterjee's (1986) critique of the originality of nationalisms in Anderson's (1983) 'imagined communities' is a classic illustration of the kinds of questions postcolonialism asks of identity politics and difference:

> If nationalisms in the rest of the world have to choose their imagined community from certain 'modular' forms already made available to them by Europe and Americas, what do they have left to imagine? History, it would seem, has decreed that we in the postcolonial world shall only be perpetual consumers of modernity. Europe and the Americas, the only true subjects of history, have thought out on our behalf ... Even our imaginations must remain forever colonised.
> (Anderson 1983)

For Chatterjee (1993: 5), however, the most creative expressions of nationalisms are those that establish 'a difference with the "modular" forms ... propagated by the modern West'. This politics of difference shares with what During (2000: 387) distinguishes as 'critical postcolonialism', which is an antagonistic and anti-colonialist category calling not just for a 'revaluation of colonised peoples' agency' but also for 'the clearing of pedagogic and research space for non-Eurocentric ways and peoples' (During 2000: 386). Postcolonialism insists on the premise that any analysis must come to terms with the legacy of Western scholarship on its objects of study.

Transposing this to the field of non-normative sexualities, postcolonial theory directly applies itself as a critical, oppositional subjectivity within the global gay discourse addressing the question of not just 'who counts as gay?' but also, as Spurlin (2001: 200) suggests, 'global according to whom?' The latter questions the Eurocentric assumptions of Western academic knowledge production implicated in questions of colonialism. Although postcolonialism can never be exhaustively accounted for, grasping the intricacies of its theoretical apparatus supplies a compelling basis for an oppositional politics in the global queer domain. This is the intellectual endeavour of the study: in tracking and underscoring the specificities of postcolonial theory's oppositional subjectivity and politics of difference, I hope to provide a way out of the limiting assumptions and logics entrenched in the early global queer scholarship and re-think the asymmetric relations between the Western and non-Western queer.

Second, postcoloniality is applied in this study as a particular historicity, heeding Loomba's (1998: 19) caution that 'if it is uprooted from specific locations, "postcoloniality" cannot be meaningfully investigated, and instead, the term begins to obscure the very relations of domination that it seeks to uncover'. The term is therefore used in this second application as an exploration and description of the historical conditions in formerly colonised societies. It is connotative of the emergence of an independent nation-state after the end of colonisation, with effects that continue through from the past into the present.

The historical dimension of the postcolonial is applied in this study through a focus on Singapore's pronounced postcolonial context. A subsequent chapter does the critical job of explaining the actual historical and material conditions of postcolonial Singapore in relation to neoliberal globalisation and domination by global capitalism, to make the case that a society caught between postcoloniality and global forces produces distinct sexual identities and practices. Maintaining this view of the actual postcolonial site puts in focus the way cultural struggles over the ascendency and authenticity of sexual meanings and values are caught up and contested simultaneously in multiple symbolic systems – between colonial legacies, postcolonial nationalisms, state ideologies and global hegemonies. At the same time, sexual identities, meanings and experiences are also caught in, and refracted through, the material conditions of the postcolonial nation-state, shaped as they are by the distribution of wealth and power in a Gramscian sense. Therefore, the application of this second dimension historicises our understanding of sexual identities and practices in a specific political and socioeconomic milieu, and locates them in webs of knowledge and power. This extends the postcolonial model of cultural difference to consider material questions of institutions, history, contact, change and power relations.

Third, as a response to the dichotomous theoretical models so pervasive in the early global queer literature, the explicit refutation of binaries in postcolonial theory holds particular application and heuristic value for global queer studies. Hall's (1995: 247) interpretation of postcoloniality directly problematises those dichotomies inherent in the cartographic and developmentalist logics identified earlier, which as we saw, continue to be taken for granted in analyses of globalisation processes in the global gay domain. Hall writes of the 'postcolonial' as 'not merely descriptive of "this" society rather than "that", or "then" rather than "now",' but instead reads colonisation as part of a 'transnational and transcultural "global" process (that) produces a decentred, diasporic or "global" rewriting of earlier, nation-centred imperial grand narratives'. The 'theoretical value' of the concept is in its refusal of the binaries of '"here" and "there", "then" and "now", "home" and "abroad" perspective'.

Instead of divides and dichotomies in the postcolonial world, it is the continuities of the past and the present and the intersections of the local and the global that define the axes for exploring the negotiation of same-sex identities. In its refusal of strict schisms, the postcolonial perspective can be broadly applied to move conceptions of non-Western lesbian and gay subjectivities away from restrictive categories. Thus, I apply these facets of postcolonial theory as a broad starting point to deconstruct the persistent gridlocks arising from the dichotomous temporal and spatial logics that, as we saw earlier, structure theorisations of global gay identities. My theoretical approach is, of course, also impelled by a search for a way of talking and thinking about the 'modern' globalised sexual subjectivities of lesbians in Singapore with neither deep nor detailed historical and cultural blueprints. Boellstorff (2005: 28) observes that:

> ... the possibility of a nonthreatening and non-antagonistic relationship to processes of cultural globalisation is almost completely absent in the literature on globalisation and non-normative sexualities and genders outside the West.

Singaporean lesbians, by their apparent mimicry of Western global forms, have been written out of antagonistic accounts based on past versus present and notions of local versus the global. By overcoming the theoretical reductionisms and schematic divides that have the effect of excluding them, postcoloniality offers a re-conceptualisation of Singaporean lesbian identities and practices. It is also in this sense that postcoloniality is a reconciliatory, rather than just a critical, anti-colonialist category (During 2000). In the more obtuse language of Bhabha (1994: 140), reconciliatory postcolonialism is:

> More *around* temporality than *about* historicity: a form of living that is more complex than 'community' more symbolic than 'society'; more connotative than 'country'; less patriotic than *patrie*; more rhetorical than the reason of State; more mythological than ideology; less homogeneous than hegemony; less centred than the citizen; more collective than 'the subject'; more psychic than civility; more hybrid in the articulation of cultural differences and identifications than can be represented in any hierarchical or binary structuring of social antagonism.

Although it is in such theoretically complex language of resisting binarism, hierarchy or telos that postcolonialism is often fused with poststructuralism, it must be reiterated that the 'postcolonial' deployed in this book is used in an historicised sense, where specific historical and political economic forces shape the postcolonial milieu. In this context, postcolonialism is not about poststructuralist notions of a 'free-floating' signifier but an historical material approach which places sexuality in a framework emphasising both symbolic meanings and structural transformations such as state and capital formation. It is the latter that delineates postcolonialism from the theoretical radicalism of poststructuralism even as it shares with it a theoretical predisposition.

Returning to Bhabha's (1994: 140) quote on reconciliatory postcolonialism, the point I want to make is that postcolonialism aims to dissolve the schematic divisions inherent in 'hierarchical and binary structuring'. Indeed, as selected quotes from Hall (1995) and Bhabha (1994) have intimated here, dichotomous thinking has been postcolonial theory's particular target. Therefore, it presents itself as a useful approach to address the teleological and cartographic assumptions and binaries underpinning conceptualisations of contemporary global gay identities to ask how one becomes 'a legitimate citizen of the present' During's (2000: 388).

The investigation of my research question takes place within the broad postcolonial frame set up above with its three – political, historical and theoretical – dimensions. To summarise the operationalisation of these three aspects of the postcolonial in my work, first, the political dimension connotes the 'anticolonialist' and oppositional subjectivity this book takes towards the universalising assumption of the dominant Western queer; second, the historical dimension plays out the condition of Singapore's postcolonial historicity and its impact on Singaporean same-sex identities; and third, its theoretical position usefully targets the static logics that have been locked in global queer studies and, in my opinion, provides a better lens through which the specificity of Singaporean sexual subjectivities can be grasped.

In what follows, I revisit two specific conceptual processes drawn from and linked to postcolonial theory, that of, 'hybridisation' and 'transnationality'. These theoretical tools, as I shall show, attend to linear developmentalist conceptions where the West is seen as the pinnacle, and unilinear flows presumed in cartographic conceptions where the West is seen as the origin. I combine both theoretical processes in a re-formulated framework to re-orient and remedy the dichotomous and limiting logics of existing analyses, thereby enabling a more productive reading of the globalisation of same-sex identities, including that of Singaporean lesbian identities.

The postcolonial orientation of queer Asian scholarships

Before moving on to the conceptual processes of 'hybridisation' and 'transnational' sexualities, I wish to briefly acknowledge at the outset that these concepts have been advanced in the queer Asia critique: a number of queer regional scholarships have demonstrated the postcolonial turn through theorisations of 'hybridised' and 'transnational' sexualities.

The turn to postcolonialism in lesbian and gay scholarship began slowly. In 1993, Weston (1993: 344) made the observation that:

> ... in the international arena, the 'salvage anthropology' of indigenous homosexualities remains largely insulated from important new theoretical work on postcolonial relations.

Half a decade later, Boellstorff (1999: 344) confirmed Weston's view to be 'distressingly valid'. However, since the turn of the twenty-first century, a growing number of studies on queer sexualities in Asia have employed notions of 'queer hybridity', 'hybridic sexualities' and 'hybridised gay identities' (Jackson 2001; Sinnott 2004; Martin *et al.* 2008; Plummer 2010; Kong 2010), as well as advanced the postcolonial-allied concept of 'transnational' sexualities (Bacchetta 2002; Blackwood 2005; Wilson 2006) to re-imagine global gay relations. Adopting the theoretical tools of the postcolonial, several studies have emerged in the various postcolonial contexts of Indonesia, India, Thailand and Hong Kong and elsewhere in the region.

My work draws on the broad postcolonial drift of these second generation global queer scholarships, which are more nuanced accounts of Asian sexual cultures and more attuned to the inequities of global gay relations compared to first generation global queer studies conceived by Altman (1989, 1996a, 1996b, 1997) and Plummer (1992). However, while queer Asian sexualities have been increasingly conceptualised as 'hybrid' and 'transnational', I contend that there is a need to re-theorise these concepts as contemporary applications since discussion of these theories has not been comprehensive, resulting in misapplications and misconceptions with a few significant exceptions (Martin 1996; Sinnott 2004; Boellstorff 2005; Garcia 2008; Blackwood 2010). This is evident, for instance, in scholarly works interpreting these theorisations as limited, static processes involving mere cultural 'meldings' and 'merging' of Western and non-Western homosexual identities (Oswin 2006: 782). While Oswin correctly reads the hybridisation processes as producing new identities – 'read not as Western or non-Western but as both and neither simultaneously' – her conclusion that 'merging rather than trumping takes place' (Oswin 2006: 782) misses important ways in which hybridisation processes 'fundamentally' interrogate the Western core. Similarly, having reviewed the literature on the globalisation of gay identities with particular reference to hybridisation, Corboz (2009: 3) asked, 'how can one explore the globalisation of sexual identities and culture without reproducing various pervasive binaries such as global versus local, modernity versus tradition?' This is puzzling because postcolonial theorisation offers just this very re-conceptualisation of fixed binaries.

The conceptual processes of 'hybridisation' and 'transnationality', as I shall show, dismantle these binaries. For Corboz (2009: 3) to pose this as a 'central question' despite her examination of the hybridisation and transnational literature on sexual identities, suggests these theories have not been adequately explained and deserve further academic attention. Inadequate elaborations and the failure to grasp these conceptual processes result in static conceptions not unlike the developmentalist and cartographic logics identified in the first generation scholarship. I argue that 'hybridic' and 'transnational' sexualities, when developed further and considered together, comprehensively address the temporal and spatial binaries that condition the existing scholarship on global queerness.

Therefore, while an identifiable body of 'postcolonial' scholarship has appeared within the Asian queer critique over the last decade, I return to Boellstorff's (1999) conclusion and take as a starting point that:

... the spectre of LGQ identities as either homogenised or fractured beyond recuperation by the forces of globalisation must give way to a more *nuanced postcolonial and translocal perspective, informed by a rubric of postcolonial LGQ studies.*

(Boellstorff 1999: 499, italics mine)

This book is an attempt to provide a more nuanced account of postcolonialism in the study of non-normative sexualities. In what follows, I delve into the processes of 'hybridisation' and 'transnational' sexuality to refresh and update the ways in which these concepts may be applied and understood within the queer Asia literature.

Re-theorising hybridisation

In 'Signs Taken for Wonders', a chapter from *The Location of Culture* (1994), Bhabha begins with this anecdote. An Indian evangelist finds a group of native men seated under the shade of trees reading translated versions of the Bible. The men think the book is a divine gift sent directly from God through an angel from heaven. The Indian evangelical, himself a convert and thoroughly co-opted, tries to convince the men that it is an English founding text originating from the divine-colonial authority of the European Sahibs. His efforts to convert the native men to Christian orthodoxy were, however, met with great resistance by the people who understand that the book is God's direct gift to them. The people say they may accept baptism one day but will not take the Sacrament as they do not eat meat. It is who they are. They will only accept the book as an authority that is mediated by their own values.

This is the moment the document is transformed and a crucial insight offered to the hybrid object: the Bible is not merely being adapted to local beliefs and context. According to Bhabha's theorisation, hybrid meanings are produced from this encounter, which transforms and disrupts the coherence of the Bible. This process of hybridisation, as Bhabha (1994: 115) states:

> ... retains the actual semblance of the authoritative symbol but revalues its presence by resisting it as the signifier of disfiguration after the intervention of difference.

While power asymmetry exists at the point of encounter – evident in how the colonial authority intervenes and repeats itself as different from the culture it seeks to subjugate – the authoritative symbol is revalued during the encounter. Furthermore, colonial power is, in effect, produced only belatedly and repeatedly in the battle for the status of the 'truth' of the hybrid object. Bhabha (1994: 108) states:

> Such an image can neither be 'original' – by virtue of the act of repetition that constructs it – nor 'identical' – by virtue of the difference that defines

it. Consequently, the colonial presence is always ambivalent, split between its appearance as original and authoritative and its articulation as repetition and difference.

Each repetition of the coloniser's differential and discriminatory discourse undermines the very claims of this discourse to a natural and singular originality. Power is diluted, compromised and hybridised at every turn – split between the coloniser and the colonised. Therefore, in Bhabha's conceptualisation, hybridisation leads us to 'the ambivalence of the presence of authority' (1994: 110).

Bhabha's theory on the ambivalence of authority, and the contingent relations and relentless negotiation between the coloniser and the colonised, offers a crucial rethinking of the relations between the Western and non-Western queer. All colonising discourses and universalising impositions in the global gay domain, in this conceptualisation, are hybridised forms, re-signified by the effects of those who receive them. In each asymmetric encounter between the Western and non-Western queer, the moment the power-laden authority makes a claim for a universal global gayness is also the moment that the singularity of the global gay is undermined.

Crucial to this point is that hybridisation is not a matter of adaptation: it goes beyond the simple melding of two distinct cultures and cultural practices to produce something different and unique. Rather, in the interaction between two cultures, hybridisation is 'the Third space of enunciation' that emerges in the contact zone, rendering the 'structure of meaning and reference an ambivalent process' and destroying the dichotomous 'mirror of representation' of self and other, modernity and tradition (Bhabha 1994: 37). It is a process that disaggregates the cultural systems of the coloniser and the colonised hitherto propped by all the binaries of 'self and other', 'modernity and tradition'. In this conception, both cultural systems are viewed as porous and permeable rather than as the binary and bounded categories of 'Western' and 'non-Western', 'modern' and 'traditional'. These begin to break down and trouble claims to utopian teleology and cultural purity as hybrid practices are reconfigured with meanings that are partially familiar, partially strange and in different proportions in both cultural systems (see Figure 2.2 for an elementary illustration of hybridisation processes).

Certainly, hybridisation points to a mutually constitutive form. In Bhabha's terms, the colonial identity can only exist in relation to the coloniser's, which it maintains and is maintained by. The process of hybridisation taps productively into the rich vein of interstitiality and interaction in the borderlands between the coloniser and the colonised. These borderlands are a place of incommensurable contradictions, an interstitial zone of displacement and deterritorialisation that shapes the identity of the hybridised subject (Gupta and Ferguson 1992).

It is within these borderlands, what Bhabha (1994: 28) terms the 'Third Space' in which 'something else besides' that 'contests the terms and territories of both modernity and tradition' and transpires as 'the transformational value of change', that I wish to locate Singaporean lesbian subjects, who, I argue, have hitherto been seen as a mimicry of the colonising Western queer and therefore mundane in the eyes of Western scholars studying Asian queer cultures.

However, in Bhabha's explication of the discourse of colonial mimicry, it is precisely this mimicry that makes Singaporean sexual identities and practices a form of menace to the coloniser, one that ultimately reveals the tensions inherent in imperialist conceptions of queer identities. This desire to see in Singapore a set of sexual identities and practices as familiar within the categories of knowledge of the West might be described by Bhabha (1994: 86) as 'the desire for a reformed, recognisable Other, as a subject of difference that is almost the same, but not quite'. This desire constitutes an attempt by the colonising power to discipline and declare victory over the 'other' place, but it is Bhabha's point that colonial mimicry inevitably highlights the relationship of coloniser to colonised, showing the limits of the colonisers' discourse when faced with its 'Other'. When read this way, same-sex subjectivities in Singapore turn quickly from mundane to menace and therefore meaningful in countering the imperialist queer.

It is my argument that the sexual identities and practices of lesbians in Singapore, and in other non-Western contexts for that matter, can be more productively understood within Bhabha's (1994) theorisation of hybridisation as:

> ... the effect of *an ambivalence produced within the rules of recognition of dominating discourses* as they articulate the signs of culture difference and *re-implicate* them within the deferential relations of colonial power – hierarchy, normalisation, marginalisation, and so forth.
>
> (Bhabha 1994: 33, italics mine)

Postcolonial hybridisation enables a study of 'modern' lesbians in Singapore to be 'more than the mimetic but less than the symbolic that disturbs the visibility of the colonial presence and makes the recognition of its authority problematic' (Bhabha 1994: 34). Through an understanding of same-sex identities and practices in Singapore as processes of hybridisation, I seek to – borrowing Chakrabarty's (2000) term – provincialise Western conceptions of what it means to be gay in the global sphere. Clarifying the conceptual term is an attempt to rethink and re-evaluate the teleological privileging of the supposedly 'modern' Western queer constructed within the static logics of earlier scholarships. My argument is that a more nuanced understanding of postcolonial hybridisation rectifies existing Eurocentric constructions that place the non-Western queer in an unproductive linear teleological pathway with the hegemonic Western model as the terminus towards which it must follow.

The process of hybridisation keeps in view instead the dialectical and productive ways in which global gay identities intersect and relate under conditions of globalisation, and in so doing, a richer picture of the complexities and historical processes that constitute global relations emerges. Re-configuring global gay relations in this way makes way for a levelling of power dynamics (see Figure 2.2

for an elementary framework). My analysis will show that lesbian identities in Singapore are more than mere adaptations or derivations of Western identity. Instead, as my data demonstrates in later chapters, the emergence and realisation of queer life in Singapore is also produced through the postcolonial history and politics of the nation, and these understandings intermingle with global queer discourses producing hybrid meanings that transform what it means to be a 'modern' sexual citizen.

Turning to 'transnationality'

Just as 'hybridisation' re-orients a teleological conception of global gay identities, 'transnationality' addresses the local and global binaries in cartographic conceptions of same-sex sexualities. Reifying the local against the global in our search for differences, as Oswin (2006: 788) argued, is to 'trap the non-Western queer in a category read as distinctly separate from an equally definable West and as only and always local'. The transnational approach overcomes this theoretical stasis.

It might be useful to begin by following the group of feminist scholars, who, as Kearney (1995: 560) observes, engaged in 'perhaps the most creative analysis of local politics and identities in transnational contexts'. Grewal and Kaplan (1994) conceptualised the term 'transnational' to move beyond the simplistic dichotomy of the local/global, and the 'transnational' has gained contemporary currency within feminist studies of sexual identities as it attends to the inequities of globalisation. This work is partly catalysed by the 'transnational turn' (Povinelli and Chauncey 1999: 439) within feminist sexuality scholarship, particularly that shift in the usage of terms from 'global' to 'transnational' to assuage the asymmetric flow of sexual meanings presumed in the globalisation process (Grewal and Kaplan 1994). The transnational, as opposed to globalisation, disrupts unilinear flows in such a way that 'the "global" and the "local" thoroughly infiltrate each other' (Blackwood 2005: 221, see Figure 2.2 for an illustration). Such a formulation cross-cuts the problematic cartographic logic and binaries of West and non-West, including all the fixities of modernity and tradition, liberation and oppression that persistently mark the global-local divide (Kim-Puri 2005). When these interplays and movements are traced in conjunction with historical processes and relations, the 'transnational' could signal 'cultural and national difference' (Grewal and Kaplan 2001: 666) not just as forms of resistance but as sites from where distinct new sexual subjects and sites of power are produced.

Two points on the 'transnational' are pertinent to this book. First, akin to postcolonial theorisations of 'hybridity', 'transnational' sexualities within feminist sexuality scholarship point to the complexity, creativity, conflict and collusion of cultural productions in the interactions of the 'local' and the 'global'. In this approach, the West is not taken as a superior cultural system that forces the non-West to change local practices in form and meaning. Rather, the a priori existence of both cultural systems is not assumed, allowing for an appreciation of contextual specificities that goes beyond futile arguments of 'them' and 'us'.

Second, the 'local' and the 'global' within the transnational frame are 'both acts of positioning, perspectives rather than mere locales' (Rofel 2007: 456). Transnational sexualities in that interlocking and interactive transnational space, such as the one occupied by lesbian sexual subjectivities in Singapore, become 'signifiers of difference' (Rofel 2007: 456) disrupting the symbol of the hegemonic global gay. Transnationality therefore moves us beyond invocations of culture and society as bounded spaces marking territoriality. Instead, the concept of culture is reconfigured as an ongoing discursive practice and an imagined invocation given meaning through specific signifying practices, including those constructed by the nation state.

In this study, the complexity of transnational circuits of meaning is comprehended through the empirical narratives of lesbians in Singapore. The theorisation of 'transnationality' in this work therefore relies on a critical empiricism that restores the subject within transnational studies, providing a corrective to a field that tends to:

> ... read social life off external social forms – flows, circuits, circulations of people, capital, and culture – without any model of subjective mediation, when, it is the travail of the subject, fashioned far afield of herself, that globalisation has yet to track.
>
> (Povinelli and Chauncey 1999: 445)

Implicit in this transnational analysis of sexualities is therefore the materiality of lesbian lives, shaped as they are by class location, the political economy and structures of power. Theorising these differences adds a material dimension to the transnational frame, addressing one of its most persistent criticisms: that the cultural is often privileged over the material in transnational cultural studies (Kim-Puri 2005: 143) as if social life is produced through cultural representations and discourses without regard for how material conditions shape the reception of these cultural meanings. This is to say, comprehending sexual specificities in a global frame entails examining how these sexualities articulate with both discursive and material productions of that particular site. By turning to the empirical realities of lesbians in Singapore, this work reveals how subjects make sense of their sexual practices and identities through both cultural logics as well as material embodiments that mediate their sexual subjectivities. The intersections of the cultural and material dimensions produce contingent forms of a 'reverse discourse' evident in the women's reconfiguration of the everyday, which the empirical data addresses.

In order to understand the production of local lesbian subjectivities, the historical specificity of Singapore and the postcolonial state is incorporated as both a material and ideological structure in the creation of lesbian subjectivities. The postcolonial state, as a number of scholars note (Blackwood 2002; Boellstorff 2007a; Grewal and Kaplan 2001), has been overlooked within a simplifying transnational equation linking the formation of non-normative sexual identities to global and cultural flows. However, Grewal and Kaplan (2001: 672) point out:

What we are really grappling with here is not just representation; it is also the emergence of new forms of governmentality with an entire repertoire of strategies, regulatory practices, and instrumentalities linking the state to bodies.

Postcolonial contexts for sexual subjects, as Boellstorff (2007a: 22) also notes, are often national in character, and such a conception gives way to an understanding of how:

> ... most nation-states make underwriting normative heterosexuality central to their practices of governance and ideologies of belonging and how in the process they inadvertently help people conjure 'alternative' sexualities and desires.

In analysing 'sexual tensions' in contemporary Singapore, Oswin (2010: 130) called for a shift in analytic attention to postcolonial governors who are 'key actors in the regulation of sexuality in the era of independence'. This book takes up Oswin's (2010: 131) argument that the postcolonial elites have been complicit in extending the colonial regulation of sexuality to 'civilise the rest of the colonised community'. This renders Singapore a case for a 'more complicated model of transnational relations in which power structures, asymmetries and inequalities become the conditions of possibility of new subjects' (Grewal and Kaplan 2001: 671). Bringing the postcolony and a critical empiricism to bear on transnational sexualities enables a re-imagination of an historicised, contextualised transversality in which the material and cultural dimensions are conjoined to shape unique sexual subjectivities.

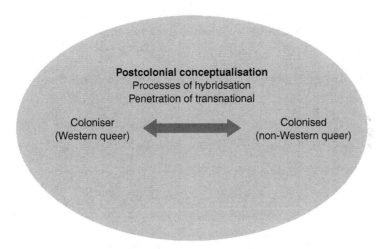

Figure 2.2 A re-theorisation of global gay relations.

Coda

I began this chapter with a review of the global gay literature, highlighting in particular the dichotomous logics that pervade scholarly discussions on global gay relations. The key objection within this debate was the assumption of a hegemonic Western queer construction symbolising the 'modern', global gay identity. In response, scholars – particularly those studying Asian queer cultures – sought various ways to address the specificity of non-Western queer identities. However, early scholarships tended to offer conceptualisations along a linear teleological logic or a cartographic conception that continue to bind the non-Western queer within dichotomous understandings privileging the Western-inflected global gay.

A later scholarship adopting postcolonial orientations began challenging these binary conceptions. However, while the concepts of 'hybrid' and 'transnational' sexualities have appeared in analyses of Asian same-sex identities and sexual cultures, they have not been comprehensively advanced. What this chapter has done is to make postcolonial theorisations of 'hybridisation' and 'transnational' approaches more explicit in their theoretical application and political orientation, and combine them into a single framework as they each address and re-orient the inherent developmentalist and cartographic understandings in the scholarship. Augmenting this framework, I have also argued for a material dimension situating these cultural processes as a set of contested practices within an historical context.

Thus, I offered in this chapter a central theoretical framework for understanding the globalised sexual subjectivities of lesbians in Singapore. These theorisations of hybridisation and transnational sexualities help to explain the confluence of conflicting and complicit Singaporean lesbian identities that can shape the meanings and lived experiences of what it means to be gay in different and unexpected ways. At the same time, the specific forms of lesbian subjectivities in Singapore provide a rich field site for the illustration and elaboration of hybridising, transnational sexualities that re-queer the global gay domain, making the case that it has been remiss of the Asian queer scholarship to leave out Singapore in its analyses. On these bases, I argue that one more meaningful contribution – the empirical case of 'modern' lesbian sexualities in postcolonial Singapore – can be made to an already well-established debate around the globalisation of queer sexualities.

Notes

1 See for example the scholarship of Jeffrey Weeks (1977), Lilian Faderman (1981), Jonathan Katz (1983), and Carroll Smith-Rosenberg (1985). In Foucault's social constructionist tradition, these theorists claim that the late twentieth-century Western concept of the homosexual is an historically specific sociocultural configuration.

3 Postcolonial Singapore
State, nationalism and sexuality

In the last chapter, I argued for a postcolonial perspective to reconceptualise global gay identities and proposed that three dimensions of the 'postcolonial' be applied. One, as an oppositional political praxis critical of Eurocentric master discourses on non-Western sexual identities; two as an historical specificity where the conditions of postcolonialism, including the forces of the political economy, the dynamics of globalisation and postcolonial nationalisms faced by the new postcolony intersect to shape sexual meanings; and three, as a theoretical intervention into the scholarship on global gay identities, which is persistently structured by binaries rendering non-Western sexual identities and practices as derivatives of an 'original' Western model, unrecognised as distinct or 'authentic' in their own forms. The first and third dimensions, namely the political and theoretical implications of the 'postcolonial', have been addressed and illustrated previously. Here, I wish to focus on the second dimension, that of the historical specificity of postcolonial Singapore, particularly its emergence as an independent nation-state after the end of British colonialism.

The centrepiece of this chapter is therefore the outline of the character and trajectory of the postcolonial developmental state in Singapore. I discuss the material conditions as well as the ideological discursive context from which homosexual discourses and practices have emerged. Then I highlight how homosexuality has been directly targeted by the postcolonial state through both legal means and the discursive practices of the postcolonial ruling elites. These repressive state measures produced forms of local resistance. The state's construction and control of non-normative sexualities and the resistance engendered by its repression of alternative sexualities brings to the forefront questions about the relationship between sexuality and nationalism. Before turning to Singapore's case of postcolonial statehood then, I want to address at the start of this chapter the intimacies between sexuality, state and nationalism, and the interrelation of these categories in a complex postcolonial context. These theorisations also provide the conceptual contextualisation for discussions in the next chapter such that, when taken together, the two chapters establish a more nuanced postcolonial context so that we can better understand the case of Singapore.

Sexuality, state and nationalism in a postcolonial world

'Sexuality' existed as an autonomous field of academic inquiry with scarcely any interaction with the study of 'state' and 'nationalism' until the mid-1980s, when scholars began to pay attention to the critical role of sexuality in the creation and maintenance of nationalisms and nation-states. If the making of national cultures involves a process of naturalisation by which the nation is imagined as natural, fixed and taken-for-granted by its inhabitants (Anderson 1983; Foster 1991; Chatterjee 1993), surely then, scholars say, the naturalness of particular sexualities becomes an easy target through which homogeneous and bounded national communities can be imagined. Many scholars therefore sought to understand how nationalist constructs are naturalised around certain ideas of sexuality. A long genealogy of scholarship, as Foster (1991) and Dwyer (2000) note, focused on the hegemonic power of the state and its national elites in privileging 'respectable' forms of sexuality and repressing 'abnormal' forms (Mosse 1985), in distinguishing 'proper' male homosociality and suppressing sexualised male-to-male relations (Parker *et al.* 1992), in idealising manly virility and female virtuosity (Foster 1991), in confining female virtue to an 'inner domain' (Chatterjee 1993), and, more broadly, in producing a shared national narrative that mutes sexual difference and masks inherent sexual violence (Enloe 1989; Bhattacharjee 1992). Sexuality is in these ways an important frame through which the naturalisation of nation-states can be understood. These accounts stress the instrumentality of sexuality and gender in the state's nationalist project. They probe how sexualities and genders are variously permitted and prohibited, incited and crushed, included and excluded, repressed and regulated in the production of the 'national culture' of nation-states, seen as the natural container of a homogeneous culture and society (Gupta and Ferguson 1992). Indeed, a growing academic corpus speaks compellingly to the imbrications of sexualities and nationalisms (Parker *et al.* 1992; Berlant and Freeman 1993; Stoler 1995; Gopinath 1997; Finlayson 1998; Puri 1999, 2004 among others). What figures prominently in this interrelationship is the central role of the state, the 'material/discursive site' (Puri 2008: 21) through which developmental programmes, policies, laws, narratives and ideologies directly and indirectly produce sexuality and gender.

Within the corpus of queer research, the state has also been moved to the forefront of analyses addressing questions of non-normative sexualities and nationalist identity politics in diverse contexts, including postcolonial sites in Asia (see for example Kinsman 1996; Aarmo 1999; Tan 1999; Puri 1999, 2004; Gopinath 2005, among others). Even in places, such as Indonesia, where the state neither regulates homosexuality through legal means nor represses it through official discourse, state power over sexual subjects is still seen as manifest through 'indirect percolations' of nationalist discourse (Boellstorff 2005: 189; Blackwood 2005). Drawing on Antonio Gramsci's (1971) theorisation of 'hegemony' and poststructuralist, particularly Foucault's (1982), insight on power and governmentality, critical queer theorists focus on the nationalist project of state-making, the policies and practices of the state in perpetuating and prescribing what is normal and natural, and how sexuality in this process is both actively and inadvertently given form and meaning by state developmental objectives and nationalist politics. Specifically, this scholarship highlights how normative heterosexuality is constructed in state practices of governance and ideologies of belonging, and how social reproductions predicated on 'compulsory heterosexuality' (Rich 1980) privilege normatively-gendered heterosexual women and men as bearers of respectable sexuality, and promulgate same-sex sexualities as threats to the social or symbolic reproduction of the nation. This scholarship forcefully theorises 'state' and 'nationalism' as agents acting upon sexuality and sexual identities.

The conceptual stance of this scholarship is relevant for Singapore, not least because there is direct and extensive state involvement in the texture of everyday Singaporean life. When it comes to sexuality, what is acceptable, what is desirable, what is respectable, under what circumstances, for which gender, for which race, at what ages, and how sexuality can be channelled towards socially-productive ends, are all key points of concern for the postcolonial state in Singapore, as Heng and Devan's (1992) compelling account on the state's intrusive efforts at fertility management illustrates. Also, unlike other Asian contexts, such as Indonesia, where homosexuality is not directly addressed but indirectly violated through a heteronormative mandate, (Boellstorff 2005: 189; Blackwood 2005), state-based discrimination and violence against homosexuality in Singapore is explicitly enshrined in the penal law and official discourse. Lesbians and gay men in Singapore are not only excluded from social policies unrelentingly predicated on heteronormativity, they are also the direct targets of negative state discourse, and, for gay men in particular, the direct objects of criminalisation under Section 377A of the Penal Code. It is through these exclusionary or violent practices that same-sex sexualities are transformed by the nationalist identity politics of the state and nationalism. Foregrounding the state and nationalism, with a focus on the sexual politics of control, repression and discrimination in postcolonial Singapore, is in this sense crucial to understanding the question of local non-normative sexualities. In particular, the globalised subjectivities of Singaporean lesbians must be understood in relation to the encompassing realities of Singapore's postcolonial context where powerful state and national elites have emerged within the political and moral economy of nation-building in Singapore to re-organise relations of sexuality.

Through tracing Singapore's postcolonial history and its particular modernity in this chapter, I bring the state and nationalism to the forefront of the analysis as a foil against which to consider the accounts of lesbian women in Singapore. In so doing, however, I wish also to caution against an analysis that unreflexively frames the state and nationalism as agents of sexual control or repression omitting further theorisations of 'state', 'nationalism' and 'sexuality', and the complex interplay between these categories (Carver and Mottier 1998; and Puri 2004), particularly in the contemporary postcolonial world (Dwyer 2000: 28).

Therefore, it is necessary to develop some aspects of the complex relationship between 'state', 'nationalism' and 'sexuality' so as to advance a more critical perspective of these categories and provide an understanding that goes beyond the assertion of the way hegemonic states and nationalisms interpellate individuals into normative discourses and shape sexualities in a one-way process.

Setting the conceptual context: 'state', 'nationalism' and 'sexuality'

Analyses of how hegemonic state power and dominant nationalism produce and shape sexual subjectivities need to be more nuanced for understanding the politics of sexual identity in postcolonial nations such as Singapore. By highlighting the hegemonic power of the state and nationalism to subordinate sexuality, critical scholars and activists draw attention to state-inflicted sexual violence, criticise state power, and hold national elites accountable for their role in privileging normative sexual patterns and penalising unapproved forms. Certainly, raising the issue of state-based discriminations against same-sex sexualities is a critical form of political intervention, which this work participates in and also seeks to further. However, in focusing on how state practices and nationalist ideologies regulate and repress homosexuality, we unwittingly reify 'state' and 'nationalism' as overarching, immutable agents acting upon sexuality, ironically imbuing these categories with further strength (Carver and Mottier 1998; Dwyer 2000; Puri 1999, 2008). This means that at the same time as we criticise state power, we reproduce it. Moreover, as Dwyer (2000: 28) warns, we 'run the risk of mistaking the desires of national elites for ethnographic actuality'.

What is necessary, then, is a 'disaggregation' of state and nationalism, and to view these categories as less coherent and unitary 'things' (Dwyer 2000; Fox 1990). Although few scholars would dispute the point that neither state nor nationalism are monolithic categories, as Puri (2008) points out, conceptually and empirically the state is often treated as an 'it'. A certain 'thingification', borrowing Césaire's (1972) term, occurs when state and nationalism are conceived as an aggregate of its apparatuses of control.

Problematising these categories through the framework of sexuality has found strong and vivid expression in feminist sexuality writing and queer theory calling for analyses to 'sexualise the state' (Puri 2008) or 'queer the state' (Duggan 1994). The former prompts sexuality scholars to lay bare the categories of 'state' and 'nationalism' and expose the complex and 'messy' sets of related structures, institutions, agencies and authorities with attention to the dissonance and fractures between these sites, rather than as monolithic agents acting singularly on sexuality. The latter argues for a perspective that exposes and dismantles deeply entrenched assumptions of heteronormativity promulgated by institutions of policy and planning, mass media, education, religion, and indeed by homosexuality itself. There is no ontology to heterosexuality, as queer theorists have long argued (Sedgwick 1990; Butler 1990; Fuss 1991). It is inherently unstable and always dependent on homosexuality acknowledged as a priori. It is always in the making by state bureaucracies and nationalist ideologies, determining and securing the nation's 'purity' and integrity in relation to, and contingent on, non-normative sexualities. 'Queering the state' is therefore to see the multiple and unstable ways in which state agents construct heteronormative orders beyond, but also always around, a sexual binary.

Insofar as state power rests on an imagined naturalisation, scholarly conceptualisations of the state hold political implications. Political intervention on our part therefore requires a conceptual and empirical demonstration of these sites as fraught and contested even, or perhaps especially, as we draw attention to the dominance and hegemony of state and nationalism as a form of critique.

Moving away from a view of state and nationalism as hegemonic agents of sexual control also makes way for the possibility that the encounter between state, nationalism and sexuality is a more complex one. State regulation and nationalist ideologies do not simply condition or impinge on citizens' sexualities in a unilinear fashion. Rather, attempts to define sexuality through nationalist discourse, legal censure, or public denunciation, insert into public culture and consciousness the full range of sexual differences and conjure up alternative sexualities and desires. Put simply, sexualities are conjured at the same time as they are contained. In this process, sexuality becomes not just a passive site of regulation but takes on an agency 'around which political debates or resistances cohere' in a dialogic manner (Dwyer 2000: 28). Indeed, state regulation and nationalist ideologies governing citizens' sexualities constitute a terrain for intense political struggle where competing agents simultaneously construct idealised images of sexual difference and press for differing political claims. This understanding draws partially from Foucault's (1978) espousal of sexuality as not just a target and locus of control, but the very site from which power unfolds and disperses in the form of a 'reverse discourse'.

Through examining two local events signifying the emerging sexual resistance in Singapore, and drawing attention to certain disjunctive ways in which the postcolonial national elites responded to these events, the subsequent chapter situates itself as a necessary counterbalance to this one where I trace, as a form of critique, the rise of the hegemonic postcolonial Singapore state. Building more critical approaches to state and nationalism upon feminist sexuality scholarship and queer theory, these two chapters underscore the state as both reproductive of domination at the same time as open to contestation in the sexual sphere. Maintaining a broad postcolonial perspective, I take these local acts of resistance not merely as reactionary to hegemonic state power and nationalism within a binary sexual framework polarising power against resistance. Rather, I see the power of state, nationalism and sexual resistance as hybridising forms, each producing, limiting, sustaining and suppressing each other dynamically through knowledge and practice. This postcolonial perspective further theorises the relationship between 'state', 'nationalism' and 'sexuality' as one of reciprocal incitation and struggle where none of these categories can be seen as either the source or subject of power in a Foucauldian sense.

These categories also need to be contextualised in the broader global context of postcolonial state-building where sexuality-related changes and national culture are not just the 'internal' domestic concerns of citizens, but also 'external' global indicators of the nation's modernity (see for example, Carrillo 2007). Postcolonial states are established and accommodated through adherence to international standards of citizenship, including sexual citizenship (Dwyer 2000). Therefore, it is crucial to view state-building and sexual contestations within a transnational frame, inflected by the nation-state's desire for recognition and membership in the global political economy. The nation's ideological positions on sexuality, as Carrillo (2007) argues, are symbolic of whether a country is modernising or not, and of its readiness for participating culturally, politically and economically in the world. These insights are exceedingly useful for interpreting 'modern' Singapore. For a nation-state with no natural resources of its own and entirely reliant on its participation in the world economy for the transaction of international labour and capital, embedding itself in global institutions and norms is unequivocally necessary for national survival, a perspective long held and frequently espoused by state authorities. This global level of influence is therefore crucial in the consideration of the local politics of sexuality and nation building in Singapore.

Furthermore, the state is not a monolithic actor entirely invested in shaping national identity and nationalism for it is increasingly constituted by a global class of elite 'transnational cultural producers and consumers who, as Breckenridge and Appadurai (1988: 3) point out:

> ... need new ideologies of state and nation to control and shape the population who live within their territories. But as these populations themselves are exposed, through media and travel, to the cultural regimes of other nation-states, such ideologies of nationalism increasingly take on a global flavour.

Disaggregating the state through this view of transcultural postcolonial elites makes the exchange between elites and masses, cultural 'producers' and consumers, ever more complex, suggesting that the capture of the dynamics between state and sexuality cannot be exhausted by describing the one-way regulatory effect of the state's discourse on sexuality and gender. How these categories are imagined, produced and represented is highly contested between the elites themselves, and by non-elites and sexual subjects who also draw from, and imagine themselves partially through, global cultural forms.

Taken together, the re-theorisations of 'state', 'sexuality' and the 'nation' within the broad framework of a postcolonial perspective allow us to better engage with the creation and contestation of nationalism and sexuality in Singapore. It is with these understandings in mind that I now turn to the historical analysis of the postcolonial state in Singapore, its nationalist and developmental projects, and its complex management and entanglement with sexual differences in Singapore.

Specifying Singapore's postcolonial historical context

Independent Singapore is the outcome of two political severances. The first one in 1959, when the British colonial office granted domestic self-governance to Singapore as part of its move to re-instate political autonomy in its Southeast Asian colonies, including Malaya. In Singapore, the newly-elected leadership, the People's Action Party (PAP) led by Cambridge-trained lawyer Lee Kuan Yew and his cadre of English-educated elites, were convinced that an independent small nation with no natural resources was a 'foolish and absurd proposition' (Lee Kuan Yew, quoted in Drysdale, 1984: 249). The PAP desired instead a merger with the Federation of Malaya, seeing in the Malay Peninsula an important economic hinterland for its own industrialisation program. Singapore, in the PAP's vision, was to be the 'New York of Malaysia, the industrial base of an affluent and just society' (Lee Kuan Yew, quoted in Turnbull, 1989: 278). Determined to swap sovereignty for economic viability, the PAP fought hard for Singapore's inclusion in the Federation of Malaya. This led to the formation of Malaysia in 1963, comprising of the Peninsula states, Singapore and the British Borneo territories of Sabah and Sarawak. This union was achieved through the support of the British colonial office, which made the inclusion of Singapore a precondition for Malaya's formation of the Federation fearing that Singapore would fall into communist hands. The British formally relinquished Singapore as a colony in 1963 when the Federation was formed. However, in just over two years, membership in the Federation proved to be politically unviable for Singapore due to ethnic friction. The state broke away from the Federation of Malaya, suffering its second political severance. Independence in 1965 was, for the PAP, an uncharted political reality.

For the postcolonial state, separation from Malaysia would result in substantial economic loss of a potential common market and its trade dependence on Malaysia.[1] Furthermore, the prospect of large-scale unemployment loomed with the withdrawal of the British military bases from its shores.[2] The failed merger also had political consequences, testing the PAP's already tenuous organic legitimacy with its citizenry. While traditional elites in postcolonial states could typically re-claim intrinsic links to the indigenous community in a way colonial powers could not, such claims made by the young British-educated PAP elites would not resonate with a population made up mainly of immigrants. Apart from the small indigenous Malay community, the growing Chinese population and a smaller minority of South Asians were the progeny of migrants who had come in search of economic opportunities when Singapore was established as a British trading post in the early nineteenth century.[3] The fledgling population was mainly economically motivated and still culturally oriented towards their respective homelands with a minimal sense of belonging to the nation. In other words, at the time of separation and independence, the founding elites had no indigenous cultural ties to resurrect or nationalistic loyalties to build on. What it had were diverse ethnic immigrants inhabiting disparate worlds. The anti-colonial Chinese had developed cultural links with left-wing unionists, which the PAP and colonial powers had colluded to crush through the 1963 merger, and the Malay community had acquired a sense of political significance in the larger union with Malaysia, only to be let down by the PAP's inability to maintain the merger. The separation was, for the PAP, both economically and politically traumatic. How was the new nation to integrate an imagined community given this fraught state of affairs?

It was in this historical context that the PAP began its invention of the Singaporean nation, inscribing an ideological leitmotif of 'national survival' and acquiring a deep developmental ethos in the process. The material question of survival, the PAP reasoned, could logically be resolved by rapid economic development. To this end, the postcolonial state pursued a relentless capitalist industrialisation program: courting Western capital to take a stake in the Singaporean economy, intervening directly in local industry and going to great lengths to ensure Singapore remained a conduit of global capital flows so it stayed plugged into the capitalist world economy. Labour relations were disciplined and citizens mobilised to create conditions favourable for foreign capital investment. The state rolled out a long litany of legislations, several of which were extended from the British colonial administration. These included the 1966 Trade Union Act, which made it illegal for trade unions to carry out strikes and industrial action without the consent of the majority of its members expressed through a secret ballot; the Internal Security Act, which conferred state powers the right to detain without trial anyone suspected of threatening national security for an indefinite period; the 1968 Employment Act, which extended the working hours of Singaporeans and reduced the number of public holidays, and annual and medical leave; and the 1966 Land Acquisition Act, which endowed the state with arbitrary powers to acquire land deemed necessary for economic development. In the name of securing economic growth, the state controlled and penetrated every segment of society. For Singaporeans, all aspects of social life became subject to the logic of the industrial economy: schools were nationalised and English formalised as a first language in order that Singaporeans be proficient in the language of trade and commerce; land dwellers were moved and local communities disaggregated to make way for the state's massive development of the city and public housing programme; racial tensions were tamed by police action and ethnic diversity flattened by meticulous social engineering; civil groups were politically curtailed[4] and population growth carefully managed. The Singaporean state grounded an imagination of a nation in a disciplined, mobile population all pulling in the same direction as state-led development towards the fulfilment of modernity's promise of progress and prosperity.

Over the span of five decades, the postcolonial state has successfully delivered a nation from 'third world to first', an achievement written in official history as 'The Singapore Story' of a 'small' nation 'overcoming the odds' to achieve massive economic and social transformations (Kuan Yew Lee 2007). The Singaporean state has demonstrated that an independent nation freed from Western imperialism can very well design its own modernisation without descending into the political or social chaos characteristic of other postcolonial societies. State provision of modern infrastructure, near-universal public housing, and quality education and healthcare has propelled Singapore quickly along the path of rapid development. The country is ranked internationally as one of the most advanced economies (International Monetary Fund 2009), attracting significant foreign investments in banking and technology. Well-placed in the league of developed capitalist nations, Singapore is highly regarded as a stable and reliable ally by first-world Western economies. The ambition is to 'benchmark ourselves against the best places in the world', said Goh Chok Tong (1998) and 'to make Singapore one of the top cities in the world not only to work in, but also to live and play in' (Goh 2000). 'Global city' became the buzzword for the new millennium. The vision included the greening of the city so it could be internationally known for both its economic success and its image as an environmentally-conscious garden city; the courting of foreign talent in the likes of professionals, entrepreneurs, professors and students; a flourishing arts and creative industry to appeal to the cosmopolitan set; the building of architecturally iconic skyscrapers and structures that catch international attention. Singapore's aspirations and accomplishments did not go unnoticed. To admirers in the West, and developing neighbours in the region, its rise has been observed as phenomenal, totally out of proportion to its physical size and the magnitude of its economy. To Singaporeans who enjoy material affluence, standards of living and literacy levels comparable to the most developed nations, the PAP became 'Singapore's best bet for the future' (Tan 2007a: 3), and it was in this way that the postcolonial state of a migrant port city with shallow historical memory culturally grafted itself onto the local community.

The PAP's hegemony has never been broken since independence in 1965. With consecutive leadership renewals from its first and longest serving Prime Minister, Lee Kuan Yew, to Goh Chok Tong in 1990, and then to Lee's son, Lee Hsien Loong in 2004, the PAP has singularly ruled Singapore, and is thus an ineluctable fact of Singapore's historical context. To the Western thesis that liberal democracy is the political inevitability of economic development (Lipset 1960; Huntington 1997 and Girling 1988), the postcolonial state offers itself unapologetically as a political anomaly. It applies only the most minimum set of democratic procedures; an electoral system of 'government by free choice of the people, by secret ballot, at periodic intervals' (Lee Kuan Yew quoted in Mauzy and Milne 2002: 129). The election process is itself limited. Campaigning time is kept to a minimum, new election boundaries are drawn late into the election cycle, and low participation from political opponents due to formidable obstacles put in place by the ruling party means the majority of electoral constituencies are uncontested, leading to PAP victories even before votes need to be counted. For almost two decades after independence, the PAP won every single seat in every election held, forming the sole political party in parliament. Only from 1981 onwards did opposition parties begin to secure a minority number of parliamentary seats. Over an unbroken reign, manifestations of state power have involved the detention of political opponents without trial, and the suppression of free speech, public assembly and political dissent through liberal uses of defamation suits. These tactics impoverished the opposition. Provoked by these illiberal practices, critics have variously called the Singaporean state 'authoritarian' (Mauzy and Milne 2002), a 'dictatorship' (Bello 1990), 'paternalist' (Chua 1995), 'corporatist' (Rodan 1989; Brown 1993) and 'hegemonic' (Castells 1988; Worthington 2003).

Instead of cowering to criticism, the PAP brandished *realpolitik*, rationalising its political tactics and social management strategies as 'necessary' and 'pragmatic' for a small nation subject to the vicissitudes of the global system. Strong political leadership and a disciplined population are 'needed' for Singapore's economic survival and success, not the liberal democracy of the West. Two ideological constructs underpin the PAP's self-proclamation. This first, 'pragmatism', is inextricably tied to the concept of 'survival' to form an encompassing ideological framework. 'Pragmatism' as an ideological concept is always relevant and renewable, providing 'in-context' and instrumental justifications for all state actions, including unpleasant and contradictory ones (Chua 1995). Be it the state's extensive political and social administration, its harsh repression of opposition forces, its pre-emptory exercising of power to prevent perceived problems, these are all rendered 'necessary' in the context of the precarious historical and material conditions facing the nation in the early years. When the state's developmental strategies began to succeed and the material lives of Singaporeans vastly transformed by the rapid economic growth it achieved, 'pragmatism' as a concept gained ideological validation and currency among Singaporeans who continue to return the PAP to power at every election The legitimacy and longevity of the PAP is one built on a deep ideological consensus with the people around 'economic pragmatism'. Despite its illiberal and anti-democratic ways, the Singaporean government is not simply an authoritarian state (Chua 1995).

The second self-defining discourse of the PAP is the binary oppositioning of Singapore in an East/West dichotomy. In this formulation, the nation is imbued with conservative 'Asian values' of thrift, industry and filial piety as a form of cultural consolidation against 'undesirable' Western influence. By the 1980s, after two decades of political independence, Singapore was rapidly prospering from the capitalist free market system. Annual economic growth rates in the double-digits, high levels of educational attainment and surplus employment in a rapidly expanding economy have generated massive increases in extravagant wealth. Singaporeans could, for example, relish in the luxury of conspicuous consumption and 'job-hop' for better salaries. In the eyes of the state, these were symptoms of Western liberalism, individualism and self-interest creeping in closely on the heels of globalisation and capitalist expansion. The state raised 'Asian values' as an ideological barricade against the penetration of these 'Western ills', which it saw manifesting in the local body politic as the loss of a unity of purpose, an unwillingness to sacrifice for broader social good and the decline of the family, among other social and cultural problems it saw as already afflicting many advanced capitalist societies in the West.

Crucially, the set of Asian values is yoked to an underlying economic instrumental rationality. 'Thrift' and 'industry', for example, are good values for the economy, and even 'filial piety' provides a justification for the state to privatise the burden of care of elderly citizens, freeing resources for the national economy. The construction of things 'Asian' flowed into a broad ideology of collectivism and communitarianism, and a set of 'Asian values' was eventually inscribed as national ideology in a White paper called *Shared Values*. 'Nation before community and society above self', 'family as the basic unit block of society', 'consensus, not contention' and 'religious and racial harmony' are to be formally adopted as national values (Singapore Parliament 1991). Also to be included is 'regard and support for the individual' but this must be carefully distinguished from the 'me-first' attitudes of Western individualism (Goh 1988) and specified as compassion for individuals who might have fallen behind in the free market capitalist system. Against the background of rising Asian capitalism in the 1990s and the growing newly-industrialising 'Asian Tiger' economies of Japan, Taiwan, Hong Kong and Korea at rates outstripping the West, the state's self-Orientalising recuperation of Singapore's place in a 'long Asian civilisation' (Goh 1988) gained much currency and made a lot of sense to Singaporeans and to Western observers. The elevation of 'Asian values' as the *sine qua non* of modern capitalist development in the region gained high ideological buy-in, and it was on this moral-ideological high ground of the East/West binary edifice that the Singaporean state would constantly 'talk back' (Ang and Stratton 1995: 66) or 'moralise' against the West for its excessive liberalism (Chua 1990: 17).

'Economic pragmatism' providing 'in-context' justifications for state intervention in the name of development continually made way for the state to operate extensively and intrusively into every aspect of society. 'Asian values', emphasising stability, harmony and community above the self, enabled the state to rationalise social discipline and economic development above political development. The effect of such formidable ideological work is that the state has been able to pursue economic openness while closing in on personal, social and political freedoms in Singapore (Chua 1995). Singaporeans are keenly aware of their lack of freedoms but have come to accept and embody the normative value system of the government. The idea that one must be pragmatic in 'our' context, and a belief in a sort of Singaporean exceptionalism arising from 'our' Asian values and culture, pervade the social consciousness.

Despite the PAP's ideological hegemony and consensus with the people, its desire to embrace global capitalist economic modernisation and determination to avoid what it sees as the pitfalls of Western individualism and liberal democracy is a tension that the PAP has had to deal with at every stage of Singapore's development. Decades of economic growth and a highly educated and socially mobile population have made the PAP's political consolidation against liberalism and democratisation all the more susceptible to external social forces. Paradoxically, contemporary political challenges facing the PAP are made from its own policy successes, and the ruling party finds itself having to navigate an evolving national modernity within a non-static global modernity. The political discursive regime of the state must therefore continuously produce ideological work.

Ideology, as Zizek (1989) philosophises, is 'a sublime object'. For ideas to become hegemonic, as Gramsci (1971) posits, the concepts must be naturalised by the ruling party's ability to deliver real material concessions to its citizens, which is what the PAP continues to do remarkably well. With the societal material transformation of Singaporean society, the ideas and interests of the postcolonial state have come to be taken for granted by national subjects as the common-sense-reality of everyday life. Local subject positions are thus heavily inflected by the political rhetoric of the ruling elite and queer subjectivities are not more immune from the constraints of normalising strategies associated with postcolonial nationalisms. Queer identities and narratives, to this extent, cannot be fully understood outside the purview of the complex national discursive context.

State policing, portrayals and pronouncements of homosexuality in Singapore

Persisting with the conception of the hegemonic state and the ideological interpellation of citizen subjects into its nationalistic fold, this chapter continues by looking at the ways in which the state has controlled and constructed homosexuality in Singapore. Even as what comes across as the strong arm of the state acting on and censoring homosexuality, I would like to keep several ideas in play. One, the Singaporean state is not a monolith and operates through a multiplicity of disaggregated structures, agencies and agents, such as individual political leaders who occupy different subject positions and standpoints towards homosexuality. Two, the policing of sexual differences is never just an internal matter of establishing social control, asserting normative standards and defending national 'purity' so as to craft a national identity. Rather, the nation's position on sexuality is also cognizant and constituent of the external expectations of significant international communities, particularly for that of a postcolonial state with ambitions to become a 'modern' global city. These ideas will be applicable as the book traces the politics of homosexuality in Singapore. In this section, however, the focus is on the state's explicit suppression of homosexuality in the law criminalising consensual sex between men, in media censorships of homosexual content, and in the public pronouncements against same-sex desires made by its postcolonial national elites.

Legacy and law

After Singapore gained independence in 1965, the PAP maintained the sodomy law left behind by the British colonial government. Statute Section 377A of the Penal Code prohibits any act, or abetment, of gross indecency between men in public or in private. If caught, the crime is punishable by up to two years imprisonment.

In an informative essay tracing the history of Section 377A, Douglas Sanders (2007a) reveals that the British parliament began legislating against homosexual acts in 1543, when laws on 'buggery' and 'sodomy' were formulated from ecclesiastical condemnations of homosexuality. While previously a church law, the prohibition of homosexual acts became a secular law under the reign of Henry VIII who wanted to undermine the Catholic church's authority partly to secure his divorce and remarriage. Were it not for his personal agenda and the power struggle between Henry VIII and the Catholic church, the formal British civil injunction against homosexuality might not have existed. The sodomy law, an artefact of a peculiar history, was later exported and applied in the British colonies, first in India as part of the 1860 Indian Penal Code, then subsequently to the other British colonies in Asia, including Singapore.

Anti-homosexuality enforcements in Singapore took the form of police entrapments in the early 1990s. In a study of local newspaper reports, a sociologist notes that 'almost every month there were news reports about men being convicted for molestation, soliciting and gross indecency' (Leong 2005: 166). Figures from public records released by the state (taken from *Yawning Bread* 2007a) and from independent research (Chua 2003; Gopalan 2007) reveal that convictions under Section 377A have been carried out almost every year between 1988–2007, with the most intense period of prosecutions coinciding with Singapore's participation at the 1993 World Conference on Human Rights in Vienna.

It was on this occasion in Vienna that the Asian values debate came to the fore with several Asian states signalling their acceptance of the Universal Human Rights Declaration while adopting a Bangkok Declaration resisting an unequivocal endorsement of universal human rights. One article of the Bangkok Declaration states that 'while human rights are universal in nature, they must be considered in the context of a dynamic and evolving process of international norm-setting, bearing in mind the significance of national and regional particularities and various historical, cultural and religious backgrounds' (1993 Bangkok Declaration, Article 8). Engaging with the discourse of universal human rights allowed postcolonial governments to paint themselves as forging an independent path. Singapore's Minister of Foreign Affairs, Wong Kan Seng, took the platform to defend Singapore's repressive laws:

> Identifying the core rights which are truly universal will not always be easy ... Every country must find its own way ... We have intervened to change individual social behaviour in ways other countries consider intrusive ... deployed laws that others may find harsh ... We do not think that our arrangements will suit everybody. But they suit ourselves.
>
> (Wong quoted in Offord 1999: 303)

Then the Minister proceeded to use homosexuality as a trope of difference 'to consolidate the imagined border' between Singapore and the West (Offord 1999: 309), declaring that 'homosexual rights are a Western issue' (quote taken from Offord 1999: 305), not one for Singapore. The state's construction of homosexual rights as a sort of neo-colonial imposition is one enthusiastically embraced by gay rights opponents in Singapore who see themselves as defenders of 'traditional' family values against the onslaught of liberal Western ones embodied by lesbian and gay Singaporeans. By transposing queer sexualities onto the Asia/West ideology with which the dominant heterosexual majority identify with and reproduce in their opposition of queer sexualities, the state effectively shores up the hegemony of the 'Asia vs. West' model of development through a rendering of homosexuality as 'queer' to Singapore.

Despite the state's anti-homosexual stance, declared so brazenly at a human rights conference, the number of 377A convictions did in fact decline towards the end of the millennium. From 2001 onwards, sodomy charges were made only where minors or extortion were involved (*Yawning Bread* 2007a). Subsequently, in 2007, the Singapore state declared it would not proactively enforce the law against consensual acts taking place between adults, in response to a parliamentary petition to repeal Section 377A. I discuss this event in the next chapter as one of the two 'reverse discourses' engendered by the repression of non-normative sexualities in Singapore. Despite the government's pledge to not enforce Section 377A, homosexuality remained a target of policing. In 2010, police entrapment of an Indian Malaysian national in a disused cemetery led to a charge of indecent behaviour (*New Paper* 2010), and a man who had oral sex with another man in a public restroom was charged under Section 377A but public prosecutors later amended the charge to that of committing an obscene act in public (*Straits Times* 2010a). Injunctions against gay persons are thus issued in different ways.

Furthermore, the existence of the criminal law perpetuates overt and subtle discriminations against sexual minorities. Being charged with a crime for having sex could set forth a series of effects, such as: losing one's job; being denied public benefits including pension, health insurance and housing; inability to obtain rights to children in custody access, adoption and fertility treatment for example; and inability to sponsor a partner in immigration law, among other injustices that activists have enumerated (Sanders 2007b: 4).

That lesbian women are simultaneously affected by the law is reflected in a report submitted by a group of women activists to the United Nations' (UN) Convention on the Elimination of All Forms of Discrimination Against Women (CEDAW). The report categorically states:

> The continued existence of Penal Code Section 377A perpetuates and condones discrimination against queer persons, including queer women.
>
> (*Sayoni* 2011: 11)

Representatives from *Sayoni*, a local queer women's group, argue that Section 377A does not just criminalise gay men, it also institutionalises unequal rights and a lack of protection for all LGBT persons. The women note in their submission that repealing the law 'would have a cascading effect to help reduce discrimination and social stigma against queer women and men' (*Sayoni* 2011: 11). But with Section 377A in place, a spectre of prosecution and prejudice looms large over sexual minorities in Singapore, casting a blanket of invisibility on issues faced by the community. Census and data on the gay community is hard to obtain because standing up to be counted is tantamount to admitting to a crime. Worldwide rates of LGBT suicides, depression and self-harm indicate the abjectness of LGBT lives, but very little is known or understood about the conditions facing sexual minorities in Singapore. Incidents of violence, abuse and bullying of LGBT youths at home and at school are addressed through the under-resourced voluntary efforts of grassroots activism. Because being gay is illegal, there are no state-sponsored institutions to address work place discrimination, family and child-rearing concerns, and issues of aging and poverty faced by sexual minorities. The effect of the law, even if not enforced, is far-reaching.

Sodomy laws in the British Empire were struck down in 1967. With the exception of Myanmar, Malaysia, Brunei and Singapore, all former British colonies in East and Southeast Asia have decriminalised homosexual conduct. Gay sex is now legal in most parts of the world. The Singaporean government's insistence on preserving the colonial-era statute makes it an outlier, especially in the developed world. The state's inertia over Section 377A sends a very wrong signal to the world that Singapore is a backward and regressive state, say gay rights activists.

In a parliamentary speech explaining why the law will stand, the Prime Minister said:

> Singapore is basically a conservative society. The family is the basic building block of our society. It has been so and, by policy, we have reinforced this and we want to keep it so. And by 'family' in Singapore, we mean one man, one woman, marrying, having children and bringing up children within that framework of a stable family unit.
> (Lee Hsien Loong 2007, parliamentary address on debate to amend the Penal Code, quote taken from Quah 2015)

Through the ideological mobilisation of a 'conservative society', the state imagines and assumes the national community to be morally conservative, and offers this as 'a convenient excuse for not going beyond what the government is comfortable with' (Tan and Lee 2007: 182). Removing the law against homosexuality would allow a liberal 'Western' influence to threaten the internal purity of Singapore's 'Asian' conservative social fabric held together by a specific heterosexual family imagined at the centre. But who, as critics have continually asked (e.g. Tan 2007), constitutes this conservative majority? It is this ongoing cultural production of a 'mythical heterosexual "moral majority" repeatedly invoked by the state' (Tan and Lee 2007: 189) and articulated alongside assumptions of heteronormativity that sustain the criminalisation and, as we shall see, the censorship and ridicule of homosexuality in Singapore.

Media prohibitions

By ideologically adopting the heterosexual family as the basis of Singaporean society, the state imagines a national community through relations and desires that are normative of the majority of the population, rendering the nation heteronormative. The point must be made, however, that normative heterosexuality in Singapore is narrowly defined. In the words of the Prime Minister, 'by "family" in Singapore, we mean one man, one woman, marrying, having children and bringing up children' (Lee 2007). Said in defence of the sodomy law in Singapore, Lee's affirmation of the heterosexual family is an assertion of notions of proper family and sexual respectability, key to colonial and postcolonial narratives of identity, civility, progress, modernity and development. Lee's response is also about procreation and raising children in Singapore. Normative heterosexuality is, for the government, a narrow model of the Singaporean family in service of a broader function of social reproduction by which the proper heterosexual family reproduces the nation. Heteronormativity is in this way foundational to nation building and development agendas.

For the colonised driven by a desire to be given status and recognition as a 'modern' civilised nation, the sexual norms of British Victorian values and laws, including the sodomy law, were inherited and adopted. Then, as a young postcolony anxious to build and reproduce a nation, shaping and perpetuating a specific set of familial heterosexual norms has been a major preoccupation. For example, heteronormativity has been institutionalised and worked into Singapore's public housing policies across colonial and postcolonial times (Oswin 2010). The British administration's housing programme re-settled the largely single male migrant population from squalid shacks and shop-houses into modernist flats to encourage family formation and reunification with their overseas family through supportive immigration policies. The postcolonial state's Housing and Development Board (HDB) programme (2008a) embedded heteronormativity into its policies by instituting 'a proper family nucleus' – centred around the very narrow heteronormative model of family singled out by the Prime Minister, namely, the married, heterosexual, procreative couple – as qualification criteria for public housing benefits. With over 80 per cent of Singaporeans living in public housing flats, the HDB is undoubtedly a major instrument of social control, inhering heteronormativity deeply within a postcolonial world driven by desires for progress, modernisation and development. Thus embedded and institutionalised, the set of heteronormative relations is internalised and expressed repeatedly, consciously and unconsciously, in the lived experiences of everyday life.

What drives heteronormativity more forcefully, and further embeds it as natural and eternal, is also the deliberate exclusion and exteriorisation of homosexuality in a sexual binary that prominently contaminates homosexuality as an 'other' in an oppositional logic (Fuss 1991). This is exemplified in postcolonial Singapore through the prohibition and negative portrayals of homosexuality in the Singapore media, and the denouncement of same-sex desires in the political discursive space to which we now turn.

In what follows, Table 3.1 highlights the role of media authorities in censoring positive images of lesbians and gays in the media, and Table 3.2 in a later section captures the public pronouncements of homosexuality made by government officials. These are by no means the only ways in which same-sex desires have been subject to the force of heteronormative logics and desires, but they are among the more vivid examples of how same-sex desires have been directly targeted by state institutions.[5]

The Media Development Authority of Singapore (MDA) is a government-appointed board overseeing the media broadcast sector. Core to the MDA's mission is to develop a globally-competitive media sector in Singapore while fostering a cohesive and inclusive society through quality media content. The MDA sees itself as integral to nation building (MDA 2011). It aspires to place Singapore media on the world stage so as to attract global capital and talent. At the same time, it sees itself as guardian of the nation's values, playing a crucial role in scripting the internal coherency of the nation according to dominant nationalist constructions. As state agent and media authority, the MDA has played an overt and direct role in guarding the sexual respectability of the nation and in preserving the hegemony of the heteronormative sexual order through its keen policing of same-sex desires. MDA film and television codes treat homosexuality as alternative to mainstream Singaporean values. These codes have placed homosexuality alongside the categories of paedophilia, incest, drug use and prostitution, all of which are subject to varying levels of censorship. Films or television programmes portraying homosexuality as normal or neutral can, in MDA's books, be seen as promoting an alternative lifestyle and thus censored or classified for restricted viewing. This is to say, homosexuality is made invisible in mainstream media unless it reflects a mirror of social problems and personal ills.

As a matter of policy then, media depictions of same-sex 'lifestyles' as positive or even neutral are either banned or censored. Innocuous gay characters in roles ranging from parents to passers-by are all deemed unfit for film or television, if these characters were not somehow portrayed as psychologically disturbed or dysfunctional or so exaggerated as to be improbable. Instances of queer figures appearing in Singapore's mainstream television have involved a lewd figure bent on seducing an innocent, handsome man (in the 1992 Chinese drama serial entitled 'A Bright Future'); a jobless, effeminate man running into all sorts of trouble and judged as 'abnormal' by a potential employer (in a 2003 infotainment series, 'OK, No Problem')[6]; and colourful cross-dressing characters in slapstick comedic routines, (such as the *Liang Po Po* caricature appearing on a prime time programme called 'Comedy Night', which ran through the 1990s and was eventually made into a film in 1999). Whenever broadcasters do not collude in portraying homosexuality negatively, they meet the wrath of MDA's hefty penalties. The negative representation of homosexuality in Singapore, to be sure, is not just a question of 'truth' distortion. In Stuart Hall's (1997) work, terms, images and messages are caught up in webs of power, and the question is one of how powerful constituencies define and conjure, in this case, the meaning of homosexuality itself, which is then avidly consumed by people in a range of affective modes including disgust and fear conforming to dominant heteronormative values. Table 3.1 presents a snapshot of the active role played by various authorities in shaping Singaporeans' understanding of homosexuality through the policing of homosexual content in the cinema and on television over the last several years.

Table 3.1 The policing of homosexual content in the media

Date	Forms of media suppression	Statements from media authorities
2003	Local television station was fined S$15,000 for featuring an interview with Hollywood celebrity, Anne Heche, who spoke about her romantic relationship with another female celebrity, Ellen DeGeneres.	'Broadcasting programmes which glamorise and promote lesbianism is considered a major breach of the Code' (MDA 2003).
2004	A gay themed romantic comedy, *Formula 17*, was banned from screening in Singapore.	The film 'creates homosexual utopia, where everyone including passersby, is homosexual and no ills or problems are reflected. It conveys the message that homosexuality is normal, and a natural progression of society' (Singapore Films Committee quoted in 'Socially conservative Singapore bans popular gay-oriented Taiwanese film', *Taipei Times*, 2004, 23 July).
2006	Leading cable broadcaster was fined S$10,000 for showing pixellated scenes of lesbian sex from an American reality show called *Cheaters* past midnight.	'While pixellation was used during the sex scenes, it was still obvious to viewers that the women were naked and engaging in unnatural sex acts. The programme also showed the woman tied to a bed in a bondage session with two other women. The visuals were deemed to be sexually suggestive and offensive to good taste and decency' (*Yawning Bread* 2006).
2007	Organisers of a two-week photo exhibition of 80 same-sex couples kissing were denied a licence. The exhibition had to be cancelled.	'The proposed exhibition, which mainly focuses on homosexual kissing, is deemed to promote a homosexual lifestyle and cannot be allowed' (MDA letter to organiser, quoted in Macan-Markar 2007).

2008	Another local television station was fined S$15,000 for airing a home improvement show, *Find and Design*, featuring a gay couple renovating a nursery room for their baby.	'The episode contained several scenes of the gay couple with their baby as well as the presenter's congratulations and acknowledgement of them as a family unit in a way which normalises their gay lifestyle and unconventional family setup. This is in breach of the Free-to-Air TV Programme Code which disallows programmes that promote, justify or glamourise gay lifestyles. MDA also consulted the Programme Advisory Committee for English Programmes (PACE) and the Committee was also of the view that a gay relationship should not be presented as an acceptable family unit. As the programme was shown on a Sunday morning, PACE felt that this was inappropriate as such a timeslot was within family viewing hours' (*Sayoni* 2008a).
2008	Leading cable broadcaster was again fined S$10,000 for airing a promotional advertisement of the Mandarin pop music video, 'Silly Child' by Olivia Yan, which showed two fully-clothed women kissing.	'Within the commercial, romanticised scenes of two girls kissing were shown and it portrayed the relationship as acceptable. This is in breach of the TV advertising guidelines, which disallows advertisements that condone homosexuality. MDA also consulted the Advisory Committee for Chinese Programmes and the Committee concurred that the commercial had promoted lesbianism as acceptable and romantic, especially when shown together with the lyrics featured' (*Fridae.com* 2008).

Although Table 3.1 indicates the extensive policing of homosexual content in the media, a few exceptions have been made, particularly when it pertains to the regulation of internationally-known and critically-acclaimed media content. Whether these exceptions indicate a loosening of the leash on homosexual content remains debatable, but the following examples nevertheless appear to buck the trend of censorship enforcements. In the late 1990s, the MDA permitted the Singapore International Film Festival (SIFF), an annual privately-organised event, to screen selected films without any cuts. In 1998, the gay film 'Happy Together', which won the Best Director award at the 1997 Cannes festival was given a once-only showing at the SIFF. In 2006, two top-grossing Hollywood films, 'Brokeback Mountain' and 'Transamerica', were given wide-release and shown uncut under an adult R21[7] rating. In 2009, 'I Love You, Philip Morris' was also rated R21 and given wide-release. Then in 2011, the Oscar-nominated American drama 'The Kids Are All Right' was given a one-release restriction by the MDA under an R21 rating. The film, portraying two lesbians and their children as a regular family, appears to overstep MDA guidelines, but in this instance, the agency 'took into account the higher level of interest in "The Kids Are All Right" following its Oscar nominations' (quote taken from the *Straits Times* 2011a). The extent of MDA's moral policing and censorships in the local media is thus subject to its desire to participate in the global circulation of cultural production, where circulating cultural goods reciprocally interact with and produce the interpretative communities that consume them (Lee and LiPuma 2002).

The apparent inconsistency on the part of the MDA drew public attention and varying opinions (*Straits Times* 2011b). For some, it heralded hopes of 'more scope for homosexuality to be examined as an issue' (gay activist quoted in *BBC News* 2006). Others are more sceptical, pointing to how state authorities have allowed homosexual content in the media only on small platforms with niche audiences and limited reach, such as the SIFF or in local theatre (Au 2009; Leong 2005). The one-release stipulation, coupled with 'an additional' restricted rating is seen by some as a 'huge leap backwards' (*Yawning Bread* 2011a). Where a wide release was given, the gay protagonists either met with a tragic ending (in 'Brokeback Mountain'), faced homophobia from family (in 'Transamerica') or were criminals (in 'I Love You, Philip Morris').

MDA's selective enforcements on fictional films parallel the censorship and self-censorship practices of the state-controlled local press on news relating to gay men and lesbians. Prior to 2004, as Leong (2005) has meticulously documented, Singapore's main English-medium daily, the *Straits Times*, portrayed only negative and stereotypical images of gay men and women. While gay criminality was routinely reported in the local news, and tended to frame gay men as 'molesters and perverts', news on women-women relationships was limited, and when these did appear in the press the women were cast as 'catty, vengeful and treacherous' (Leong 2005: 165–166). Over the same period, same-sex marriages across Europe started to gain recognition (*BBC News* 2000), the head of a German political party came out of the closet (*The Times* 2001), and Taiwan's first public gay marriage obtained blessings from the mayor of Taipei (*Fridae. com* 2006a). These major strides made by gay men and lesbians around the world made global news, but none of these were reported in the *Straits Times*. Thus, media observers concluded at that time that the newspaper was incapable of sympathetic coverage of gay rights (George 2000: 70) or that if 'one were solely dependent on the *Straits Times* for hard news concerning gays and lesbians in the world, one would get the impression that the world was basically straight, with not much happening in the lives of gays and lesbians elsewhere' (Leong 2005: 163).

If this was the world's perception of LGBT lives in Singapore, the impression was corrected by no less than the Prime Minister. In a highly reported *Time* magazine interview Goh gave in 2003, he voluntarily brought up the issue of gay Singaporeans. To the journalist's question that Singapore might come across as too rigid to attract global talent, Goh said his was a less inflexible government employing openly homosexual Singaporeans in sensitive positions. 'In the past, if we know you're gay, we would not employ you but we just changed this quietly', he told the magazine. Homosexual acts, however, would remain illegal in the country. Goh's statements lifted the mantel on lesbian and gay media reportage in local and international news. From 2004 onwards, print news on lesbian and gay issues started to appear in the *Straits Times*, especially after 2007, when the topic of homosexuality received wide public attention through the parliamentary debate on Section 377A. News reports on global gay rights and anti-gay laws began to appear with some frequency (see for example *Straits Times* 2008b, 2009a, 2009b, 2009c). Alongside these, however, were news articles continuing the trend of portraying Singaporean lesbians and gays negatively. A cursory scan of headlines in the main broadsheet is revealing: 'Woman committed obscene acts with girl' (*Straits Times* 2011c), 'Drugs turn gay sex romp into fatal affair' (*Straits Times* 2010b), 'Surge in HIV cases among gay men' (*Straits Times* 2008c), 'Man gets jail, cane for molesting two boys in his flat' (*Straits Times* 2007a), among others. The roots of these prejudiced media portrayals on screen and in print media are located in the 'continued criminalisation of (male) homosexuality in Singapore' and 'the self-defined role of the mainstream press as agents of law and order' (Leong 2005: 165). The internet has been the only media space that is left relatively free from state-control, and thus cyberspace is where lesbian and gay subjectivities emerged, a point I will discuss in relation to the identity formation of Singaporean lesbians in subsequent chapters.

Official attitudes and pronouncements

When positive images of non-normative sexualities are censored, all that are left are 'images that injure' (Lester 1996). Postcolonial state elites participate in this sexual violence in the public pronouncements they make associating homosexuality with negative images of 'infection', the 'paedophile' and the 'psychopath', as italicised in Table 3.2. In addition, it is yoked to the nationalist rhetoric of

Table 3.2 Statements made by government office holders in selected speeches

Context	Name	Office*	Statements
1993, United Nations World Human Rights Conference	Wong Kan Seng	Foreign Minister	Homosexual rights are a Western issue, and not relevant … (taken from Offord 1999).
2000, at a seminar, titled 'Fostering the Renaissance spirit', for Pre-University students, May	Lim Swee Say	Minister of State	… I do not believe that a single group of people in Singapore has the right to publicise its lifestyle and impose it on others. I am an avid golfer, but I do not hold a forum on golfing to say how much I love golf and convince others it is good (taken from Sa'at 2007).
2003, in an interview with *Time* magazine	Goh Chok Tong	Prime Minister	… it's more than just the criminal code. It's actually the values of the people. The heartlanders are still conservative … (*Time* magazine 2003).
2005, address at Parliament during Budget debate, 9 March	Balaji Sadasivan	Minister for Health	We do not know the reasons for the sharp increase of HIV in the gay community. An epidemiologist has suggested that this may be linked to the annual predominantly gay party in Sentosa – the Nation Party – which allowed gays from high prevalence societies to fraternise with local gay men, seeding the infection in the local community (taken from *Fridae.com* 2005a).
2007, Reuters Newsmaker event, 24 April	Lee Kuan Yew	Minister Mentor	They tell me, and anyway it is probably half-true, that homosexuals are creative writers, dancers, etcetera. If we want creative people, then we got to put up with their idiosyncracies so long as they don't infect the heartland … We are not promoters of it (homosexuality) and we are not going to allow Singapore to become the vanguard of Southeast Asia (taken from *Yawning Bread* 2007b).

2007, at a meeting with the youth wing of the People's Action Party, 21 April	Lee Kuan Yew	Minister Mentor	So why should we criminalise it? So what do we do? I think we pragmatically adjust, carry our people. Don't upset them and suddenly upset their sense of propriety and right and wrong … So you have to take a practical, pragmatic approach … (taken from *Fridae.com* 2007b)
2007, at a Pre-University Seminar, 22 May	Lui Tuck Yew	Senior Minister of State for Education	My position is that I'm not so sure I subscribe to those arguments … Even if it's a medical condition, do you excuse paedophiles and psychopaths and people that who can likewise claim to have a medical condition? If you say homosexuality – you are not doing harm to anybody, it's only between the two of us … Well, there are lots of relationships between either a person and maybe even an animal, or between a person and another person, perhaps incestuous in nature, that are between the two of us and we are not doing harm to anybody else. To me, there are certain norms in society and before we make major shifts to those norms, it is important that we sit down, deliberate, and think through it carefully and move at a pace that society allows us to move (taken from Sa'at 2007).

Note
* Refers to office held at time of speech.

'Westernisation', seen as a frivolous 'lifestyle', and an 'imposition' on 'conservative heartlanders'. It was therefore 'pragmatic' to retain Section 377A. The fusing of nationalist rhetoric with anti-homosexual discourse is evident in underlined statements in Table 3.2.

In these elite discursive productions, homosexuality is seized as a lynch pin merging the multiple systemic ideologies of 'Asian values', an East/West opposition and 'pragmatism' into a master nationalist narrative. The fusing of political ideologies with deeply ingrained cultural heteronormativity was a clear play for hegemony. Anti-homosexual rhetoric served an Althusserian ideological state apparatus within modern nationalist discourse. State power is in this sense manufactured through same-sex desires in a transparent strategy that does not require much ideological work for 'no postcolonial nationalist myth is more pervasive than the belief that homosexuality is alien ... and the outcome of Westernisation' (Puri 2008: 10).

The tone and content of these official pronouncements are, however, not always consistent. For instance, official attitudes appear sympathetic at times to the belief that homosexuals are born gay rather than choose a gay lifestyle. Consider the statement of Lee Kuan Yew, the retired Prime Minister given the role of Minister Mentor, whose views remain influential:

> I have asked several doctors this – that you are genetically born a homosexual because that's the nature of the genetic random transmission of genes, so you can't help it. So why should you criminalise it? It's a genetic variation.
>
> (Lee 2007, taken from Sa'at 2007)

Lee's public view was seductive. The perspective that sexuality is not a choice, but a way people are born, has become a compelling cause and a great triumph for the global gay rights movement. As such, Lee's view was received as pro-gay and progressive by gay and liberal constituencies. Legitimising same-sex desires as a biologically-determined identity, Lee made further remarks that the acceptance of homosexuality is an 'inevitable force of time and circumstance' (Lee 2007, taken from Sa'at 2007) and 'it's a matter of time before it's accepted' (Lee 2011: 247). While Lee's 'born this way' perspective of homosexuality may appear progressive and well aligned with contemporary global gay politics, the idea is, however, based on troubling homophobic and erroneous understandings of sexuality framed in terms of a nature versus nurture dichotomy. The nature versus nurture argument is one the anti-gay camp often wields to place the onus on gay people to prove that homosexuality is biologically determined. When evidence shows up in research, for example in brain structure and genetic differences for gay men, (LeVay 1991; Hamer *et al.* 1993) published in premier scientific journals no less, the findings are met with dominant scepticism and opposition. The enterprise, rooted in homophobia, is always futile. Furthermore, historians and anthropologists have long documented the diversity of sexualities across time and place. Heterosexuality along with homosexuality, pederasty, pan-sexuality, polygamy, transgender and third-gender expression are all incontrovertible historical and social facts. What is in fact 'natural' is the diversity of sexualities and genders, even as some practices are more difficult for contemporary Singaporean sensibilities to comprehend. Whether these are biologically-determined or culturally-driven practices are a moot point, say social scientists. The nature/nurture binary is a false one, for sexuality is always connected to biological impulses yet always also expressed through human culture to produce a diversity of sexualities and genders.

Notes

1 Trade with Malaysia accounted for almost a third of Singapore's exports and imports in 1960 (Peebles and Wilson 1996: 10).
2 British military bases had accounted for 20 per cent of national growth and 25,000 local jobs in the mid-1960s (Turnbull 1989: 294).
3 At the time of independence, the Chinese made up 75 per cent of the population, the Malays 17 per cent, and Indians 7 per cent, with the rest falling into the residual category of 'Others'.
4 See Chua's 1993 article, 'The changing shape of civil society'.
5 See for example *Sayoni*'s 2011 report on the 'Discrimination against Women in Singapore based on Sexual Orientation and Gender Identity' for a comprehensive account of how state-based discrimination is applied in every sphere and 'stage of life' (*Sayoni* 2011: 5) of queer women in Singapore.
6 Although 'OK, No Problem' was meant to be a 'documentary' educating the public on the kinds of prejudices and difficulties faced by homosexuals in Singapore, with a focus on work discrimination, the 'gay' figures in the 'educational' skits were the stereotypical two-dimensional, comedic characters that cannot be taken seriously, perpetuating images of queer people in negative ways.
7 Audience must be at least 21 years of age.

4 Sexual politics in Singapore
Sodomy law and lesbian resistance

In Singapore, the Media Development Authority censors positive depictions of homosexuality while allowing negative and stereotypical images to be broadcast freely. Politicians deliver anti-queer propaganda in the public sphere, speaking about homosexuality in the language of 'infection', 'psychosis' and 'paedophilia'. Being gay is illegal so public policies and services, whether it pertains to housing, immigration or marriage, are designed according to a heteronormative logic and explicitly exclude same-sex couples. Local activists and academics have pointed to the ways in which the state disciplines and punishes homosexuality through laws and regulations, legitimised through the continuous criminalisation of male same-sex relations (*Sayoni* 2011; Au quoted in Sanders 2007b; Leong 1997). In such a context, numerous works have treated the Singaporean state as a singular authority and regulator of bodies, subjectivities, activities and places associated with non-normative sexualities (Au 2009; Lim 2004; Offord 1999), and sexuality has been analysed as the site for the production and reproduction of state power and nationalist projects in postcolonial Singapore (Heng and Devan 1992). Lesser attention has been paid to how sexuality, in turn, shapes and structures state form and practice. One recent illustration of this is Chua's (2014) 'Mobilizing Gay Singapore: Rights and Resistance in an Authoritarian State'. Although the category of the state is foregrounded in the title, its account of lesbian and gay politics does not explore the form and character of the state in any sustained or explicit way. For all its sophistication in analysing the local LGBT movement, the state is taken as a stable 'authoritarian' entity wielding 'domestic hegemony' over its sexual subjects and to which lesbian and gay activists adapt a strategy of 'pragmatic resistance'. It is understandable that Singapore is not a context likely to generate accounts of a multifaceted, nuanced state within sexuality and queer research, given how the PAP has ostensibly oppressed non-normative sexualities.

While it is important to critically identify the ways in which the state overtly and indirectly shapes and regulates sexuality, as local research and activism have done, what is also necessary is attention to how questions of sexuality probe the ways in which the power of the nation-state and the premises of official nationalisms are sustained in postcolonial Singapore. As foreshadowed in the previous chapter, developing a one-sided conceptualisation of state-sexuality relations runs the risk of reproducing the state as an over-arching monolithic authority controlling and regulating sexuality. How might we re-think the nexus of state-nationalism-sexuality to interrogate notions of a singular and hegemonic state? What insights about the state might we gain from a more critical understanding of sexuality?

Foucault's theory on the specificities of power, within a framework of the governmentality of sexuality, provides a re-entry into the conceptualisation of state-sexuality relations established in the previous chapter. His work addresses the dialogic relationship between 'state' and sexuality' – adding to the theoretical economy of feminist sexuality studies, queer, poststructuralist and postcolonial theories established earlier – to advance an understanding that sexuality is not shaped in a straightforward unilinear process by the hegemonic state. Rather, sexuality also operates instrumentally in the dispersal of power, inciting forms of a 'reverse discourse'. But this aspect of Foucault's work is often overlooked in hasty dismissals of his theorisations as overly deterministic of the sexual subject. He writes:

> By power ... I do not understand a general system of domination exercised by one element or one group over another, whose effects ... traverse the entire body social. It seems to me that first what needs to be understood is the multiplicity of relations of force that are immanent to the domain wherein they are exercised, and that they are constitutive of its organisation; the game that through incessant struggle and confrontation transforms them, reinforces them, inverts them; the supports these relations of force find in each other, so as to form a chain or system, or, on the other hand, the gaps, the contradictions that isolate them from each other; in the end, the strategies in which they take effect, and whose general pattern or institutional crystallisation is embodied in the mechanisms of the state, in the formulation of the law, in social hegemonies.
>
> (Foucault 1978: 121)

First, rather than view the state as a singular source of power, the production of state power is dispersed among the set of state structures located within a matrix of governmentality in which the state's institutions, agencies and relations function as 'dense transfer points for relations of power' (Foucault 1978: 103). This framework usefully approaches the state in its disaggregated form, and allows for 'gaps' and 'contradictions' between these points of transfer while accounting for the pervasiveness of power over sexualities.[1] Second, in Foucault's formulation, even as state agents emerge as dense transfer points of power and regulation, they are not the only ones. The discursive and material aspects of sexuality – medicine, jurisprudence, identities, desires and practices – are also inserted into the dense matrix and thoroughly infused by relations of power. Although these sites are saturated with discourses of what is 'respectable sexuality', and complicit in the proliferation of power through the production of knowledge and 'truth', their appearance also 'made possible the formation of a "reverse" discourse: homosexuality began to speak on its own behalf, to demand that its legitimacy or "naturality" be acknowledged' (Foucault 1978: 101). These aspects of Foucault's framework fit neatly into contemporary feminist sexuality and queer theory's 'sexualisation' (Puri 2008) or 'queering' (Duggan 1994) of state-sexuality relations.

In what follows, I examine two such 'reverse' discourses in Singapore, each one incited by the advance of social controls over homosexuality. These events ushered in an unprecedented visibility of same-sex sexualities in Singapore. The first is the mobilisation against the male sodomy law in Section 377A. The second is the leadership tussle in the women's advocacy group, the Association of Women for Action and Research (AWARE), over the alleged lesbian leanings of its incumbent leadership. Through an analysis of these positions of resistance, this chapter calls for a rigorous scrutiny of the state and its institutions in both coercing and conjuring same-sex sexualities. Although earlier discussions on media prohibitions and official rhetoric on homosexuality have provided preliminary glimpses into how the state is a non-unitary site, fractured by contradictions and inconsistencies in the exercise of power, the two events examined in this chapter provide further insights into the intricacies of state-making: its mundane and routinised effects, its unanticipated and surprising turns, its consistencies and inconsistencies, its hegemonic and contested aspects, as well as its location in a postcolonial world where boundaries are blurred and political agency is oriented both inwards and outwards. While the previous chapter has traced how the postcolonial state has powerfully grafted itself onto the body politic and operated on a specific mode of heteronormativity through the perpetuation of what queer theorists call a heterosexual/homosexual binary, this chapter also cautions against a straightforward reading of state practices as always already impinging and homophobic. Instead, this chapter persists with the theme of postcoloniality by eschewing binaries and re-articulating the links between state, sexuality, citizenship, governance and modernity. Specifically, what is at stake here is a more tangled and complex postcolonial national context from which Singaporean lesbian subjectivities emerged, which makes way for not only a more nuanced understanding of the formation of women's non-normative sexualities, but also paves the way for the introduction of individual agency, as will be evident in the women's accounts we encounter in subsequent chapters.

A parliamentary petition against Section 377A

In 2007, when the Singaporean government carried out a review of the Penal Code installed by the British administration in the nineteenth century, a set of amendments was proposed: Section 377 of the Penal Code, the law banning oral and anal sex between men and women, will be repealed, whereas Section 377A, which criminalises oral and anal sex between men, will remain. With these revisions, Section 377A now stands codified in the Singapore Penal Code between the new law on necrophilia (the revised Section 377) and the law on bestiality (Section 377B), reconsolidated under a different schedule of punishments.

The move did not go unnoticed. Lesbian and gay activists and supporters mobilised to petition for the removal of the British sodomy law, sparking a counter lobby from religious and conservative segments. The clash drew widespread attention from within and across the nation. On blogs, online discussions and letters written to the press, Singaporeans began to take sides in a battle to repeal or retain the law. Finally, the petition was debated in parliament. For the first time in Singapore's independent history, the presence of homosexuals in society was openly acknowledged in parliament. It was also only the second time ever that a petition has been presented to parliament for debate.[2] The 'rare petition' (*TODAY* 2007) and the public arguments it engendered opened up a wide discursive space for Singaporeans and foreigners to articulate and interpret the 'state' of Singapore.

In parliament, the arguments ran the gamut from equality to legality to morality. Nominated Member of Parliament (MP), Siew Kum Hong, who delivered the petition in parliament on behalf of the gay community, built his case on the principles of equality, and the rule of law and democracy. First, the amendment to Section 377 permitting heterosexual oral and anal sex, and the retention of Section 377A criminalising the same acts between men, treats sexual minorities and heterosexuals unequally, Siew argued. Citing Article 12(1) of the Constitution, which provides that 'All persons are equal before the law and entitled to the equal protection of the law', Siew said that amending 377 without also repealing 377A is unconstitutional. Second, the preservation of Section 377A in a Penal Code seeking to maintain the safety and security of society is illogical, for 'how does the private and sexual conduct of consenting adults make Singapore unsafe?' Siew asked. Furthermore, the function of criminal law is the protection from, and punishment of, harmful behaviour, but neither 'harm' nor 'culpability' can be logically established in private, consensual sex. Third, keeping Section 377A only to 'signpost' the values of a conservative majority – an argument the state had used to justify the retention of Section 377A during the Penal Code review – runs the risk of enforcing the tyranny of the majority, going against fundamental democratic principles enshrined in the Singapore Constitution. Furthermore, Siew made it clear that 'sign-posting' public morality is never the objective of criminal law, and even if it were, the selective flagging of gay sex and not other affronts to public morality is discriminatory. Adultery, for example, is commonly viewed by society as immoral, yet Section 498, the law making it 'an offence for a man to entice, take away or detain a married woman with intent of having illicit intercourse with her' has been removed from the amended bill. Laying bare the principles of criminal law and the rationale used by the state to justify retaining Section 377A threw into sharp relief a set of inconsistent and irrational practices found on the sexual fringes of the Singaporean state and nation. For a government often emphasising its leadership, efficiency and performance as grounds for its political longevity, the irrationality over 377A is inconsistent state practice. Siew (2007) urged the House to 'do the right thing' and signpost:

... fairness, justice, non-discrimination, openness and inclusiveness fundamental to a secular democracy ... endorse the view that our people should feel free to express diverse views, pursue unconventional ideas, or simply be different ... if those words sound familiar that is because those were the very words of the Prime Minister in his swearing-in speech ...

Critical public discourses and competing ideas made by the country's highest officials revealed, through these sexuality debates, how attitudes, values and policy positions are scarcely unified among the ruling elites. Three MPs from the dominant party broke ranks by speaking up in favour of repealing Section 377A, thus fracturing the state's official stand. MP Baey Yam Keng, who spoke partly in Mandarin to address the traditional Chinese ethnic majority, recounted his experience of living in London where he saw first-hand how the acceptance of homosexuality did not prove disastrous for heterosexuals and their families. MP Hri Kumar questioned the legal ambiguity of having a law in place but not in force, highlighting the potential difficulties for enforcement agencies to interpret the unclear legal position, and the issue of inconsistent punishments meted out to consenting homosexual men but not to heterosexual adults. Furthermore, repressing gay sex would hinder the state's efforts to respond to the threat of HIV/AIDS. MP Charles Chong urged the house to show leadership and not hide behind the views of the conservative majority. The debates in parliament revealed the intrusion of sexual politics into state territory producing disagreements and disunity. Even within a dominant state, there is no coherence in ideology, especially since PAP MPs are themselves transnational elites influenced by global discourses, practices and understandings of sexuality, and their differing positions on homosexuality reflect disjunctive ideas on what Singapore is, and what being Singaporean means.

The arguments of progressive advocates were met with objections from conservative MPs. Thio Li Ann, a Nominated MP, was the most vociferous in her support of Section 377A. Defending the legality and constitutionality of 377A, Thio argued that maintaining the law is not a case of discrimination against gay men but one of 'valid differentiation' since '377A does not target any specific actor; it would cover a heterosexual male experimenting with male sodomy'. There is 'demonstrable harm' as 'anal-penetrative sex is inherently damaging to the body and a misuse of organs', said Thio. In a fit of barely-disguised contempt, Thio further likened gay sex as 'shoving a straw up your nose to drink' before she went on to provide in her parliamentary speech lurid details of gay sex and its 'adverse health implications' such as 'gay bowel syndrome' and 'anal cancer'. Harm, in her opinion, can also be intangible, hurting the moral sensibilities of third parties. Section 377A is therefore beyond legal reproach in how it protects public health and public morality, so her argument goes. Thio also offered a puzzling interpretation of 'secularity' as one where 'Religious views are part of our common morality. We separate religion from politics but not religion from public policy,' as if it was possible to separate public policy from politics. Although the arguments were more rhetorical than reasonable, all but a few of the country's highest officials thumped their seats in approval of Thio's parliamentary speech.

These arguments echoed far beyond the chambers of the parliamentary hall, and set forth a series of contestations in the public sphere. The concept of 'secularism' as propounded by Thio in parliament was subject to rebuttals and criticisms in numerous commentaries. One published in the national broadsheet, for instance, was titled '377A debate and the rewriting of pluralism'. In the article, the Singaporean writer Janadas Devan poked fun at Thio's definition of 'secularism', 'I had always assumed that it was necessary to separate religion from politics as well as public policy', Devan wrote (*Straits Times* 2007b) but not before he launched into a disparaging critique of Thio's concept of 'pluralism':

> ... we had believed 'pluralism' meant ... 'autonomy ... for individual bodies', a 'society in which ... minority groups maintain their independent cultural traditions', 'a system that recognises more than one ultimate principle or kind of being', as the Oxford English Dictionary puts it ...

However, Thio's version of democratic pluralism seems to be 'whatever passes for the majority at any moment', said Devan. Published in the national broadsheet and widely circulated on the internet, critiques such as Devan's ignited popular discussions on 'secularism' and 'pluralism'. These terms have been abstracted from local vernacular and the ideals and values they stand for are seldom articulated or debated in public discourse. However, through the sexuality debates inside and outside parliament, these concepts gained some force and traction. At a public seminar, for instance, a local theologian of the Free Community Church catering to lesbian and gay worshippers, announced to listeners, 'Singapore is a pluralistic society ... there must be spaces for it' (*Fridae. com* 2007c). On social media, blogs, notes and letters to the press circulated widely, several Singaporeans wrote and wondered aloud the implications of allowing a conservative majority to regulate the private activities of sexual minorities. Was this not a form of majoritarianism politics, and what would this mean for other minorities and the social cohesion of Singaporean society? Discourses such as these have remained largely unarticulated and abstracted from public culture, fixated as the nation was on economic development and an imagination of the country's 'vulnerability' as a small nation subject to the vicissitudes of globalisation. 'Survivalism' and 'pragmatism' were thus dominant discursive frames manufactured in official narratives and embedded in popular imaginations of Singapore. But Section 377A and its concomitant politics obliged the state to open up and be scrutinised along democratic principles, and the values of non-discrimination, fairness, justice and inclusiveness.

The sexuality initiatives also brought into the public sphere a series of arguments concerning the status of 'modern' Singapore in the international arena. While priding itself as being at the forefront of modernisation in the region, critics pointed out how Singapore remains one of the last few countries in Southeast Asia – alongside Malaysia, Myanmar and Brunei – to preserve this specific piece of British colonial relic. Former British colonies, Hong Kong and Australia, have long repealed their sodomy laws. Although not pro-actively enforcing 377A might be the government's attempt to avoid being 'out of step with the modern world,' observed the Law Society of Singapore, its existence even in the absence of enforcement 'risked bringing the law into disrepute' (quote taken from Siew's parliamentary speech).

Discourses on 'modernity' were reinforced by public statements made by foreigners such as the famed British actor, Ian McKellen, who was on tour in Singapore for his theatre plays. Appearing in an online video titled *Ian McKellen supports IndigNation*, McKellen states, 'Let me come to the one thing I don't like about Singapore, which is 377A. It is a British law and why the hell you have not got rid of it I am not sure ...' McKellen apologised for 'those dreadful laws that we British left behind' and urged the Singapore government to 'treat us with respect like we treat everyone else'. A few days later on a local television news programme, McKellen announced, 'I am a gay man and I'll be looking for a gay bar (in Singapore), if there is such a thing' (*Fridae.com* 2007d). McKellen's position on homosexuality in Singapore is significant in the context of the state's global city ambitions and its courtship of a 'creative class', which, according to Richard Florida (2002) is the driving force for economic development in a post-industrial, knowledge-based economy – precisely the system the Singaporean government has been cultivating since the Asian financial crisis of the late 1990s. Taking seriously Florida's postulation that members of a creative class tend to settle in places that are 'diverse, tolerant and open to new ideas' (Florida 2002: 249), government officials have been fostering a creative cultural industry where queer cultural productions such as lesbian and gay bars have been allowed to flourish as part of an overall drive towards achieving global city status (Oswin 2014).

The PAP has shown remarkable leadership and adaptability in restructuring Singapore's economy to capture global opportunities. But when intersected with the question of sexuality, it would seem that the government no longer assumes a clear policy or singular right to dictate ideologies and practices. 'We will let others take the lead', said the Prime Minister (Lee 2007), 'we will stay one step behind the front line of change; watch how things work out elsewhere before we make any irrevocable moves'. In a country where leadership has traditionally been authoritarian, autonomous and unapologetic, this shift can hardly go unnoticed. It was just over a decade ago that the Foreign Affairs minister, Wong Kan Seng, brazenly announced Singapore's exceptionalism at the UN conference on Human Rights. Singapore must find its own way 'that suit ourselves', Wong had said (quote taken from Offord 1999: 303). But contentions over homosexuality have led to a different policy paradigm. 'You either go with the world and be part of the world, or you will find that we become a quaint, a quixotic, esoteric appendage of the world', remarked Minister Mentor Lee Kuan Yew on the existence of Singapore's gay law (*Fridae.com* 2007b). Not only was this a sharp contrast to earlier nationalist constructions of Singapore, it would seem that the state has relinquished its once absolute authority, allowing that the entry of transnational forces into the sexual terrain is not a matter over which it can exercise control.

Indeed, mobilisations over Section 377A widened across Singapore with clamours of protests enacted by advocates and opponents of the repeal. The gay community and its supporters created a 'Repeal 377A' website gathering over 8,000 signatures while opponents countered with a 'Keep 377A' website that attracted thousands more. Members of the local arts fraternity – actors, actresses and musicians – produced a rap video urging to 'Repeal 377A Singapore!' while opponents wrote letters to the local press and deployed the power of the pulpit speaking against the repeal at church sermons. Generally, advocates and opponents produced arguments well-rehearsed in controversies over the acceptance of homosexuality. Advocates argued on the principles of equality, civil liberty and human rights, and that the retention of the legislation is a contravention of the Singapore constitution. The opposition's quarrel was that removing the law will lead to the moral degradation of Singaporean society, and to changes in laws and policies such as those pertaining to sexuality education in schools, gay marriages and child adoption. Allowing homosexuality would also threaten the 'conservative majority' in Singapore, lower the nation's already precarious birth rates, and endorse a Western homosexual agenda imperilling Singapore. Collectively, what these efforts demonstrate is how Section 377A served as a predominant symbol of power around which a broad coalition of individuals and groups rallied to reverse and reinforce discourses around Singapore, which were once dominated by the single-party state's monologues. Through the sexualised prism of Section 377A, state power is fragmented and dispersed in a milieu where all sorts of power, besides state power, are also at work. The event plays out the multiple nationalisms sexuality entails.

The typically resolute state eventually settled on a paradoxical and contradictory position. The sodomy law will be kept but it will not be enforced. 'We just leave it' said Prime Minister Lee Hsien Loong in the closing of the parliamentary debate. It would 'be better to accept the legal untidiness and ambiguity. It works, don't disturb it' (Lee 2007). If gay activists were to push for the repeal, there will be backlash from the conservative camp. The state will 'strive to maintain a balance, to uphold a stable society with traditional, heterosexual family values, but with space for homosexuals to live their lives and contribute to society' (Lee 2007). Claiming deference to a conservative majority and the defence of sexual minorities, the government decided to 'leave things be' with the promise that it would not proactively enforce the law, and would change its stance along with changes in public opinion. Section 377A was thus left without resolution, and in this ambiguity lies a 'queering' of the state as disaggregated across its multiple positions and myriad of agents, revealing perceptible instabilities.

The retention of Section 377A led easily to the conclusion that the entire episode was 'purely symbolic politics' (Chua 2007: 60). Much as the parliamentary petition may be read as political posturing and a failure, such readings tend to emphasise the state as hegemon, acting singularly on sexuality. The episode of the parliamentary petition of 377A nevertheless provides valuable insights into how state policies and practices are often inconsistent. Laced with what appears to be a conciliatory logic with many loopholes, the government's response towards the law gives us necessary glimpses into a number of points of fractures and inconsistencies that help undermine the reproduction of state power over homosexuality. Consequently, instead of being set back by this failed attempt to remove the law, lesbian and gay activism took off in Singapore.

Neither can the state's maintenance of Section 377A be read as homophobia. While heteronormativity undergirds almost all its social policies, the state's position, as this event evinces, is more tangled than the mere expression of homophobia. The PAP's uncharacteristic ambivalence towards its position and policy on same-sex sexualities, as discussed, must be understood in the context of the postcolonial elites' navigation of a Singaporean 'modernity' and its global city ambitions. In competing for global capital and skilled labour, postcolonial elites must, on the one hand, produce an image of Singapore meeting international commercial standards and adapting to global norms and values where a more tolerant attitude towards liberal lifestyles have become normative. On the other hand, postcolonial nationalism requires the construction of a 'national culture' that is 'stable' and cohesive bulwarking against global disjunctive flows. On Section 377A, the government would refrain from exercising power and taking leadership. Instead, it would look cautiously for cues, as the Minister Mentor's (Lee 2011) reflection revealed:

> I would hesitate to push it through against the prevailing sentiment, against the prevailing values of society. You're going against the current of the people, the underlying feeling. What's the point of that, you know, breaking new ground and taking unnecessary risk? It will evolve over time, as so many things have, because after a while my own sort of maturing process will take place with other people. You don't just live and then you cut off your ideas after a certain time. You keep on living and you watch people and you say, 'Oh that's the way life is'.

This is not to say that state power was wantonly given up. Despite the state's conflicting position on 377A, that it would not proactively pursue consenting homosexual activity, there have been several charges of Section 377A since 2007. A 377A injunction was issued against two gay men caught for sex acts in a public toilet. Given the ambiguous parliamentary conclusion, a human rights activist and lawyer filed an application in the High Court challenging the constitutionality of Section 377A by pointing to the irregularity of the laws and rights applied to gay men in Singapore. In response, the Attorney-General Chambers amended the charge to that of committing an obscene act in public, and both men were convicted under this revised charge. This episode suggests that if homosexuality is not prosecuted by an impotent law it will be persecuted by the discretionary powers of public prosecutors. However, what this challenge against the Singapore Constitution does – after the wide-ranging debates over the repeal of Section 377A in 2007 – is to re-stage the inconsistencies and disaggregations of the state. A critical queer reading of the state reveals once more that law enforcement and the courts, rather than the monolithic state per se, are also battle sites on which the legitimisation of same-sex sexualities is fought. The tussle with religious Christian Right groups in Singapore, explored in the next section, proves to be another contestation site. Placing the power collisions and collusions, tensions and tactics between and across state institutions, agencies and other sexual sites under the analytical lens offers a more critical framing of how same-sex desires are both defined and defiant in the postcolonial context of Singapore.

A leadership tussle over lesbianism

It was Saturday, 2 May 2009, at the city Town Hall. Dana Lam, the re-elected President of the Association of Women for Action and Research (AWARE), raised her hand in victory to loud cheers from a raucous crowd of over 2,000 women. This would be her third term as President. The 'old guard' were jubilant over the wresting back of leadership at AWARE from a new Executive Committee (EXCO) who themselves had seized leadership at the organisation a month earlier.

The story began when unfamiliar faces appeared at AWARE's election day to contest and elect the next Executive Committee of the 28-year-old organisation. Eighty of the 102 members who attended AWARE's election day had signed up to join the organisation only three months earlier. To the surprise of long-term members, a group of professional Chinese women, barely acquainted with the organisation, were voted in as the new leaders of AWARE. The unexpected change sparked suspicion among long-term members that the new team had hidden agendas. When it emerged that most of the 'new guard' were from the same Anglican Pentecostal church with 'trenchant anti-gay and anti-abortion views' (*TODAY* 2009) and that the Christian leaders had marshalled supporters from the church to participate in AWARE's general elections, it became clear that this was a quasi-religious take-over of Singapore's most established women's advocacy organisation. AWARE's foundational values, which are liberal, inclusive and secular, were suddenly at stake. The perceived threat to AWARE's ideological direction became all too real as the new guards proceeded to install surveillance and change the locks to the centre's doors, terminate the headships of AWARE's sub-committees, ban the practise of allowing ex-Presidents to attend meetings, and fired the centre manager with a replacement hired from the same church. This seizure of the well-established women's organisation led to a great public outcry, and ignited public discussions of religion, multicultural secularity and what constitutes 'national culture' in contemporary Singapore through, what turned out to be, the unlikely issue of female same-sex love in Singapore.

Under public pressure, the new committee called for a press conference announcing that the liberal old guards at AWARE had taken 'a gay turn' (*Straits*

Times 2009a). AWARE had sponsored a lesbian-themed film called 'Spider Lilies' at its charity gala, held a Mother's Day event featuring mothers and their lesbian daughters talking about relationships, invited 'a famous homosexual activist' (*Straits Times* 2009b) to talk about HIV, and helped a female transgender group, SG Butterfly, to raise awareness and reach out to the transgender community. Most alarming on AWARE's litany of queer transgressions was the comprehensive sexuality education (CSE) programme it provided to public schools for 12- to 18-year-olds, which conveyed homosexuality in neutral, and not negative, terms. The new guards cited as evidence the following incriminating terms used in AWARE's CSE teaching guide:

> Anal sex can be healthy or neutral if practised with consent and with a condom.
>
> Avoid using the term 'husband' and use 'partner' instead, so it is more inclusive. For example, homosexuals have partners, not husbands.
>
> (Taken from *Straits Times* 2009b)

'Are we going to have an entire generation of lesbians?' asked Dr Thio Su Mien, a senior lawyer and former dean of the Singapore University law faculty, who identified herself as 'Feminist Mentor' to the newly-elected Christian new guard. Claiming to be the mastermind behind the new guards' seizure of power, Thio accused the old AWARE of becoming a 'single purpose organisation overly concerned with promoting lesbianism'. Her goal, she proclaimed, was to return AWARE 'back to the original purpose' (*New Paper* 2009). Thio's allegations would go on to mark the start of the most publicised mobilisation over women's same-sex desires in the history of Singapore.

What was an internal tussle over the so-called lesbian leanings of AWARE turned into a very public scuffle played out in the media. The old leadership called for a press conference to respond to the new team's allegations (*Straits Times* 2009c). If AWARE had held activities that involved lesbians, said a founding member to the press (*Straits Times* 2009d), it was because these women were already present in society. Although the women's organisation has organised a handful of events for lesbians in Singapore, never before has the presence of female sexual minorities in Singapore been so openly acknowledged by the women's organisation. The issue of lesbianism 'exploded into national consciousness' and led to debates on whether faith-driven groups should be taking over secular organisations (*Straits Times* 2009e). With the media fully drawn into the controversy, these debates had wide reach. Despite the calls for restraint and 'objectivity' by political leaders, these went largely unheeded. Even reporters from the *Straits Times*, the main government-controlled broadsheet, pursued the AWARE saga with much vigour, unmasking the anti-homosexual stance of the new EXCO by producing all the anti-gay forum letters the women had previously written to the newspaper.

With the media fully drawn into the controversy, the episode attracted wide interest. Battle lines were drawn between supporters of the liberal old guards and the conservative Christian new guards. Liberals objected to the hijacking of a women's organisation over the single issue of lesbianism; conservatives expressed shock at AWARE's CSE programme; death threats and character assassinations were exchanged between both sides; fear-mongering was rife, with concerns of a religious takeover on one side and of a homosexual movement seeking to infiltrate Singapore on the other. The Anglican Pentecostal church threw its weight behind the new leaders with the pastor urging his congregation to 'be engaged' in support of their 'sisters' in the new EXCO. 'There's a line that God has drawn for us', the pastor said, 'and we don't want our nation crossing the line' (Hong 2009). Nationalist sentiment was thus fused with religious fervour in the battle against women's same-sex love. The pastor's attempts to mobilise his church drew the ire of the National Council of Churches, a regulatory body, which issued a public statement announcing, among other things, that it did not condone the use of the pulpit to get involved in politics. Subsequently, the pastor issued a public apology.

These public quarrels culminated in an extraordinary general meeting called by the old leadership to remove the new team. Thousands of Singaporean women signed up for AWARE membership to participate in the proceedings. The women came from all walks of life – working professionals, students, mothers, daughters, netizens, lesbians, Muslims, Hindus and Christians. Eventually, outnumbered by the supporters of the old team by about 1,400 to 700, the new EXCO leadership was ousted and the re-elected leaders took office amid buoyant cheers. These public displays made visible the role of sexuality in the formation of national public culture.

In stark contrast to the staging of these public cultural spectacles was the scant involvement of the state as the AWARE event unfolded. For the most part, state agents and authorities stayed on the sidelines, save for a few official comments warning about the divisiveness of religious politics in multi-cultural Singapore and the need for a moderate civil society. The Deputy Prime Minister, Teo Chee Hean, was one of the first to address the issue. In a newspaper article titled 'Keep religion above petty politics', he was quoted as saying:

> It is important in Singapore that all groups make sure that when they have a point of view to put across that they do so in a way which is tolerant of other groups ... we should operate in Singapore in a way that is respectful and tolerant of other's views.
>
> (*Straits Times* 2009f)

Rebuking the Christian conservatives' unfriendly takeover of the women's organisation and warning the group against pushing too hard is a sharp contrast to how state trope, usually reserved in the past to curtailing LGBT demands for a place in the national community, is now used to urge for respect and tolerance of sexual 'others'. Subsequently, in a similar reversal, the Minister for Community Development, Vivian Balakrishnan, addressed the Christian conservatives' anti-gay views with the same rhetoric the PAP used to justify keeping Section 377A:

> ... there will always be some issues where you cannot get everybody to agree on. We must be able to live and let live.
>
> (*Straits Times* 2009g)

The lack of a clear, direct and explicit intervention is somewhat surprising. The postcolonial elites did not rush in to play the role of the arbiter of sexual rights, or to moralise over the issue of sexuality. Perhaps the postcolonial elites no longer desired to take the initiative on these socially divisive matters. Chong (2011) argued that this event demonstrates the PAP's retreat from its role as a moral guardian of society, creating a 'moral void' which Christian conservatives rushed to fill. The AWARE saga and the sexual politics that followed seemed to have given new shape to the dynamics of nation building and nationalism in contemporary Singapore.

Only when pressed for a direct response by the media did the other Deputy Prime Minister, Wong Kan Seng, reiterate the state's stand on homosexuality:

> The way for homosexuals to have space in our society is to accept the informal limits which reflect the point of balance that our society can accept, and not to assert themselves stridently as gay groups do in the West ... Government policy on homosexuality is settled.
>
> (*Straits Times* 2009h)

Unravelled and then reassembled towards a certain course, the seeming finality of the government's position towards homosexuality underscores the point that inconsistency, unpredictability and a lack of a coherent position may characterise a state, but they certainly do not always imply an undermining of power. It is notable, however, that the expression of this power is not unrelentingly homophobic. The government's hesitant entry into the fray, its 'soft' rebuke of the Christian conservatives' actions, and its unreconciled positions suggest that state practices and sites can be messy, fraught and contested arenas with the potential for resistance and transformations.

The AWARE episode was significant for several other reasons. Not only did it provide a forum for the recognition of the existence and legitimacy of lesbian women in Singaporean society, it called attention to the production of a sexual truth regime that goes beyond state politics and power. Appropriating queer theory is instructive at this juncture. The battle for homosexuals in Singapore, and elsewhere for that matter, is not simply one of demanding democratic representation from the government. Nor is it simply a struggle for inclusion and belonging to a core nationalist identity invented by the modern state. Rather, the battle is also about wrestling control over multiple and competing discourses concerning hetero- and same-sex sexualities, and the opponent is not just the state, but other constituencies attempting to define discourse and 'normative' sexuality. Queer theory keeps us alert to multiple sources in a field of power relations where variously constituted communities – in the case of AWARE, the heterosexual Christian right, and the homosexual community – interact with administrative units (Patton 1993: 173). This bears strong congruence to Foucault's formulation of power relations, and critical feminist theorists' clarion call to undermine monolithic structures. Taken together, sexuality, from these theoretical perspectives, is reproduced and repressed at multiple sites, transverses relations of power, with each site or unit surfeited not just with power but also agency.

Coda

I have argued for modes of investigation which strip bare the state into its distinctive processes and forms. Sexuality scholars call this the 'sexualisation' or 'queering' of the state. Key to these conceptions is the notion that the state should no longer be seen as an entirely homophobic, monolithic entity acting singularly on sexuality, but one disaggregated into its related set of generative processes, structures, institutions, agencies and authorities. Through focusing on the messiness and inconsistencies across its operations of power, the image of the state as an impenetrable leviathan can be undermined, making way for a more dialogic state-sexuality relationship.

The sexuality debates and mobilisations around these two events have provided unwonted interpretations and re-imaginations of the Singaporean state through a few discursive prisms. To summarise: first, there is the constitutional rendering of the state wherein the national community is re-imagined into being as open, diverse and inclusive, and the state's role is to uphold the fundamental protections afforded by the Singapore Constitution. Second, there is the inflection of the Singaporean state through democratic principles of equality and plurality, with contesting interpretations offered by advocates and opponents of the homosexual debate. Third, there is also the inflection of the state through religious doctrine where the concepts of 'religion', 'national culture' and 'secularity' have fused, producing tensions around the ways in which Singaporeans of all institutions – the church, lay citizens and state builders – approach these terrains. Fourth, there is a majoritarian view where the state acts not on its own initiative as it did before but is directed by a supposed conservative majority 'silently' making policy and ideology. Finally, there is a view of Singapore as an international actor in an international arena of states, where technologies of power in global economic and cultural systems operate in relation to sexuality to 'queer' the state by highlighting its lack of omnipotence in re-shaping sexual ideologies and practices in Singapore.

The danger of leaving the state 'unqueered' and unravelled in an overarching, immutable form is that we tend to easily fall back on the assumption of the state as all-powerful, all-pervasive and always already homophobic, especially, and ironically, when we critique its dominance and discipline of non-normative sexualities. Disaggregating and re-imagining the state are therefore ways to interrogate state power without inadvertently reproducing its power. When so disaggregated, the dissonance and fractures of power become visible, and it is through these fissures that forms of a 'reverse discourse' and resistance rise to the fore. Therefore, we can argue alongside Foucault (1978) and critical sexuality scholars that sexuality enters the system of governmentality not just as a site of repression, but also as a site of resistance. Power and repression engender politics and resistance, which reared strongly in the two local mobilisations against the discriminating male sodomy law of Section 377A, and over the issue of lesbianism in AWARE. There is thus a politics of sexuality not reducible to a binary polarising of power against resistance. This brings us to the realisation that the powers of the state and queer resistance are hybrid forms: each producing, limiting, sustaining and suppressing each other dynamically in a field of continually interconnected power relations. In this dialectic relationship, subject and object are intimately bound together in such a way that the latter is produced by the former in a reciprocal struggle, and in this inversion and transformation, it is no longer determinable what is the source or subject of power. This postcolonial perspective is pertinent within the re-formulated state-sexuality relationship.

In the previous chapter, I made the point that paying analytical attention to the state's hegemonic power is necessary as a form of critique and political intervention against state-led violations of same-sex sexualities. But equally crucial is a more nuanced understanding of state-sexuality relations. If analyses of sexuality do not sufficiently 'sexualise' or 'queer' the category of the 'state', these same analyses criticising state power also become unwittingly complicit with the constitution of state power itself. In such a situation, the project of scholarly critique turns counterproductive.

In this chapter, the events of the parliamentary petition against Section 377A and the AWARE saga play out the co-production and complexity of state-sexuality relations. These events expose how state policies and laws are not only sites of sexual repression, they are also sites of sexual resistance. Operating within a sexual truth regime, the state, its agencies and self-proclaimed representatives coerce and subjugate sexual subjects at the same time as they hail sexual subjects into being and on whose bodies the nation is imagined. Informed by this more complex understanding of the local-national context from where same-sex sexualities in Singapore have emerged, we now turn to the agentic and creative ways in which lesbians in Singapore negotiate their globalised sexual subjectivities and construct their sexual identities around local-cultural forms.

Notes

1 This latter aspect is often deployed in critical queer scholarships focused on the pervasiveness of power over sexuality: through its capillary operations, which certainly involve state institutions, an 'omnipresence of power' is 'produced at every instant, at every point, or moreover in every relation between one point and another' (Foucault 1978: 122). However, by not attending to the conceptualisation of the state within the matrix, the scholarship tends to reproduce the assumption of a monolithic system of domination.
2 The parliamentary petition to repeal Section 377A is only the second ever in the history of independent Singapore to be presented to Parliament for debate. The first parliamentary petition was presented in 1985 when one Sivadas Sankaran, who was sued for defamation on a memorandum he submitted to a Select Committee of Parliament, petitioned for Parliamentary privilege. Member of Parliament, J.B. Jeyaretnam, presented the petition, which was denied.

5 Transnational politics of local queer activism and lesbian activists

In the previous chapters, the postcolonial Singaporean nation-state was first analysed as a central material and discursive site through which hegemonic codes of sexuality are produced. Although there are numerous ways to grasp state power over sexuality, I focused on the postcolonial state's developmental project, its intersecting discourses on nationalism and sexuality, and its repressive practices against homosexuality in the law, in the media and in the public rhetoric of its postcolonial elites. But as repression is enforced and extended, so is resistance unequivocally engendered. The lobby against the male sodomy law in 2007 and the leadership tussle over lesbian issues in 2009 are two compelling events demonstrating evidence of a 'reverse discourse' in the very sites where strong social controls over homosexuality have been advanced. In the state-affiliated media and among individual state actors, homosexuality has been acknowledged, if not legitimised, sometimes in the same language and rhetoric by which it has been disqualified. As the unfolding of these events demonstrated in the previous chapter, the state is characterised by an uneven set of discourses, apparatuses and institutions that serve to regulate and yet reinforce same-sex sexualities in Singapore. Examining the PAP's legal discourses, its control over the media, and the various positionalities undertaken by its postcolonial elites towards homosexuality helped make apparent their multiple and contradictory scripts of sexuality. In the ensuing analysis, thus, the state was problematised as a unitary, coherent source of social enforcement producing hegemonic codes of sexuality with an immutable force. Unravelling the state enabled an analysis that threads through the gaps and contradictions between its institutions and agents. Indeed, as evident in previous chapters, the postcolonial Singapore state has at significant times tolerated, if not supported, the proliferation of differences from unruly sexual citizens.

These re-conceptualisations of the state and state-sexuality relations help set the stage for this chapter, for it is through the fractures and interstices of multiple points of power that queer activism and lesbian activists emerge. Local queer scholarship has captured the growing visibility and contours of lesbian and gay communities in Singapore, as well as pointed to the apparent contradictions in the government's methods of social control, noting for instance the 'U-turns – ambivalent, schizophrenic, and unpredictable responses of the government' towards homosexuality (Tan and Lee 2007: 182). However, existing analyses have tended to view these contradictions as the result of 'cautious liberalisation' on the part of the government (Tan and Lee 2007: 183) or the 'illiberal pragmatic' governance of the state (Yue 2007: 105). By describing these state-directed effects in the absence of a re-formulation of state-sexuality relations, these analyses have only painted a picture of state power, lending it further strength. Thus, in Tan and Lee's (2007: 183) analysis, no 'real changes' have been made to challenge the state's authority over sexuality:

> How far the government is willing to go at each juncture is largely a function of strategic calculations to maximise state power and, in materialistic Singapore, the economic gain required to transform this power into authority.

What was perhaps intended as a critique of state authority ironically ends up reifying the state as an immutable force when, in fact, the politics of sexuality in Singapore have commandeered new nationalisms that the state has struggled to keep pace with and take charge of. As I examine the growth of queer activism and lesbian subjectivities in the following discussions, my endeavour is to avoid falling back on the assumptions of the Singapore state as omnipotent. Instead, I wish to continue asking after the points of penetration, the sites of fracture, the intersections and inflections in the clash and collusion of state-sexuality relations in postcolonial Singapore.

In the last two chapters, I have focused on the 'internal' material and ideological context of Singapore from where lesbian subjectivities and practices have emerged. Moving into the next two chapters, I wish to consider and analyse the sexual subjectivities of local lesbians in postcolonial Singapore by locating them 'externally' in the global context. Just as I have argued that queer narratives and identities cannot be understood outside the purview of the complex national discursive context, my primary premise is that same-sex sexualities, especially that of middle-class, educated lesbians in Singapore, cannot be analysed without taking into account the effects of global flows. My aim in this latter part of the book is to turn the lens onto the subject positions and narratives of lesbian women in a transnational context. It thus becomes useful to bring all these theorisations – of state-sexuality relations, and hybridisation and transnational subjectivities – into one analytic field as we make sense of the accounts of the Singaporean lesbian women we are about to examine. Are same-sex-desiring women in Singapore merely mimetic of Western gay models? Are they meek same-sex subjects of the nation-state? What happens when the globalised sexual subjectivities of these middle-class lesbian women meet and intersect with dominant discourses of localised nationalisms, and vice versa? As we examine the women's lives, aspirations and desires, keeping these questions in mind will help us make sense of what it means to be gay in postcolonial Singapore.

This chapter looks at the growth of queer organising generally and the lesbian groups within that, and considers the subject positions of local lesbian activists in Singapore. The next chapter examines the accounts of local non-activist queer women. What does being lesbian mean in their daily lives from the perspective of both groups of women? Dividing my respondents into these two chapters will delineate how the women, from the vantage point of their different affiliations to the global and local politics of sexuality, are interpellated in transnational cultural discourses and the ideologies of the postcolonial nation-state. Situating their narratives in separate chapters will also highlight the tensions and contradictions of the women's alternative sexualities from these two subject positions, which, as I shall argue, hold political implications and real-life consequences for both activists and individual queer women in Singapore.

Lesbian activists in Singapore gained prominence through their work alongside gay men in umbrella queer organisations. As such, this chapter begins with a general analysis of queer activism in Singapore in which lesbian activists played prominent roles in queer organising. Then, paying closer attention to lesbian activism, I turn my attention to the politics and subject positions of prominent lesbian activists in Singapore who are firmly located in global circuits of queer knowledge production, but at the same time attempt to articulate the specificities of their location as Singaporean queer women.

Fostering queer consciousness in fraught discursive tropes

Lesbian and gay community groups started to organise from the 1990s amid transitions in the socio-political sphere. The handover of leadership in the PAP, from Lee Kuan Yew to Goh Chok Tong in 1990, led analysts to observe that the political culture in Singapore had become more open and consultative compared to the authoritarian rule of the regime's predecessor (Welsh *et al.* 2009). Goh himself promised a 'softer' style, 'more in keeping with the mood of the day' (2001 National Day Rally speech). But other analysts, such as Rodan (2009), warned against overstating the transformation. Recognising that social pluralism had inadvertently accompanied economic prosperity in the city-state, Goh pre-emptively designed state structures to co-opt diverse political views, effectively curtailing independent political participation by organisations and individuals.[1] In Rodan's (2009: 61) assessment, this was the equivalent of the 'structural and ideological refinement of authoritarian rule' rather than its dilution.

The socio-political context was confounding for lesbian and gay subjects. In 1997, Goh announced in parliament the launch of 'Singapore 21' (S21), a government-led public consultation exercise to deliberate on the nation's future in the new millennium. In keeping with his proffered consultative and inclusive style, Goh's S21 initiative involved over 6,000 Singaporeans participating in the collective task of forging 'a new vision for a new era' (Goh 1997). In his parliamentary speech, Goh warned that globalisation in the twenty-first century will 'mean more intense competition'. He urged Singaporeans to be 'like the US' in producing 'more ideas and innovation', to 'respect and accept greater diversity in ideas', and 'respect the different cultures in our midst'. Departing from the

PAP's typically authoritarian politics, Goh invited Singaporeans to 'participate actively and become involved in community and national issues'. The Prime Minister's open invitation for greater social and political participation was an opportunity for the LGBT community to latch onto the shifting nationalist rhetoric of the ruling party. People Like Us (PLU), the main LGBT lobby group of that era, decided to take the discursive tropes of S21 to task. Seizing the sudden 'liberal' tone of the government, PLU applied for a license to hold a public forum titled 'Gays and Lesbians within Singapore 21'. This was a calculated move. From PLU's perspective:

> If a licence was given, there would be a forum where PLU could bring gay issues to the public attention. If a licence was refused, it would be proof positive of empty promises by the government, and the negative publicity would exact a price by damaging the government's PR efforts.
>
> (People Like Us 2003)

The application was eventually turned down. According to the authorities, the 'mainstream moral values of Singaporeans are conservative, and the Penal Code has provisions against certain homosexual practices' (Mah 2000). It was not unexpected. What deserves attention, however, is PLU's act of resistance, particularly in how the contention against the government was framed in terms of a no-loss outcome. Even though the application to hold the forum was denied, resistance in this instance took the form of the mutation of state power by highlighting the inconsistency and hypocrisy of state authorities. It is possible to make too much of the 'victory' registered by the PLU here. After all, the end result did not detract from the continuing, almost Gramscian, hegemony of the postcolonial PAP state over homosexuality. However, the greater loss would be to make too little of the PLU's attempts to snare the state for a place within the national community. To view this exchange as merely another instance of how 'homosexuality and its representations have been the subjects of prohibition in postcolonial, communitarian Singapore' (Tan and Lee 2007: 180) would serve only to entrench state power over sexuality. What is needed is a more sustained focus on the strategies and contentions claimed by the nation's sexual dissidents. In the reclamation lay the possibilities of a re-orientation from hegemonic state oppression in the direction of sexual empowerment and agency.

In 2003, following another government-led national consultation exercise called 'Remaking Singapore', PLU closed in on new overtures made by Goh to the local queer community. In an interview for a *Time* magazine cover feature titled, 'The Lion in Winter', Goh said his administration would now hire homosexuals to 'sensitive positions' in the government. 'In the past, if we know you are gay, we would not employ you. But we changed this quietly' (*Time* magazine 2003). This policy reversal was inspired in part by the state's desire for a Singapore makeover. In the wake of the dotcom bust in North America and the protracted Asian financial crisis, 'Remaking Singapore' was launched to transform Singapore's 'dull image' as a 'famously uptight city-state' (Associated Press

2003) into a vibrant, open city where talented Singaporeans would be enticed to stay and foreign professionals lured in for work and play. Singapore will do 'whatever it takes' to attract talent, said Vivian Balakrishnan, the Minister in charge of the Remaking Singapore Committee tasked to makeover Singapore. 'There are a sprinkling of gay bars, and many dance clubs set aside one night each week for gay customers', reports the *Time* article. Goh went on to say:

> ... in time the population will understand that some people are born that way ... we are born this way and they are born that way, but they are like you and me.
>
> (Quoted in *Time* magazine 2003: 4)

Within hours of the *Time* feature appearing on the magazine's website, the gay community was abuzz with excitement. 'My eyes zoomed in on the word "born", for this marked a profound change in the government's stance', wrote Alex Au, a leading activist and one of the founders of PLU, on his widely read blog (*Yawning Bread* 2003). Au and his contemporaries received Goh's 'born that way' comments as 'remarkably positive'. In a place where same-sex desires are treated as morally reproachable lifestyle 'choices', and so little else has been said about homosexuality in the public realm, this was for the community, 'a bolt from the blue' (*Yawning Bread* 2003). Goh's remarks can be read with scepticism in at least two ways. First, it places the discussion of homosexuality once more within the limiting terms of the nature versus nurture debate; the dichotomy imposed to demand proof of homosexuality's naturalness on the one hand, and assume heterosexuality as an unproblematic a priori 'natural' fact on the other hand. Second, the sudden openness towards homosexuality merely demonstrates once more the state's economic rationality and strategic pragmatism; 'queerness' is deployed as a 'technology' for economic goals on the one hand; and abstracted from issues of human rights on the other hand. Audrey Yue theorises this as the 'illiberal pragmatics' (2007, 2012) of sexual governance in Singapore, where the state desires only those who 'do' gay at the gay bars and dance clubs, and not those who wish to 'be' gay following Western rights-based politics. But such scepticisms were elided by 'indefatigable optimism' (*Yawning Bread* 2003). Reading Goh's comments alongside the Senior Minister's earlier remarks to the US National Public Radio that homosexuality could be a 'DNA problem' (Lee, quoted in *Yawning Bread* 2000) led to the conclusion that homosexuality has finally been acknowledged as having a genetic basis by both leaders. Moreover, official thinking has 'progressed' from seeing homosexuality as a 'problem' (Lee, quoted in *Yawning Bread* 2000) to an understanding that 'people are born that way' (Goh, quoted in *Time* magazine 2003). The shift in government position has been foreshadowed, wrote Au optimistically on his blog (*Yawning Bread* 2003).

PLU quickly agitated for action. On the Singapore Gay News List (SiGNeL), an email forum run by the PLU, subscribers were mobilised to write letters of appreciation to the Prime Minister as well as letters of appeal to the press seeking for wider social acceptance in light of Goh's apparent acquiescence. A

SiGNeL participant declared, 'a window has been opened ... for us to stand up and make our voices heard' (quote taken from Tan and Lee 2007: 194). Analysing Goh's *Time* magazine comments in their article titled, 'Imagining the Gay Community in Singapore', Tan and Lee (2007) underscored how queer activists strategically organised themselves in and through the state's inconsistent rhetoric, rising up to assert themselves through changing discursive contexts.

Also of interest and relevance is their account of how queer activists had urged gay Singaporeans to:

> ... come out, and not just from the closet but from the safety of the private 'gay scene': only by expressing themselves in the public sphere can they fight for greater diversity and acceptance in Singapore society.
>
> (Tan and Lee 2007: 194)

'If you do not', as Tan and Lee (2007: 194) quoted an informant, 'I think you lose the right ever to complain about Singapore being an unaccepting place'. Similarly, a female activist was also quoted:

> So, if you, as a GLBT (gay, lesbian, bisexual, transgendered) person, are not going to take up the challenge now, then forever hold your peace, because YOU (the gay girl who is happy partying ... or the gay boy who is happy at all the saunas ...) chose to give up that right.
>
> (Tan and Lee 2007: 194)

A conscious mode of 'being gay' that bears commitment to Western gay liberation is differentiated from 'doing gay' in these activist responses. Evident in these discourses is also the centrality of a politics of visibility and 'coming out' – the political ethos and strategy of queer communities in the West. Although it was left unsaid, the evidence presented in Tan and Lee's (2007) account signals how the local queer movement has engaged with a global gay discourse to articulate their demands. For both the writers and their activist informants, the realisation of gay rights in Singapore is one tied to a model of Western sexual identity politics wherein gaining visibility is paramount. Those who do not respond to the 'positive call' to come out and speak, as Tan and Lee (2007: 195) write, are 'discursively highlighted as passive, apolitical, sceptical, and *frivolous* gay Singaporeans' (italics mine). On this point, the writers conclude that closeted gay Singaporeans 'constituted a threat to the potential fulfilment of a liberated and recognised gay community claiming its rightful place among other legitimate communities in Singapore' (Tan and Lee 2007: 195).

What is left unquestioned in this analysis is the particular political trajectory the activists and the writers envision for the local gay community. It raises the question of whether it is possible to opt for a queering of culture that does not rely on these particular strategies of unmasking and declaring one's sexual identity. How are we to understand postcolonial queers who do not want to speak out publicly about their same-sex identities? A further insight into these same-sex subjectivities will be provided in the next chapter when we examine the sexual subjectivities of individual lesbian women. Here, the characterisation of closeted gay Singaporeans as 'frivolous' and 'unliberated' because they do not conform to hegemonic assumptions of queer visibility returns us to the problematic of privileging an Anglo-American same-sex model as global, universal and inevitable. To what extent is local activism imbricated in a global gay discourse, and how does this implicate their politics? I will attend to these central questions in the subsequent sections of this chapter. As we begin to look more closely at local queer activism in Singapore, the point I wish to re-assert here is that our lens must necessarily be bifocal. As analysts celebrate the opening up of opportunities for sexual minorities, and as activists challenge for political and social space through deploying particular strategies of activism in local contexts, both the analyst and the activist must also pay attention to the incursions of imperialist sexual politics with respect to a global postcolonial world order. The former is a question of sexual nationalism, the latter of sexual colonialism. But for an ever-vigilant and insecure postcolonial state, sexual colonialism from the West could be turned into a convenient nationalist discourse to rationalise its agenda of sexual nationalism.

Certainly, the postcolonial state has been keenly sensitive to the resonances between dominant Western modes of sexual identity politics and local queer activism. It sought opportunities to frame same-sex rights as a 'Western issue' alien to a postcolonial Singapore instilled with 'Asian values'. Links with the Western gay movement thus situate local same-sex sexualities as a prime site for the state to consolidate its nationalist anti-Westernisation narrative. In the language of its Prime Ministers, 'Western countries went for experimental lifestyles in the 1960s – the hippies, free love, all the rage' (Lee 2007) with 'bad Western values' such as the 'me first, society second' attitude and the 'trend towards promiscuity, fun-loving, free-loving kind of society' (Goh quoted in Koh 1989: 744). In contrast, 'good Eastern values' represent opposite terms, and above these, an attitude of 'society first, me second' (Chua 1995: 158). Westernisation of Singaporean society has been an abiding worry for the state's ruling elites. The economic success of Singapore and the material affluence enjoyed by Singaporeans will inevitably breed individualism and excessive consumerism. Furthermore, the institutionalisation of English as the lingua franca of the nation meant that while Singaporeans became proficient in the language of commerce and could participate competently in the global capitalist economy, a largely English-educated population also meant a certain risk of 'deculturalisation' (Goh 1978), leaving Singapore vulnerable to the forces of Westernisation. Thus, the discursive binaries of a 'moral East' versus an 'immoral West' were consciously and continuously imagined by the postcolonial state as part of its nationalist consolidation against the global reach of the Western economy and its cultural apparatus. Within this ideological formulation, same-sex sexualities are cast in the camp of the 'Western Other' – a figure of excess and bodily indulgence in opposition to the disciplined 'Asian' subject (Yao 2007) – so as to buttress the state's moral nationalist discourse.

Subsequently, on the employment of gay civil servants, which created battle-lines in the public sphere between supporters of the queer community who strategically positioned themselves within the new liberalising rhetoric of the state versus the moral conservatives who opposed what they saw as a state sacrificing its moral leadership in pursuit of economic growth and global city ambitions, Goh made the following announcement at a National Day Rally speech:

> As for my comments on gays, they do not signal any change in policy that would erode the moral standards of Singapore ... Singapore is still a traditional and conservative Asian society ... the more (gays) lobby for public space, the bigger the backlash they will provoke from the conservative mainstream.
>
> (Quote taken from *Fridae.com* 2003)

By yoking the issue to the trope of 'conservative', 'Asian' morality and culture, Goh demonstrates the state's well-cultivated instinct to turn to a reverse-Orientalist discourse that constructs Westernisation as undesirable in Singapore (Hill 2000). The gay community is thus interpellated as subjects of the government's broader ideological discourses, standing in as abject representations of the state's East/West and Asianism versus Westernisation binary constructions. Despite the negative legal and social milieu, queer Singaporeans have not been as much banished from the postcolonial state's imagined nation, in Anderson's sense (1983), as they have been subalternised to the sidelines of society. The subaltern class, as Spivak (1988) has argued elsewhere, is necessary to both colonial rule and postcolonial nation-building. In the case of Singapore, state ideology re-functions lesbian and gay subjects as subaltern structures to support and validate the postcolonial elite's control of political and cultural capital.[2]

Sidelined as they have been, the local queer community has nevertheless carved out vibrant and visible social spaces. By the early 2000, 'gay ghettos' started to appear and a 'new gay pulse' became palpable in partitioned areas, such as around the local Chinatown (Ammon 2002). Gay and lesbian establishments such as bars, bathhouses and karaoke lounges draw local crowds and foreigners. Between 2001 and 2005, annual queer parties, called the *Nation*, attracted thousands of gay visitors to the country and brought in so much tourist revenue that it was nominated for a national tourism award.[3] Described by the local media as an 'unparalleled alternative party' and dubbed by the foreign press as Singapore's 'coming out', the *Nation* parties were organised by Singaporean-owned *Fridae.com*, the largest gay and lesbian social networking and news portal in Asia. In the local theatres and niche film festivals, homosexual themes are portrayed with increasing frequency, along with the appearance of creative queer cultural productions such as contemporary gay fiction and lesbian night-life in Singapore (Yue 2007). However, these developments do not amount to a steady expansion of queer spaces. The *Nation* gay parties were banned by 2005 after four consecutive years. Invoking a medical discourse and citing an epidemiologist, the Health Minister warned of an 'AIDS epidemic' spreading through foreign gay visitors who were 'seeding the infection in the local community' (Sadasivan 2005).[4] The Prime Minister later reiterated that his comments do not signal a change in policy that would encourage a 'gay lifestyle', and Section 377A continues to loom large as the legal encoding of the postcolonial state's anxiety towards homosexuality. However, on the internet, the borderless sphere that remains a conundrum for state control, lesbian women and gay men have developed networks with both local and global queer communities fostering a specific queer consciousness, as will be subsequently shown.

Queering Singapore: local to transnational spaces for lesbian and gay organising

Any attempt to understand the emergence of queer activism in Singapore must not only take into account the local dynamics of political discursive processes but how queer politics have been shaped and normalised by global cultural discourses of sexuality. This is particularly so for the highly porous postcolonial context of Singapore. I have previously demonstrated how local lesbian and gay activists have begun to assert themselves through fraught discursive constructions on nationalism. I also foreshadowed how they have drawn elements from the global gay discourse to articulate their visions for the local community. Here I wish to consider further the degree to which, and to what effect, queer activists have engaged with transnational lesbian and gay practices and politics by observing the rise of Singaporean queer activism, and highlighting in particular the moments and markers in which articulations with a Western-centred global gayness have appeared.

In 1997, at an arts centre where a private forum was being held for lesbians and gay men who had learned of the event through word-of-mouth invitations, Alex Au, widely regarded in the local community as the 'founding father of Singapore's gay activism' (Wikipedia contributors in *Singapore gay personalities* 2010), rose to give a talk on 'Gay Culture in Singapore'. In it, Au made the statement and the explicit connection that the 'emerging gay culture is largely inspired by the progress achieved in the West' (quote taken from Offord 1999: 309). No further details of Au's talk were supplied by Offord (1999), whose point was that local queer activism's close affiliation with Western gay politics, as evidenced in Au's explicit statement, made the government both anxious and defensive. Similar to the point I made earlier about how homosexuality has been strategically re-functioned within the East/West discursive dichotomy, Offord argues that homosexuality operates as a trope of difference for the government to not just 'demonise' homosexuality but denounce Western human rights discourses as alien to the postcolonial nation. This, as Offord states, is precisely the 'burden of (homo)sexual identity in Singapore' (1999: 301).

This assertion from a leading gay activist does draw attention to how local queer activism has imagined a political trajectory established by sexual movements in the West. I was neither privy to the actual proceedings of the event, nor are transcripts available for an assessment of Au's (1997) view of, and vision for, Singapore's queer culture in the late 1990s. But it is possible to get a glimpse into an activist's account of, and aspiration for, the local queer community in Russell Heng's article titled 'Tiptoe Out of the Closet' (2001). Heng, an academic and Au's close contemporary, provides a self-reflexive account of how homosexuals in Singapore had progressed from 'a gay scene' in the 1960s to a 'nascent sense of community' by the close of the twentieth century (Heng 2001: 90). Based on his memory and experience, Heng (2001) records that homosexuality in the 1960s found its expression in the transsexual nativist figure of the 'ah qua' who offered entertainment and sex in the vulgarised public spaces of the carnivals and brothels of Bugis Street; by the 1970s, homosexuality transformed into the Westernised and English-speaking 'Orchard Road queens' who were regulars in the gay-friendly bars and discos frequented by foreigners; and one decade after the sexual revolutions in the West, 1980s Singapore was, in Heng's assessment, the point at which gay organising began to take shape:

> The late 1960s and early 1970s was a time when the gay liberation movement erupted in the West, and information about gay people getting together to affirm their identity, support each other, and struggle for their rights became available to Singapore homosexuals.
>
> (Heng 2001: 82).

Heng's account of queer Singapore was considered chronologically against queer political developments in the West. His linear tracing of a movement from 'scene' to 'community' has been criticised as following the 'progressive logic of Western gay liberation' (Yue 2007). In describing the 'ah quas' and 'Orchard Road queens' as figures constituting an early 'gay scene' and comparing them with a later rights-oriented 'community', the activist has imposed a particular trajectory and 'a hierarchical rendering of two different practices that are equally sustaining to the reality and vibrancy of gay lives' (Yue 2007: 151). In so doing, 'Heng's account has inadvertently delegitimised the indigeneity of local gay sexuality' (Yue 2007: 152), and benchmarks instead the local queer movement to a Western standard, placing the former in a position of belatedly catching-up with the latter. Predictably, this led Heng to conclude that the gay movement in Singapore would progress only slowly 'over a long haul' for the majority of gay Singaporeans remain uncomfortable with more assertive forms of gay activism, such as the 'radical activism and large-scale mobilisation that was witnessed at the birth of gay liberation movements in counties such as the US or Australia ...' (Heng 2001: 95). In summary, Heng's article begins by rehearsing in its title the Western queer trope of the 'closet', and concludes by lamenting the slow and quiet 'tip toe' nature of homosexual Singaporeans in asserting their sexual identities and coming out.

If tip toeing characterises the way in which homosexuals came out to organise as a community, it was mainly on the AIDS platform that the community found its first footing. In 1985, *Action For Aids* (AFA) was formed to provide counselling and support services for AIDS patients, and although it is technically not a gay organisation, the AFA was helmed almost entirely by queer women and men. Thus, it was under the auspices of AFA that lesbian and gay activists organised themselves into an official non-governmental organisation (NGO) with a public health mission.

Groups with a more explicit LGBT mission were not allowed to register formally as an organisation. In a country with an array of internal security acts and discretionary laws about what constitutes unlawful assembly, organising activities for the community puts lesbian and gay activists at risk of imprisonment. The PLU tried to register itself in 1997, but was denied. It strategically timed its second attempt in 2004, taking its cue from what it saw as an evolving discursive context following Goh's remarks and the liberal rhetoric of the *Remaking Singapore* exercise. Once again, PLU's efforts were unsuccessful. Despite the positive signals given by political elites, another authority, the Registrar of Societies, rejected PLU's second application, citing the old official discourse on how the 'mainstream moral values of Singaporeans are conservative ... it is hence contrary to public interest to grant legitimacy to the promotion of homosexual activities and viewpoints at this time' (Registrar of Societies, quote taken from *Yawning Bread* 2005).[5] As an openly gay group with an explicit mission of seeking equality for sexual minorities in Singapore, no one in PLU really believed that registration would be granted. Nevertheless, if the parameters of a lesbian and gay community were to expand beyond the AIDS discourse it was, in Heng's words, 'important to try':

> Even if it were bound to be rejected, it would be a way of getting an official explanation of why such a grouping had to be proscribed, and this would initiate a form of dialogue between the State and the gay community.
> (Heng 2001: 89–90)

Despite the impasse, PLU has been in existence for years since 1993 when Au, Heng and a small group of friends began meeting to discuss issues concerning homosexuals in Singapore. The group's private discussions soon attracted other lesbian and gay Singaporeans, and interest grew so quickly that its small clandestine gatherings in private homes soon gave way to large planned meetings in an arts centre. By the early 2000s, PLU's discussions were drawing so much interest that it decided to move operations online. The group started an email list called the Singapore Gay News List (SiGNeL) and registered over 2,000 subscribers within a few years. Despite its informal status, PLU has nevertheless consistently and creatively championed its twin causes of public education and advocacy. It has over the years functioned as an integral platform through which various lesbian and gay initiatives were launched.

Pink Dot

Eileena, a Singaporean lesbian activist, stood by as her mother spoke in Mandarin:

> 上天赐给他们的就是这自然的条件,我想。。。这些人他们自己要走这条路是很痛苦的,所以我们身为父母的我们必须跟他同在一条线来挑战这个社会。[6]

Then taking centre stage to convey what her mother had just said, Eileena, addressed the 4,000-strong crowd:

> Mum says that she knows that there are a lot of people that are still not accepting of LGBT people, and so in order for all of us to live in light, mum decided to come out together with me.

Both mother and daughter were speaking at *Pink Dot 2010*, a public LGBT-supportive event held for a second consecutive year at Speakers' Corner in Hong Lim Park, a free speech zone modelled after London's Hyde Park. Created in 2000, Speakers' Corner is an open invitation for Singaporeans to make public speeches on any day with no limit on the length or number of speeches made, but subject of course to certain restrictions. Speakers must be Singaporeans, they must be registered at the local neighbourhood police station, their speeches must not provoke racial or religious sentiments, and they are not guaranteed legal immunity, which means speakers could be sued for defamation for instance. Although civil society activists welcomed Speakers' Corner eagerly, their interest also waned quickly (Mauzy and Milne 2002), especially as the internet had become the space for digitally-connected Singaporeans to discuss their views and opinions. For a country with a modern info-communication infrastructure connecting almost one hundred per cent of the population,[7] the internet has enabled civic engagement across the local population and beyond. Tight controls over the freedom of expression no longer seemed sensible, and new ways to 'let off steam', to use the Prime Minister's words, (Lee quoted in *The Star Online* 2008) were deemed necessary. Thus, in 2008, the state relaxed a number of regulations governing Speakers' Corner, and the most remarkable of these is the liberalisation of Speakers' Corner into a space for public demonstrations.[8] All groups, including gay rights groups, were suddenly allowed to demonstrate.

Seizing the opportunity immediately, a prominent figure in the PLU-SiGNeL circle made plans to stage Singapore's first queer demonstration almost as soon as changes to Speakers' Corner were officially announced. Inspired by pride parades in the West, the enthusiastic participant had envisioned holding up placards and marching to civil rights anthems à la Mardi Gras-style. Discussions on the online group became rife with possibilities about what a local gay demonstration might look like with imaginative suggestions of marching around the park in pink finery, drag flamboyance and skimpy swim trunks while singing popular English songs that are identified with the gay community.

A loosening of laws on public gatherings coupled with the possibility of a first-ever gay rally made for ground-breaking news in Singapore. The prospect of an LGBT demonstration in a national park enthralled the media, and developments were followed keenly by various sources (see for example *New Paper* 2008; *Straits Times* 2008d), including an online news report reproducing tentative plans from the community's online group discussions. Key organiser, Roy Tan, was quoted as saying, it did not matter how many were going to support the event or if it was well-organised, the goal was 'to establish a precedent'.[9]

However, given the level of publicity it was generating, more circumspect members of the community warned against a laissez-faire approach, urging instead for a more strategic modus operandi. Organisers should take charge of the event, seize the lever of media control from the state, create well-timed and thought-out strategies for pictures, videos and soundbites, and use the opportunity to create a positive representation of the community. In addition, there must be back-up plans against potential backlash from church-organised groups. Should the pride event be overshadowed and outnumbered by a counter demonstration, what would happen to the media representation of the event and the gay cause then, asked concerned members. Others proposed creating a spectacle and adopting protest tactics 'much like the stunts that (the US queer group) ACT UP is famous for,' said one participant (SiGNeL 2008).

These views were among hundreds of posts exchanged on SiGNeL discussing plans for the community's first pride event. The initial goal was to make a statement for equal rights, even if it was for that one brief moment of symbolic rupture as envisaged by Tan. But further discussions led to a more integrative strategy with specific targets in mind, namely, the state and the media. The intent was to influence and transform public sentiment and popular perceptions of the local queer community shaped by dominant sites. Central to the strategies was a rights and recognition-based politics, which adopted once more the progressive logic of Western gay liberation. Indeed, Western inscriptions of queerness appeared all over the discussions and plans for Singapore's first pride demonstration. From the fun and flamboyance of Mardi Gras parades in the West, to the antagonistic and anarchistic tactics of US queer groups such as ACT UP, *Pink Dot* turned out to be the product of all these deliberations in the local community's vision of a pride demonstration. What then, one might ask, is the specificity of *Pink Dot*?

Staged less than a year after Speakers' Corner was liberalised, *Pink Dot* mobilised up to 2,500 lesbian and gay supporters in what was the first public demonstration in Singapore. The number is meaningful on its own given the rarity of public rallies in the country. But it also registered a new record for the largest demonstration ever seen at Hong Lim Park, a record that *Pink Dot* would continually hold as it became an annual event growing in size and number each year.

Canvassing on the theme 'Freedom to Love', *Pink Dot 2009* was a well-coordinated showpiece of the local queer community. Demonstrators were told by organisers to dress in pink clothes as a show of solidarity, and even though a sea of pink swept through the park that morning, the uniformity barely concealed how the young and the old, straight people and homosexuals, parents, couples and children formed part of the crowd. Volunteer ethnic groups put up cultural performances, and activists led in song and dance as theatre actors and actresses made impassioned speeches about the right and freedom for all Singaporeans to love:

> Too many of my gay friends have left these shores because of intolerance. Let's make a change today. My father is here too today in support of *Pink Dot*. He too wants to make a change!
> (Singaporean actress Neo Swee Lin speech, quote taken from *Pinkdotsg* 2009a)

Even though imaginations of queer protests in the West provided early inspiration for the organisers, *Pink Dot* turned out to be a family-friendly parade aimed at cultivating familial ties and friendships, and bridging the hetero-homo divide rather than targeting the oppressive privileges of heterosexuality. Such an approach is distinct from Western queer advocacy, which takes the hetero-homo distinction as a key organising principle. *Pink Dot* activists and protesters emphasised cohesion instead of conflict in their strife for inclusion.

The carnivalesque atmosphere of *Pink Dot* did not simply rehearse the 'traditional' party parades of Mardi Gras in New Orleans or Sydney, but appeared to replicate instead the local National Day parade. Youths dancing to upbeat tunes, and cultural groups dressed in their respective costumes playing traditional instruments and producing a medley of tunes are remarkably reminiscent of repertoires drawn from the yearly state-sponsored national celebrations in Singapore. State carnivals in Singapore essentially purvey nationalist depictions of Singapore as a young, cosmopolitan city composed of racially plural groups finding social solidarity in the modern ethos of progress that the developmental state secures (Goh 2011). In these carnival spaces, the movement and intermingling of bodies elide and gloss over internal tensions, including racial-class anxieties, in a suspension of time. Thus, the carnivalesque conjured in National Day celebrations, as with *Pink Dot*, serves to tap into popular sentiment and collective solidarity, perpetuating a simulacra of national harmony. It is something of an irony, in its mimicry of a national carnival, that *Pink Dot* had unwittingly reproduced the disciplinary regime of the state, preserving state power on the one hand, as it attempted to resist it on the other. Despite their continual marginalisation, lesbian and gay Singaporean subjects appeared in this instance to be strong testimonies of nationalised subjectivities.

The *piece de resistance* of *Pink Dot*, activists insist (Wikipedia contributors 2011), is the formation of the human pink dot. Hours of carnivalesque merriment would culminate in the thousands of participants huddled into a giant spherical spectacle as a symbol celebrating inclusiveness, diversity and the freedom to love in Singapore. An aerial photograph is taken of the demonstrators dressed in pink and lifting pink umbrellas, and the resulting image is then disseminated to, and carried by, the media. While simple in its aesthetic formulation, the evocative scope of the pink dot was vast. Activists explain the layers of meanings that make up *Pink Dot*:

> It references the term, Red Dot, which is often used to describe Singapore. Pink, instead of red, because it is the colour often associated with LGBT (think: pink dollar and pink feather boas), but *more importantly*, it is the colour of our national identity cards and it is what you get when you mix the colours of our national flag. Yes, we are a patriotic bunch!
> (*Pinkdotsg* 2009b)

To contextualise, the 'dot' is an epithet for the reality of Singapore's land area of no more than 704 square kilometres; it is also how the country is marked on many world maps as just a dot. This geographical image of the dot has been used in nationalist narratives of the postcolonial state as a reminder of the fragility and vulnerability of the small nation. The discourse serves at least two functions: one, it creates a self-serving fiction that vindicates the postcolonial state's use of power in the name of national protection; and two, it reiterates the success story of a small nation surmounting its physical limitation to develop a highly successful economy. Singaporeans by and large consume the latter discourse with pride, as the queer community's symbol of choice reveals. By appropriating the red dot and colour coding it pink, marginalised queer subjects in Singapore re-assert their sexual citizenship in the heteronormative nation and re-territorialise it with national pride.

The influence of national discourse is explicit in the queer cultural production of *Pink Dot*. So too are global LGBT symbols borrowed and appropriated, such as all the pink paraphernalia adorning the local pride demonstration. As earlier discussions have shown, nationalist rhetoric is often regurgitated by postcolonial elites to curtail and contain the growing demands for recognition by homosexuals in Singapore. Nationalist discourse is, in this sense, structured in competition with global gay-affirming discourses. In the quest for inclusion then, lesbian and gay activism in Singapore must carefully thread a local nationalist discourse that pits Asian versus Western values at the same time as it negotiates a global gay discourse to fashion a local code of action instrumental for national inclusion. This requires a critical balancing act. Otherwise, the movement risks interpellation into naïve essentialisms of homosexuality. What is also important to recall is that all these competing cultural constructions and interpellations of gayness do not crudely supersede or dominate the other, but operate as shifting, variegated planes engaging in a process of hybridisation and establishing new transnational spaces for queer activism.

Pink Dot thus represents an agentic and creative form of engagement. From early signs of mimicry to the eventuality of cultural hybridity, it did not end up as a 'bad' copy of the 'original' but a demonstration of the wide possibilities of sexual politics, one no less powerful than the other even if it skirts the outright politics of the West. For instance, the two identified focal themes of 'Freedom to Love' and 'Focusing on the Family' are different from the radical activism of, say, America's Queer Nation. Local activists were also quick to assert that *Pink Dot* 'was not a protest or political rally' (quoted from Leyl 2009, *BBC News*) and they were not sending any overt messages to the government. However, by creatively interrogating and interpreting local nationalist discourses of belonging and inclusion, *Pink Dot* reproduced many nuances of sexual citizenship, which appealed to a wide audience.

Activists were originally focused on courting the attention of the local mainstream media with the aim of transforming their negative representations in the public sphere. This aim was achieved as gay-supportive stories began to appear in local mainstream news (see for example *Channel NewsAsia*'s coverage at *Pinkdotsg* 2011a, reports in the local dailies, *TODAY* 2011 and *Straits Times* 2011d). Exceeding expectations, *Pink Dot* also quickly caught the attention of major international news carriers with reports of the event syndicated via global wire services (see for example, the *BBC News* report by Leyl 2009, and the *New York Times* 2009 filing of the Associated Press report). Consequently, with the confluence of these multiple forces, support for the local lesbian and gay demonstration in Singapore grew exponentially from over 2,500 participants in 2009 to a turnout of over 4,000 in 2010, and in its *annus mirabilis* in 2011, *Pink Dot* received the support and sponsorship of Google Singapore, staging a more spectacular show involving a concert, musical acts and professional dancers. Since 2011, other global corporations have become increasingly vociferous in their support for *Pink Dot*. By its seventh annual staging in 2015, *Pink Dot* had grown to a record-breaking 28,000 participants, backed by leading institutions of global finance and media, such as Twitter, Bloomberg, JP Morgan, Barclay, and Goldman Sachs. *Pink Dot* was thus transformed into a global LGBT symbol and exported as a model to various parts of the world.

The reverse implantation of *Pink Dot*

The successful local pride movement is now being distributed, produced, and consumed in the United States, Canada, the Philippines, Hong Kong and Taiwan. Singaporean-style *Pink Dot* campaigns have inspired pride parades in London, Okinawa, Alaska and New York. In October 2011, over 2,500 LGBT supporters in Salt Lake City, Utah, gathered at the local baseball field to form the US version of the giant human *Pink Dot*. The imported model of *Pink Dot* Utah was constructed as an exact replica of the Singaporean 'original', espousing similar themes and deploying the 'dot' symbol, mascot, props, marketing materials and demonstration strategy.

The mimicry is most blatant in the Utah reproduction of *Pink Dot* Singapore's promotional video (*Pinkdotsg* 2011b). Produced by an acclaimed local film director, Boo Junfeng, the storyline of the Singapore promotional video is based on the premise that the majority of heterosexual members of Singapore society are in fact already aware and accepting of lesbian and gay Singaporeans in their midst. However, this awareness remains unexpressed, and results in regret on the part of straight friends, colleagues and family members. The video captures these sentiments in a montage of the heteronormative spaces of the military, the workplace, and the family: the army soldier who regrets not standing up for his platoon mate after he was 'outed'; the bride who looks knowingly at her gay brother when he made excuses to inquisitive relatives about why he is not getting married; the young mother who misses an opportunity to affirm her colleague's sexuality; the elderly father who wonders quietly to himself if his transgender son knew how much she means to him; the motherly housewife who knows but does not let on when she sees her son and his companion returning home. Acknowledgement of homosexuality in each of these scenes is subtle and implicit. Although the video accurately reflects common cultural responses to homosexuality in Singapore, a point which finds further validation when we examine the lives of individual Singaporean lesbians in the next chapter, reflecting this state of affairs is certainly not the sole point of the video. The video is also an expression of the subtle and not so subtle longings of local activists for all gay Singaporeans to take courage and come out. Thus, when announcing the promotional video of *Pink Dot* to the local queer community, the call could have been for the queer community to build ties with already accepting heterosexual allies, which is *Pink Dot*'s apparent mission, but activists spoke only of the 'poignancy' of the 'scenarios LGBT Singaporeans often find themselves in on a day-to-day basis',[10] with the unspoken implication that it is ironic for lesbian and gay Singaporeans to remain in the closet when social acceptance is just waiting to be given.

The campaign video for *Pink Dot* Utah draws on the same script and content, with each scene transposed onto more relatable US scenarios. So, for example, the Singapore army boys' altercation is replayed as a college locker room incident between white schoolboys in the Utah version. Although it is an almost scene-by-scene imitation of the original promotional video, there is one last scene in the US version that stands out as remarkable. This involves a fatherly figure exchanging greetings with his son and his partner as the couple walk hand-in-hand returning home. Here, in the final scene of *Pink Dot* Utah's campaign video, we are confronted with an explicit acknowledgement and open acceptance of a same-sex relationship that in the Singaporean version was assumed and desired, but never directly addressed or demonstrated. Nevertheless, *Pink Dot* Utah is committed to the vision and mission of its Singapore-made precedent. On its website addressing the question 'What sets *Pink Dot* Utah apart?' the American activists explain *Pink Dot*'s specificity:

> Our audience: All straight allies that want to do something but don't know what, where or how, *Pink Dot* Utah does not support any political cause or party ... This is about love and respect for ones' fellow beings. There is no other agenda.

The surprising and ambivalent reversal of flows of a local queer cultural artefact to the West exemplifies the complicated reckonings of the relationship between the two. The ways in which Singaporean activists continue to push for a Western gay politics of 'coming out' and 'visibility', and how the Americans have appropriated the specificity of a Singapore-defined, non-politicised queer demonstration, are not only instances of a discursive reversal or transgressive re-inscription, but also of the operations of postcolonial hybridity and transnational relationality which reconceptualises the coloniser and the colonised as both caught in a mutually constitutive economy of fantasy and desire. Both are seen within these theoretical paradigms as non-static, anxious positions, held in an existence that maintains and is maintained by the other.

Such a conceptualisation of an ever-shifting mode of existence held in suspension in a co-constitutive relation to the other, lends very well to an understanding of queer organising and activism – in Utah or Singapore, or anywhere else for that matter – as competing and conflicting, non-homogeneous struggles. Although 'coming out' and 'visibility' are dominant representational modes of Western queer activism, linking these singularly as the 'political discourse' and 'experience' of the West is to obscure how 'coming out' is also extremely difficult for many Western homosexuals. The arduous reality of 'coming out' in the West has been documented by researchers as early as the 1990s (Rhoads 1994; Markowe 1996; Whisman 1996), about the same time as an idealised 'out and proud' global gay identity and all its Western essentialisms took hold of our imaginations of what it means to be gay through the successes and notoriety of queer activism in the West. Conceptualising a Western gay model as hybridising and constantly transforming unravels the idea of a monolithic West as an imposition from without, revealing instead the mutual constitution of differences within the object of global queer politics. Through a postcolonial lens, it is possible to grasp the intersections and inter-relationality to visualise a solidarity politics linking queer organising internationally from Utah to New York to Alaska.

Reflections on the local queer movement

In Singapore, the hybridised product of *Pink Dot* Singapore – one which found inspiration in Western queer politics but in a postcolonial twist re-territorialised Western understandings through the engendering of a local nationalist discourse – achieved a specificity that led to its very success and eventual export to neighbouring countries and further afield in the West. But its success both locally and globally ran the risk of an emerging new orthodoxy with particular assumptions and language about what being gay is. Consequently, there will be those who take these assumptions as dogma and cast all dissent as enemies of the cause, leading to an all-out war. Such nativism emerges from a kind of hubris that refuses to see that the very survival and success of the movement is made possible precisely by differences and contradictions, which sustain its hybridising, intersecting, changing quality.

Was *Pink Dot* susceptible to its own success? Following its *annus mirabilis* in 2011, the clash that ensued between *Pink Dot* advocates and a well-known local playwright and poet, Alfian Sa'at, seems to suggest so. Sa'at, who had previously lent his support to *Pink Dot* demonstrations by appearing in a promotional video and turning up for the celebrations in a pink *baju kurung* ethnic Malay costume, decided to boycott the 2011 demonstration for, in his view, it has become dominated by the privileges of race and class. Posting on his Facebook page, Sa'at publicly announced:

> I'm staying away from PD[11] this year because it is become too big and homogeneously so. It started out as a beautiful idea, but like so many things in Singapore, has ended up reproducing the power structures that it should aim to challenge.

Not one to shy away from controversy, Sa'at posted this comment made by a friend he identified as an 'Indian professional':

> *Pink Dot* is as much a celebration of the LGBT community to love as it is a display of the self-love of Chinese, middle-class, English-educated liberals. What is inclusive in the term 'LGBT' is problematised by the fact that what is supposed to stand for the queer community in Singapore is almost exclusively CMEL!

Post-*Pink Dot*, Sa'at continued to write facetiously:

> ... I'll give a week for the *Pink Dot* self-congratulatory overkill to die down. People on my newsfeed are going enthu apeshit as if they just repealed 377a, legalised gay marriage and allowed adoption by gay couples, all in one fell swoop. Them gayz sure know how to market a colour-coordinated picnic.
>
> (Quotes taken from a Facebook discussion thread, accessed on 10 April 2012)

Sa'at's postings provoked hundreds of angry responses from *Pink Dot* supporters who felt that Sa'at had undermined the local queer movement. There were threats to boycott his plays, accusations of his personal vendetta, insults hurled at his 'self-absorbed' 'hand-wringing' and 'vitriol' in an endless stream of defensive testimonies as to how *Pink Dot* was in fact made up of an ethnically diverse crowd. Finally, a challenge was thrown at Sa'at to 'put up or shut up', that is to step forward with an alternative vision and mount an equally, if not more, impactful demonstration:

> It's simplistically and intellectually lazy to attack the 'feel good' face of something like *Pink Dot*, when it's blatantly obvious that the event itself is working strategically to make points and open dialogue for further steps

that are ahead. No, you can't have a gathering of 10,000 people calling for repeal of 377a. So ... do nothing? Do you really deny that what took place on the weekend can have any further effects, can be a stepping stone to a campaign for freedoms?

('Deer', online post in response to Sa'at)

To put it more bluntly, for me, there has to be a point to discussing the limitations of current gay activism. Is it about how to do it better, how to do it differently, or even how to do it without ostensibly doing it? But discussion for discussion's sake doesn't work for me. It is too much like intellectual masturbation. Which ironically replicates the self-absorption that it purports to critique.

('Kum', online response to Sa'at)

All the interiority forced upon *Pink Dot* – its intrinsic value as a movement to eventually repudiate the criminalisation of homosexuality in Singapore, its relay of love and diversity for all, and its realisation of liberal ideas of gay equality – has turned *Pink Dot* into an object of over-determined investment. The reified symbol is then avidly consumed by the local queer community in a range of affective modes including identification, aspiration and desire, leading to the congealment of a new homonormativity defined by dominant Chinese middle-class English-educated liberals (CMELs).

Sa'at's views certainly drew the ire of the Chinese, liberal queer activists. Responding to why CMELs seem to be overrepresented in *Pink Dot*, Alex Au took to his blog to make several arguments in general disagreement with Sa'at's position (*Yawning Bread* 2011b). First, since *Pink Dot* was conceived by privileged English-educated liberals, the movement should reflect the 'primary cause' of this constituency; it is not fair to expect any movement to 'expend precious energy and resources' on other causes. Second, since this is a largely Western-acculturated group influenced by liberal ideas in the West, it is to be expected that the primary cause of *Pink Dot* is 'gay equality'. Furthermore, Au said:

> ... fighting for gay equality is one of those self-actualisations that Abraham Maslow theorised about at the top of his pyramid. .. it should therefore be totally expected that the more privileged segments of our society are over-represented in the *Pink Dot* movement.
>
> (*Yawning Bread* 2011b)

Third, since Western acculturation and 'self-actualisation' are the vectors that connect the privileged to wider causes, Au adopts a colour-blind perspective to suggest that too much fuss has been made of the racial composition of *Pink Dot*. The primary denominator of the local queer movement or any social movement for that matter 'is not ethnicity, it's social class', said Au, ignoring the important intersections between race and class that led to *Pink Dot* being occupied by CMELs. In any case, what is ultimately important is that social movements beget change and '*Pink Dot* is on its way', Au concludes (*Yawning Bread* 2011b). Such a response teases out three barely disguised assumptions. One, that the strength of a social movement will be diluted if it attempts to broaden its base; let queers with the power of privilege 'punch above their weight' to effect change, argued Au. Two, change is to be prioritised as long as it achieves the (single-issue) objective of the (dominant) group; the marginalisation of 'other' queers is 'unfortunate' and 'unintended', said Au. Three, the liberal fight for gay equality sits at the top of a gay evolution process; those who neither initiate this fight nor participate in it are less developed queers who have not progressed along the Maslow hierarchy of needs and therefore not reached the apotheosis of Western global gayness.

Ironically, Au's response confirms Sa'at's criticisms of *Pink Dot* as constituting 'a gay mainstream seeking acceptance from the straight mainstream' via a politics that was not universally shared by minority queers in Singapore. 'And a gay mainstream', Sa'at adds, 'is often not very nice to the minorities within its own ranks'. His statements, Sa'at clarified, were meant as a discursive validation of 'the experience of people who feel excluded by *Pink Dot*'s "big Chinese party pretending to be a Singaporean one".' *Pink Dot* cannot be taken as 'truly representative of the actual diversity of queer experiences and diversities in Singapore'. But the diversity critique Sa'at put forth is not targeted at *Pink Dot* organisers. It was not his wish for *Pink Dot* to fail.

> ... I sincerely want to see the dot grow larger each year. I just feel like asking aloud whether one cares or not who are the people forming that dot, who feels left out of the dot, who's not part of the dot, and why not.
> (Quotes taken from a Facebook discussion thread, accessed on 10 April 2012)

Unfortunately, all the nuances of Sa'at's political position were lost on defenders of *Pink Dot* who reduced Sa'at's criticisms as 'bitter' or coming from a 'hater'. That is, they took issue with Sa'at's character rather than directly engage with his views. This was a missed opportunity, leading to a disappointed Sa'at concluding that 'a thin-skinned liberal movement that brooks no dissent casts into serious doubt what the term "liberal" really means'. I am sympathetic towards Sa'at's position, not least because I myself was once the target of criticism from a CMEL lesbian queer activist for daring to suggest that not all Singaporean lesbians share a similar liberal agenda of coming out. I will relate this episode in a subsequent section because I want to close this one off with some reflections. Activists and defenders of *Pink Dot* were adamant that Sa'at's perception of the local queer movement was flawed, that in fact *Pink Dot* was ethnically diverse. Defenders pointed to the song and dance shows put up by ethnic groups as part of the carnival and to photographs and video images of ethnic minorities enthusiastically participating in *Pink Dot*. But the question is really not about whether race and class were equally represented in *Pink Dot*, or how and whether the goal should be about attracting and including minority groups.

Rather, the question is how and in what ways we might recognise and acknowledge, rather than try to explain away, the problematic dominance of a particular privileged group, and why minorities might feel excluded. Dialogue and discussion appears to be one meaningful way forward in changing the dynamics and interrogating the power structures, but the one initiated by Sa'at was disparaged and dismissed by so-called liberals defending the intrinsic value of *Pink Dot*, which disconnects local queer activism from the intersectional struggles of minority groups. A more demanding critique, rather than a defensive closing down, of what *Pink Dot* means is needed. Unfortunately, this is not going to happen if *Pink Dot* becomes a space immune to critique and privilege checks, and if its supporters are unable to discuss even candidly the limitations of existing efforts and paradigms.

Returning to that mild Sunday afternoon, as Eileena and her mother spoke in English and Mandarin to the large, cheering crowd, we might do well, just as Sa'at did, to ask aloud if the socialising and camaraderie we see at *Pink Dot* teeter towards a brand of activism with certain assumptions, understandings and language of what being gay means to the exclusion of other meanings. Inclusivity is not just about diversity in numbers or mere representativeness. It ultimately rests on the extent to which activists can connect their struggles with others, incorporating and taking in criticisms, conflicts and contradictions rather than rejecting and rationalising away questions of differences and diversity. Although the local queer movement achieved its level of success through a coherent and unified symbol that is *Pink Dot*, it is in the interest and nature of successful social movements to become complex adaptive systems with adroit flexibility so as to continually expand its scope of relevance, in this case, to 'other' constituencies of lesbian and gay Singaporeans.

With these reflections in mind, I turn my attention to local lesbian activism, moving in reverse time in order to arrive at and uncover evidence of early lesbian activism in Singapore in the mid-1990s, prior to *Pink Dot* serving as a movement and focal point for the imagination of the local queer community in Singapore. The same issues and considerations discussed of local queer activism thus far are useful reflection points for us to now understand the agency and initiative of local lesbian activists, the interaction between female same-sex sexualities and state authorities, the women activists' translocal queer connections and their particular sexual politics in postcolonial Singapore.

Early lesbian agency in Singapore

The significant involvement of lesbians in activist organisations and projects establishes their central and public place in local queer activism. Lesbian women's early involvement with queer activism, starting from the late 1980s onwards, was with the AIDS cause and PLU, arguably Singapore's first queer activist group. Although these organisations were dominated by gay men, lesbians took up prominent roles and from the vantage point of their positions propelled themselves into activism and organising specifically for women who love women. From the late 1990s onwards, a number of lesbian groups began to appear online. Lesbian activism found its first footing in the world of cyberspace before taking up visible roles in Singaporean civil society.

In 1998, the lesbian email news list, RedQuEEn (*http://redqueensg.blogspot.com*), was set up by Eileena Lee to engage queer women in Singapore. RedQuEEn is similar to SiGNeL but caters specifically for women. Membership is strict and male applications are always turned down. The news list functions as a safe space for lesbians to discuss personal issues, share stories, exchange opinions and plan meet-ups with other women. Before long, RedQuEEn attracted a broad participation from lesbians in Singapore, numbering over a 1,000 in the new millennium. Connecting online as a community allowed the women to identify their shared concerns and coalesce around various causes. Several women soon stepped out of the safety and anonymity of cyberspace to venture into the public realm, offering a number of support services, including counselling for lesbian women in distress, face-to-face discussion groups for women, and social networking. RedQuEEn developed a network of subsidiary organisations, such as *The Looking Glass*, a counselling service for lesbian women and *Women's Nite*, a monthly meet-up session where the women show up for support and socialising over discussions, conversations and 'potluck' meals. Eileena spearheaded many of these initiatives but later focused on managing and operating the *Pelangi* Pride Centre, a local resource space and library offering LGBT literature, guidebooks and HIV-related materials to the local LGBT community. The centre was so-named because *Pelangi* is the Malay indigenous term for 'rainbow', the global LGBT symbol.

Another mailing list, SAMBAL (*http://groups.yahoo.com/group/sambal/*) which stands for Singaporean and Malaysian Bisexual and Lesbian, was formed in the late 1990s by Madeleine Lim, a Singapore-born filmmaker who was running an underground lesbian newsletter in the mid-1980s before she moved to live in San Francisco. Similar to RedQuEEn, SAMBAL operates as a dedicated women-only interactive email forum offering an assortment of activities – dialogue, announcement of community events, news and networking – but caters for a broader regional base of queer women in Malaysia and Singapore. While attending the San Francisco State University's filmmaking program, Madeleine formed the Queer Women of Color Media Arts Project (QWOCMAP), billed by an international lesbian foundation as 'the only organisation in the US dedicated to giving voice and agency to queer women of colour through film and video' (Astraea Foundation 2011). QWOCMAP offers free film workshops for queer women of colour and has produced over 60 films. Bringing her brand of queer activism into a foreign land, the genesis for QWOCMAP was when Madeleine realised she was the only queer women of colour in her film class. In San Francisco, Madeleine created '*Sambal Belachan*', a film still banned in Singapore for its exploration of race, sexuality and nationality. Her earlier short film titled 'Shades of Grey' explored the issue of lesbian domestic violence and was played in seven major film festivals (*Fridae.com* 2001a). In 2001, both the women founders of RedQuEEn and SAMBAL were featured in Asia's largest queer news portal, *Fridae.com* (2001a, 2001b), making Eileena Lee and Madeleine Lim the first two public faces of lesbian activism in Singapore.

A third widely known lesbian activist is Jean Chong, co-founder of the group *Sayoni*. Started by six women in 2006, *Sayoni* differentiates itself from other community groups as one focused on advocacy for lesbians in Singapore. It is a volunteer-run organisation with 50 to 70 volunteer participants. *Sayoni*'s mission to 'empower queer women towards greater involvement in the community' (*www.sayoni.com*). The women organise educational talks, training workshops, and self-development retreat camps for the community, in addition to hosting regular social activities, such as dinner parties, sports games and coffee sessions. As an advocacy group with a desire to reach out to queer women in Singapore and raise awareness on issues faced by the community, *Sayoni* began to gather data on queer women in Singapore through biennial surveys (*Sayoni* 2006, 2008b and 2010a). These surveys subsequently developed into a broader National LGBT Census (2013) carried out in collaboration with other LGBT community partners, namely, *Pink Dot* and Oogachaga, a gay counselling centre. *Sayoni* surveys cover the women's coming out experiences, their relationships with friends, family and partners, their sexual desires, their physical wellbeing and socio-economic status with the aim to 'ameliorate the dire lack of information on queer women in Singapore' (*Sayoni* 2006, 2008b and 2010a). The women's group also produced a coming out guide entitled, 'What If I'm Gay?' (*Sayoni* 2010b), with the core section of the guide providing step-by-step guidance on coming out to oneself, then to friends, colleagues, schoolmates and family. In addition to organising social events, planning outreach activities and coordinating research projects, *Sayoni* founders also expend significant efforts in lobbying for LGBT rights on regional and global platforms, and forging links with international queer communities. Jean, for instance, travels around the world giving presentations at the International Lesbian, Gay, Bisexual, Trans and Intersex Association regional (ILGA-Asia) conferences, is a key member of the ASEAN SOGIE (Sexual Orientation, Gender Identity and Expression) Caucus, and participates actively in global human rights conventions, documenting and filing reports of discrimination faced by local LGBT communities to the Universal Periodic Review of the Human Rights Council in Geneva, and to the United Nations (UN) Convention on the Elimination of All Forms of Discrimination Against Women (CEDAW) in New York.[12]

Attending to *Sayoni*'s participation at the 2011 CEDAW meeting provides some insight into the group's advocacy work and engagement with global human rights. In 2011, facilitated by the International Gay and Lesbian Human Rights Convention (IGLHRC), Jean led a three-woman team from *Sayoni* to a CEDAW convention reviewing the Singaporean government's progress with eliminating discrimination against women. CEDAW is one of two international human rights conventions that the Singaporean government has ratified and pledged to fulfil, thus it was for *Sayoni* an important venue for queer women's issues to be raised and included as resolutions, which the state is then obliged to ratify. With

IGLHRC's assistance, *Sayoni* activists prepared and submitted a country shadow report titled 'Report on Discrimination against Women in Singapore based on Sexual Orientation and Gender Identity' (*Sayoni* 2011) to the CEDAW committee made up of experts on women's human rights from around the world. In it, the report documented the various discriminatory state policies against sexual minorities in Singapore, highlighting violations of the rights of queer Singaporeans in the media and in state policies concerning education, employment, health and family. Intensive, round-the-clock lobbying at the CEDAW event, where *Sayoni* members had to be tactical – identifying allies, initiating conversations, being opportunistic, writing and re-wording resolutions – to gain maximum attention from CEDAW experts who would, on behalf of *Sayoni* and Singaporean LGBTs, speak power to truth by raising sexual orientation and gender identity (SOGIE) concerns with the Singaporean government. Prepped by *Sayoni*, several CEDAW experts probed the state's UN representatives on a wide range of issues. Are lesbians' rights to housing and employment indirectly affected by the criminalisation of homosexuality in Singapore? Is public health support available to women in same-sex partnerships so they can access medical benefits, financing and family planning? How is the banning of positive or even neutral depiction of lesbianism by the Media Development Authority compatible with the state's ratification of CEDAW's articles prohibiting all forms of discrimination against all women, including on the grounds of sexual orientation and gender identity? Are sexual minority women encouraged to take part in political and public life? Are lesbians engaged as stakeholders for policy formulation? How does the state support women's movements for sexual freedom and for gender parity? CEDAW's interrogation highlighted the intersectional injustices faced by female sexual minorities in the areas of housing, health, marriage, employment, and political life (Poore 2011). The questions, pointed and pertinent, were however met with reticence. The state's representatives did not provide explicit responses, turning instead to blanket tropes of Singapore being a conservative society and the equality of all Singaporeans before the law, no matter what their sexual orientation is. Although there was no direct engagement with any of the questions posed at the CEDAW convention, the exchange between CEDAW's gender experts and the Singaporean government was registered as an important victory by the activists. Not only was *Sayoni* able to put up for redress the injustices and abject conditions facing female sexual minorities previously existing outside of formalised frameworks, it was able to do so in an international norms-setting forum, where SOGIE discriminations would be reflected in CEDAW's final comments and recommendations to the Singaporean government. By the state's 1995 UN ratification, it is obliged to honour these recommendations. For all its efforts and successes at linking local LGBT issues to global human rights mechanisms and discourses, *Sayoni* was officially recognised as an international civil society organisation (previously called an NGO) by the UN.

Whether as early participants in the global AIDS cause, or in the establishment of queer communities online, or in their attendance at international conferences and engagement in global human rights conventions, lesbian activists came to prominence through their transnational activism pursued on the largest of scales. This raises the question of how and to what extent do Singaporean lesbian activists identify with the global queer movement, an inquiry I will now turn to.

Transnational lesbian activism

Articulate and outspoken, the English-speaking women activists are educated, well-travelled and au fait with technology, thus well connected to global circuits of queer knowledge and cultural production. A cursory scan of the websites of lesbian community groups suggests that the women readily identify with global queer symbols, with evidence ranging from their earnest explanations of the rainbow flag, its history and significance for the global queer movement (see for example, *Sayoni* 2007) to the ways in the way local lesbian activists commemorate International Coming Out Day on October 11, a date chosen in 1988 by US gay rights advocates to mark annual celebrations of National Coming Out Day (NCOD). As with most US queer cultural artefacts, NCOD has since become an internationally observed day celebrating individuals who embrace coming out as a cultural rite of passage of their sexual selfhoods. Marking the 2011 International Coming Out Day, lesbian activists in Singapore participated in, and helped circulate, an 'It Gets Better Singapore' video, a local adaption of the US 'It Gets Better Project' started by an American gay couple in response to the disturbing number of suicides among LGBT teenagers in America. The local video featured Singaporeans sharing testimonies of their coming out struggles. In denial of their homosexuality in the past, these homosexual Singaporeans say they have suffered, among other things, bullying, self-harm, conflicted behaviour, a failed marriage and other broken relationships. The message was clear: things got better when they came to terms with their homosexuality, reiterating the central place one should give to coming out, just as lesbians and gay men do in the West. This, if the reader recalls, repeats the linear, liberationist message found in Singapore's first lesbian documentary, *WWLW* (2006), discussed earlier in the book.

The avid consumption of Western queer cultural artefacts and adoption of coming out as crucial to queer selfhoods suggest a desire on the part of local lesbian activists to identify with dominant queer ideologies and politics in the West. However, in my conversations with Singaporean lesbian activists, I found their political motivations to be more ambivalent. In 2009, when I first met and conducted interviews with the women, a number of them did not regard themselves as 'activists' nor see themselves as leaders of the local queer movement despite their active involvement in championing LGBT issues and spearheading community projects. The women's self-effacement did not stem from fears of political reprisal: the activists I spoke to were either insistent that I use their real names in my research or were indifferent to my use of pseudonyms. 'The government are aware we are around', one activist said to me, 'it doesn't matter'. Indeed, information on who the women are, photographs of these women, and statements they have made in response to LGBT issues are readily available online, and very easily accessed in a nation with ubiquitous internet connection. The women's disavowal of the 'activist' label seems to stem from their aversion towards dominant images of LGBT activism as militant and subversive. This was not the motivation. Lesbian activists explained to me that their involvement with the local community was the outcome of personal struggles and search for clarification on what it means to be gay in Singapore. A few lamented the lack of local role models. 'We only had Western role models back then', said one informant, 'I had to take things into my own hands'. Western understandings were sought through the internet and books because local resources were scarce, if non-existent. 'Where else to find literature?' asked Eileena. A dominant Western queer knowledge complex does inevitably shape local lesbian activism as disaffected Singaporean lesbians reach across to the 'other' side of the world to understand their queerness. Jean's response captures these sentiments:

> I was going through difficult times, not having role models, not having supportive resources. I also saw a lot of conflicted Christians and gay people. I can't sit around and wait for people. I got sick of waiting. I started to look around to see what I can do …

Lesbian activists' subjectivities are in a very practical sense crystallised around addressing specific local needs rather than through global discourses of what it means to be lesbian. Not simply motivated by Western queer developments and discourses, the women were spurred on by the impoverishment of queer knowledges and networks in Singapore to seek and create lesbian communities. The women turned 'inwards' looking for Singaporean lesbians online, and then 'outwards' to supplant the lack of local knowledge and cultural resources, no doubt enabled by their positions as educated, English-proficient women with unhindered access to travel and technology. Unlike diasporic, Western-educated, Indian lesbian feminists who, for example, helped develop activist networks in India by drawing on their transnational experiences, ideas and connections, the lesbian activists in this study are born and bred in Singapore, and did not begin their activism offshore; apart from short-term holidays, student overseas exchange stints or work-related travel, the women received a significant part of their education in Singapore and had spent the majority of their lives in the city-state within which their sexual subjectivities were shaped.

The benign beginnings of lesbian activism in Singapore would change quickly. By 2010, the same women I was speaking to a year earlier had grown into their activist roles, and began identifying as 'out-and-proud' activists. While the women would frown and cringe whenever I referred to them as activists in the past, they were now very visible in civil society, taking on LGBT concerns and beyond. *Sayoni* activists, for instance, have openly engaged with the Minister for Home Affairs and Law on the issue of institutionalised discrimination against LGBT persons in Singapore; protested at a European Union (EU) seminar on human rights when Thio Li Ann, known for her virulent anti-gay speeches and stance, was giving a presentation at the EU Centre in Singapore, and participated at the Universal Periodic Review of the UN Human Rights Council in Geneva, alongside other civil society activists campaigning against the death penalty, gender, sexual and migrant worker injustices in Singapore. Developing a global lesbian feminist politics and language, the women activists have been articulating concepts of patriarchy, privilege and intersectionality in the public sphere, and establishing networks with international and regional queer organisations.

Negotiating these transnational ties, Jean tells me, is always an ambivalent process, complicated by the multiple simultaneous scales in which Singaporean lesbian activism is situated in global queer organising:

> Lesbian organisations in Singapore do not receive much financial support from international NGOs as they cannot be legally registered. Funding groups perceive Singapore as too wealthy. They are very interested in Third World countries like Indonesia, Vietnam and India and don't realise that strict laws in Singapore restrict groups from seeking funds publicly.

Implicit in international NGOs' hierarchical rendering of nations is the assumption that Singapore's successful neoliberal capitalist system has unleashed an economic force that erases homophobia. Such a discourse participates in what Jasbir Puar (2007) has influentially described as 'homonationalism', whereby LGBT rights are assumed to be synonymous with modernity and civility. Caught out by the old binaries of civilised/savage, developed/less developed wherein neoliberalism is yoked to a 'civilising' anti-homophobic discourse, first world Singaporean queers are all too easily seen as not requiring rescue and attention. Thus, local queer activism suffers from a certain dislocation from international and regional queer networks, as exemplified by the politics of transnational lesbian activism in Singapore.

Politics of 'coming out' and 'gaining visibility'

The political strategy of lesbian activists in Singapore revolves quite centrally around the tropes of 'coming out' and 'gaining visibility'. In Western queer politics and popular imagination 'coming out' is central to the narration of homosexual experience and identity (Humphreys 1979; Jay and Young 1992; Signorile 1995) and taken as a cultural rite of passage in the development of gayhood. According to this narrative, the homosexual achieves a liberated and complete sense of self through the act of coming out. But coming out is not just for the satisfaction and well-being of the gay individual. A public declaration of one's sexual identity also normalises and legitimises homosexuality to the benefit of all gay people. Conversely, concealment of same-sex desires implies not just 'self-alienation and inauthenticity' (Seidman 2004: 256) but also complicity with the oppression of the gay community. This discourse has taken on an undeniably hegemonic force shaping the desire and aspirations of activists around the world. In Singapore, significant activist constituencies have enthusiastically embraced 'coming out' as a political ideology and strategy. At an interview with an international women's advocacy group, Eileena, was quoted as saying:

> ... my solution to end bigotry is simple – if all of us gay people can just come out to our parents or work, that's half the problem solved! I can ... give visibility to something that has been rendered invisible ... provide positive visibility to oppose the negatives and, hopefully, normalise homosexuality.
>
> (Quote taken from Marte 2006)

The strategy is thus for individual gay and lesbians to come out as part of globalising queer mission. Interestingly, when I first met Eileena for an interview in 2009, I found her politicised views softer and more emollient, laced with a certain pragmatism about coming out in Singapore. I had suggested to her that lesbian women in Singapore generally avoided coming out to their families not out of fear, but out of a sense of duty and protection towards their elderly parents. 'They don't need to know', individual lesbian respondents have told me. I shared with Eileena these narratives to which she turned and asked with concern, 'Until when? Until when, you know? It's very hard to live like that'. Being closeted within the family was not judged by this activist as an act of political capitulation but posed as a genuine question of how one might pragmatically live with one's family. The hegemony of 'coming out' in global queer politics has, in this instance, been reconfigured through a nationalist state discourse on pragmatism along the lines of what I had outlined in an earlier chapter, but the end result is still the binding of lesbian and gay subjects into a universalising imperative, that of folding queers into a dominant ideology.

Nevertheless, paying due attention to these nuanced understandings of prevailing constructions, and the complex, hybridising transcultural ways in which sexual subjectivities are formed sometimes in conflict and sometimes in complicity with global queer circuits lend emphasis to the agentic aspects of meaning-making, moving away from a view of local actors as 'passive receptacles' who mechanically and uniformly reproduce the 'norms, values and signs of transnational power' (Mattelart 1983: 4). An agent-centred view is not just a theoretical implementation, but a political imperative, as my following social media encounter with a local lesbian activist and a Singaporean lesbian will illustrate.

Political significance of hybridising, transnational sexualities

As one of the privileged, socially mobile CMEL I wrote about earlier, I found myself speaking on national television in Australia. The programme was a face-to-face open discussion televised forum, and the topic for the evening was

'Gay in School'. The audience was mainly Australian, comprising a number of supportive parents with gay teenagers who spoke positively about how 'coming out' in school not only required self-confidence, it also resulted in heightened self-confidence. The message from these 'out' gay students, some of whom were attending private schools, seemed to be this: if you are being bullied for being gay, coming out is the solution. It liberates you from the bullying because once the declaration is made, the school bullies will have nothing more to say and the oppression will go away. This is global gay logic replayed in the school compound: the prioritising of gay visibility is the way to normalise homosexuality. 'Coming out' as both liberating and fulfilling for the homosexual individual is classic Western queer narrative. Informed by my own research work on gay Singaporeans, I responded to this discussion by countering how 'coming out' is not such an uncomplicated process leading to the achievement of self-confidence and liberation. I stated that far from feeling liberated, gay Singaporeans sometimes faced increased surveillance, pressures and forms of passive aggressiveness from family members they came out to wishing instead they had not come out. On the show, I took the position that young gay people should only come out when they are ready to deal with the intersected forms of pressures and oppressions that come with coming out. I also offered a counter paradigm of 'coming home' (Chou 2001), describing how some gay Singaporeans bring their partners to live in the family home, where they share the same room and one bed, and no questions are asked. There is tacit acceptance among family members, no explicit declaration of 'I am gay', and the outcome is nevertheless a safe and viable one. Sharing these views stemmed from my effort to interrogate and resist singular understandings of oppression, liberation and what it means to be gay and lesbian.

Barely a few days later, I found my debut television appearance in Australia circulated online by an influential lesbian activist in Singapore whom I had interviewed for my research. She had found the programme on YouTube, posted it on social media, and on her post she tagged and chastised me for what I said on the show:

> Shawna Tang, I must say I have to disagree with what you've said in the show. Just as coming out has consequences, not coming out too has its consequences. And Singapore as I've said in my interview with u, has changed and will continue to change. And change will never happen if we sit and wait.

When I explained that while my views did not reflect what she said to me, but it was certainly the experience of a number of respondents I had spoken to, she challenged the representativeness of my study and argued that I was imposing and generalising my findings. It seemed to me that she found my contingent stand on coming out as an act of political capitulation, which was upsetting and unacceptable in a 'modernising' and 'changing' Singapore, and thus sought to invalidate my views:

> 'Shawna – when u say 'a number of my Singaporean respondents etc.', it really does not say much. Depending on how we seek for respondents, the demographic of these people can skew a certain way. I think it's dangerous when we try to generalise our perspective. It seems like you are viewing the situation from a lens tinted by your own experience as a gay person. Nothing wrong with your experience, just that we must be clear to state clearly where we are coming from. From your response, you seem to be imposing your experience as a generalised Singaporean experience. And it is not. Because it is certainly not this Singaporean's experience, even if I am a minority.

So singular was the activist's aspiration for everyone to come out that this turned into an allegation of me skewing my findings a certain way, and so singular was her insistence on coming out that she did not pause to consider if I desired to be 'outed' in a public discussion. Her argument that Singapore is changing and modernising participates in a developmentalist conceptualisation of queer identities as evolving along a linear pathway marked by the same old binaries of past/present and traditional/modern, where modernity is yoked to the achievement of liberation and complete gay identities. In such a framework, if one does not aspire towards that 'modern' pinnacle, then one is simply not gay or lesbian enough.

Thankfully, it took the timely intervention of a third participant, another local lesbian whom I did not know, to validate my findings. 'Shin' posted:

> Actually I do agree with what Shawna said, perhaps it doesn't apply to all the gay people in Singapore but it does apply to a large number of people I know. A lot of us born in the 1980s do believe in achieving financial stability first before coming out for fear of being thrown out of our homes. Family ties are very important in the Asian culture and many of us do not want to hurt our families though it may be obvious to them who we really are. They know but they can't handle the truth. It's easier to just not tell them in their face.

The activist reacted to 'Shin's' comments and posted:

> I think a lot of this is self-imposed.

The activist then quickly deleted the post and re-posted:

> 'Shin', I'm not sure what your expectations are for the community here? At least for me, every bit of a small step is progress. As well, I always say, I am Asian, my culture is Asia, honesty is part of Asian values, and so, living without the need to hide who I am, is an Asian value.

The activist's first response is to take offence at 'Shin's' apolitical position, motivated by what she saw as a form of self-imposition. Her second response invokes the difference of Western and Asian values, a self-Orientalising manoeuvre that, despite her attempt to assert 'Asian values' as 'honest' and superior, does not subvert but in fact subscribes to a colonial logic.

Two ironies are inherent. First, there is some 'truth' in the activist's assertion that, 'I think a lot of this is self-imposed'. Indeed, this was an imposition of the self in all its complexity. 'Shin' is presumably young (born in the 1980s), has not yet achieved financial stability, is interlocked by her age and class location, and facing multiple oppressions and constrains within these conditions. 'Shin' is not just a gay person. She is also a daughter, possibly a young working professional trying to gain economic independence. All these multiple identities interlock to structure her sexual selfhood. Therefore, the activist was, ironically, correct to say that this was an imposition of the self in all its intersecting and interlocking categories. But a second unintended irony is evident here: in calling for queer women to engage in a politics of recognition and visibility and in denying the multiple categories that define gay people, she inevitably erases the very identities of the persons she claims to represent and fight for. What is lost in an uncritical acceptance of 'progress' and 'change' is the agentic ways in which individual Singaporeans lesbians have negotiated their globalised sexual identities around local cultural codes and norms reproducing nuanced transnational sexualities. Therein lies the particular political significance of the hybridising transnational: the manner in which transnational processes of identification are imagined, as Rofel (1999) has so astutely pointed out, shapes the kinds of identities we recognise or fail to recognise. Imposing a model of coming out built on the local-global binary edifice of tradition versus modernity, oppression versus liberation, ironically, alienates rather than liberates the local lesbian.

Notes

1 Some of these structures were crafted by Goh even before he had become Prime Minister. The Non-Constituency Members of Parliament (NCMP), the Group Representation Constituency (GRC), the Nominated Member of Parliament (NMP), and the Elected Presidency are some examples. For critical assessments of these systems, see Rodan (2009: 63); Chin (2009: 72–73, 79); Mutalib (2009: 86–87); Latif (2009) in Welsh *et al.* (2009), and Chua (2007: 918).
2 Bunzl made a similar albeit more eloquent point for the case of Austria, observing that 'homosexuals became central players in the social drama of modernity. Constituted as always already outside the margins of respectability, their abjection gave coherence to the fiction of German nationness' (2004:13).
3 The parties were dubbed by foreign press as Singapore's 'coming out' and declared as Singapore's 'unparalleled alternative party' by local media (Tan 2006).
4 'We do not know the reasons for the sharp increase of HIV in the gay community. An epidemiologist has suggested that this may be linked to the annual predominantly gay party in Sentosa – the Nation Party – which allowed gays from high prevalence societies to fraternise with local gay men, seeding the infection in the local community. However, this is a hypothesis and more research needs to be done' (Minister for Health, Balaji Sadasivan, Speech in Parliament, 9 March 2005).
5 Reply by Registrar 31 March 2004 sent to PLU published on PLU's website, https://plusg.wordpress.com/2003/08/08/history-of-the-gay-movement-phoney-liberalisation-and-the-banned-forum/).

6 The direct English translation reads:

> This is God's gift to them. I think to thread this road alone is not easy for anyone. So as mothers we should stand by them to overcome social prejudice.
> (Translation taken from *Pink Dot 2010 – from the heart* online video)

7 According to statistics from the Infocomm Development Authority of Singapore (IDA), over 80 per cent of households in Singapore access the internet.
8 For example, Singaporeans no longer need to register for a police permit to organise a demonstration, Singaporeans and PRs can also participate in demonstrations organised by the former, but PRs wishing to organise demonstrations must first register with the police. Basic regulations regarding demonstrations involving race or religious issues remain.
9 Online discussions between organisers of the inaugural Pink Dot have been recorded here: https://sgwiki.com/wiki/Sequence_of_events_leading_to_Pink_Dot
10 Please see online discussions between Pink Dot activists here: https://www.blowing-wind.io/forum/profile/9300-pinkdotsg/content/
11 'PD' is the shorthand for *Pink Dot*.
12 As background, the Convention On The Elimination Of All Forms Of Discrimination Against Women (CEDAW) was adopted in 1979 by the United Nations General Assembly, and is regarded as an international bill of rights for women. The Singapore government ratified CEDAW in 1995, and is therefore committed to submitting a national report to the UN CEDAW Committee every four years, documenting the steps they have taken to comply with CEDAW's international set of legal standards for women's rights. In addition to the report CEDAW receives from the state, the CEDAW Committee also reviews Shadow reports from NGOs to get a more comprehensive picture of women's lives, including the reality of lesbian women's lives. After receiving the official and Shadow reports, the UN CEDAW Committee submits concluding observations to the country in question.

6 'Modern' lesbian lives in postcolonial Singapore

Prelude

In the apartment of one of my respondents where I had just sat down to chat after a group interview with her lesbian friends, one of them, someone I will call Anna, began digging into her purse as her loosely worn, shoulder-length hair fell over her face. Anna possesses a kind of effervescence that is infectious. 'Want to see an old photo of me?' she looked up, whipping out her old driver's licence. Before I could respond, Anna was holding up the card to my face as the group of women closed in to take a look. I was taken aback by how masculine Anna appeared in her driver's licence photo.

'My hair used to be cropped and my style was butchy,' Anna said.

The other women around me nodded in confirmation, and one of them whom Anna used to date, quipped, 'Anna used to be cuter!' The women dissolved into giggles, rather awkwardly, as I came to understand from the other friends that their group dynamics have been affected by the 'on and off' dalliances between Anna and Judy after the end of their three-year relationship. For a brief moment, I caught both women looking uneasy. Were Anna and Judy still in a relationship, they would have been the kind of couple who had grown into a familiar likeness of each other; both tanned, feminine and lean in their attire of tight-fitting tee shirt and jeans. Seizing the silence that had befallen the room, I asked Anna what inspired the makeover? Judy took up my question, probing, 'Yes, share why, when and how did you turn so feminine?' Without hesitation, Anna said:

> When I was younger it was easier to dress as I pleased. But when I went out to work, it just became more convenient to look more feminine. It invited fewer questions. Your colleagues don't stare at you. I became more lady-like to fit in at the work place.

Anna's answer raised even more questions. Her work place is the military where she is employed as a uniformed officer. Would a masculine presentation be out of place in a male-dominated environment? Would not donning the uniform – the one incontrovertible sign of 'authentic' masculinity (Schneider 1997) – be well suited for Anna's desire to be masculine? Would not the function of the uniform – as a concealer and leveller of social disparities and incongruities as research has long shown (Joseph and Alex 1972), resolve Anna's dilemmas about inclusion and belonging at the work place? In short, being masculine, I would imagine, ought not to be too problematic in the military where Anna worked. Why did she see the need to 'dress up' or put on display her femininity? Anna's response was both surprising and illuminating:

> Precisely because I was in a male-dominated profession, I had to play up to the gender dynamics in the organisation. Most of the bosses and your colleagues are men and you have to play up to male ego. It is easier to get by than looking manly. Worse if they know I am lesbian. But once you have reached a certain level in your career, you have to be masculine ... because you have to show that you are in power. A number of high-ranking women officers are single who are able to dedicate themselves to long hours at work, or they have to play down their feminine and family side to show that they are as capable as the men taking on those high power positions. There are butchy-looking women in powerful positions! For me, after a while, I just became more comfortable wearing women's clothes even outside work. My style changed and I guess in a way I have changed too ...

On Anna's last note, I observed Judy looking away, wearing an expression of unresolved longing. The spontaneous exchange between Anna and I, and the subtle tête-à-tête between Judy and Anna, provide several useful reminders as well as entry points for the exploration of lesbian lives in postcolonial Singapore. First, in Anna's negotiation of her gender and sexual identity at work, we are reminded not just of how gender and sexuality are mutually defining categories, but also of the impingement of normative gender categories and patriarchal regimes in the structuring of the women's gendered and sexual selves. By having to dress and represent herself as feminine at work, it seems Anna's career is dependent on her being not just heterosexual, but a heterosexual *woman*. This brings us back to the point raised by queer feminist scholars that women's same-sex subjectivities are shaped by the ideologies of womanhood in the local cultural milieu they are embedded in, requiring attention in their own right. Thus, this chapter focuses on the women's same-sex experiences, addressing the specificity of their sexual lives. Two, Anna's attempts to avoid being seen as lesbian at her work place also points to how queer women selectively choose not to unmask and declare their sexual identities but still consider their same-sex subjectivities as 'authentic'. In the wake of lesbian activists' allegations and invalidations of the same-sex practices of queer women who choose to stay in the closet despite a 'changing' and 'modernising' Singapore, it is imperative to explore the diverse and multiple ways in which 'modern' same-sex-desiring women in Singapore opt to enact their queer identities without relying on the core and hegemonic trope of 'coming out'. Three, Anna's reference to her 'butchy' past reveals a familiarity with the 'butch' and 'femme' categories, which were the stable and core identity markers of lesbian communities in San Francisco and elsewhere in the United States prior to the 1970s. But these terms have fallen into disfavour (Blackwood 2010: 8). The masculine-feminine pairing of butch and femme is no longer normative: global queer discourse now assumes modern lesbian couples to reflect gender sameness. On the one hand, Anna's present-day usage of the term 'butchy' as a descriptive of the type of lesbian she was, and no longer is, points to the destabilisation of 'butch' as a fixed identity category, signalling how local lesbians' understanding of themselves and their desires continue to reflect and sustain evolving global queer definitions of what it means to be lesbian. On the other hand, Judy's facetious remark about Anna's 'cuter' masculine characteristics also indicates a subtle heterogenderal preference for a relationship between a masculine and feminine woman, situating lesbian Singaporeans in a 'premodern' queer space before 'modern' global imaginations of lipstick lesbians' as 'women who love women' took hold. These observations, taken together, hint at how Singaporean lesbian subjectivities are at once a part of the global and the local, the past and the present, the then and the now, connected and reconfigured by the vectors of local, national and global circuits to produce at first glance, surprising, if somewhat contradicting, same-sex desires and identities.

Analysing Singaporean lesbian women's experiences

This chapter is about individual lesbian lives in postcolonial Singapore. In the last chapter, we saw the rise of the local queer movement and analysed the strategies, visions and aspirations of a number of prominent activists with a focus on lesbian activism. Although lesbian activists are vested in fighting for the political and civil rights and wellbeing of individual queer subjects, queer politics runs the risk of veiling the specificities of how lesbian lives are lived behind a global queer discourse of LGBT rights and recognition. Therefore, this chapter focuses on the longings and desires, aspirations and recollections, relationships and estrangements of same-sex loving women, such as Judy and Anna, to re-tell the stories of different types of 'queer', even as their sexual subjectivities are always already globalised. These stories, when considered against the grain of hegemonic global gay discourses may at times seem conforming and familiar. Yet, at other times, they seem contradictory and unexpected. Taken together, they reveal in important ways how lesbian lives are lived in the postcolonial context of Singapore.

Through the personal and at times provocative stories of 'modern' lesbian women in postcolonial Singapore, I seek to analyse the particular experiences and meanings these women give to their same-sex sexual subjectivities. I focus on the narratives of middle-class urban lesbians in Singapore. Seen stereotypically as cosmopolitan, English speaking, educated and well-travelled, Singaporeans lesbians can appear so mundane in Western eyes: as un-exotic, un-ethnic, unmarked, and therefore unremarkable categories, 'modern' Singaporean lesbian sexualities, as I have argued, have been excluded from academic scholarships. In the absence of nuanced understandings of the women's same-sex lives, their particular 'modern' ways of being can be misunderstood and misappropriated in activist strategies. This is a case of double jeopardy.

My argument is that the specificity of female same-sex sexualities in Singapore can only be grasped by attending to the ways in which intersections of global queer discourses with local cultural interpretations produce much more complex and layered sexual and gendered subjectivities than a single, universalising narrative of 'sexual identity' suggests. It is important, on the one hand, to recognise the effects of global queer discourses in defining and normalising the same-sex subjectivities of middle-class Singaporean lesbians. On the other hand, it is also necessary to pay attention to how local codes of gender and sexuality intrude into dominant ideologies and understandings to re-shape the women's sexual subjectivities. Put differently, the bodies of middle-class lesbians in Singapore are sites on which local, nationalist and transnational hegemonic codes unevenly crisscross, and the women's sexual subjectivities illustrate these layered processes of regulation. I argue that the ways in which the women make sense of, negotiate, and construct their sexual subjectivities within these systems of power represent that moment of resistance and interrogation of universalising assumptions made of their sexual identities. My interest is therefore in how middle-class lesbians in Singapore transfigure dominant conceptions of their sexuality and gender identity, and how these concepts are taken up and lived in the postcolonial context of Singapore, where a wide array of regulatory codes of sexuality and gender are embedded.

Agency, subjects and structure

Before we begin to examine how subjects take up their particular sexual and gendered subjectivities within various structures of power, it is necessary to briefly address the concept of 'agency', which I have used several times earlier in addition to various iterations of the concept through terms such as 'agentic', 'transform', 'take up', and 'construct'. Indeed through the usage of these terms I have already begun with a conceptual framing of the sexual selves of Singaporean lesbian women as agentive, or, in other words, as capable of empirical social action that will never be completely structured or determined. Yet this is not to suggest some pure Kantian transcendental will or autonomous rational self (Kant 1956, 1965) is at play here: human agency is never entirely free from structure.

The theorisation of agency has been a longstanding struggle and concern in social theory, involving scholars from traditions as different as rational choice theory and poststructuralist theory, all mulling over the age-old problem of free will versus determinism (Emirbayer and Mische 1998).[1] Are social actors, scholars ask, capable of freely choosing and constructing the conditions of their lives if all individual actions are constituted within social structures? How do we theorise this relationship between social structure and social action to allow for notions such as 'individual negotiation', 'construction', 'choice', 'transformation', 'freedom', 'intentionality' and 'initiative' on the part of the subjects we discuss? Anxieties over agency have prompted a vast and vibrant scholarship rethinking the relationship between the social and the subjective.

For the purpose of this book, I turn briefly to two seminal sociological works providing resolutions. The first is Bourdieu's (1977, 1990, 2001) theorisation of habitus, which critiques dichotomous understandings of subjectivism and objectivism, and sees these instead as reciprocally constituting a unified social process. In this conceptualisation, everyday, routinised practices – not necessarily involving conscious strategising – are the ways in which one enacts one's practical sense of the world; agency is constituted through the habitual and repetitive interplay of self and structure. Thus, subjects take up and construct their sexual and gendered subjectivities through their repetitive everyday enactments of power that do not necessarily require conscious thought. Blackwood calls this 'practical enactments' (2010: 23), building on Bourdieu's theorisation that when subjects occupy normative social categories – as in the case of Anna taking up the culturally-defined normative model of womanhood for instance – a certain power or efficacy is gained rather than lost. The second is Giddens' (1979, 1984) theory of structuration, which characterises structure and agency as mutually constitutive and inseparable elements. In this conceptualisation, structure is seen as both the constraining and enabling condition of action at the same time as it is 'accomplished by, and consisting in, the doings of active subjects' (Giddens 1976: 121). These two theories of practice, though not without critique,[2] make possible empirical research that underscores the agency of subjects within normative systems, even if these actions are taken for granted by the actors themselves. The conceptualisation of agency and structure as fundamentally intermeshing, compatible with the claims of postcolonial theory to mutuality and co-constitution, best characterises my use of 'agency' in the examination of the subject positions of Singaporean lesbian women.

In what follows, I turn to the empirical reality of lesbian lives in postcolonial Singapore, and throughout I discuss their freedom and choice in constructing, negotiating and taking up their sexual and gendered subjectivities within systems of power. I consider the effects of nationalist and transnational hegemonic codes in normalising and regulating the women's lives, and I explore in the women's narratives how they contend with and undermine these normalising and disciplinary effects.

The women share accounts of their love lives, their friendships and family relationships. They speak to me about what matters to them and what it means to be lesbian in Singapore. They recollect how they came to recognise and accept their non-normative sexualities. They talk about their longings and desires, and their expectations for the future. Their narratives provide important insights into the question of what happens when localised subject positions meet dominant global understandings of what it means to be lesbian, and vice versa. Given the daunting breadth of these life stories, I focus on salient aspects which best allow me to explore the interconnections and penetrations of local women's same-sex subjectivities with global gay discourses in a foundationally co-constitutive relationality. Specifically, my interest is in the circulation and reception of global queer knowledge among my group of globalised, middle-class, local lesbian respondents, and how these women appropriate and reconstitute these understandings to fit particular meanings that make sense to them, offering these as legitimate conceptions of their same-sex identities.

Thus, this chapter is organised along two main themes: one, labels the women identify with and the ways in which they organise their sexual subjectivities around gendered roles; and two, 'coming out' in postcolonial Singapore and the women's response to and management of their sexual and gendered selves in various social spheres. In exploring these themes, I hope to provide insights into the women's sexual selfhoods: their understanding of their sexual identities, their sense of community with individuals like themselves, how they came to their sexual subjectivities through their relationships and individual desires.

Taken together, I argue, these aspects of lesbian lives reveal the women's complicated and contingent models of hybridising, transnational sexual subjectivities (Tang 2012), which underscore the range as well as the specificity of Singaporean lesbian lives. As we shall soon see, lesbians in Singapore tap into the global circulation of discourse on gay rights, desires and freedoms in forming their sexual subjectivities, but their de-localised conceptions are remoulded in the force field of overlapping local, national and global contexts, producing distinct sexual identities and practices in a co-constitutive relationality to Western queer sexualities. The same-sex practices of Singaporean lesbian women, I argue, are no less 'authentic' for even as they draw from Western queer discourses, they transform and develop new understandings that redefine ways of being gay.

In the final analysis, I argue that the emergence of these complex modes of hybridising, transnational sexualities neither assume a position of local resistance nor global gay embodiment, but a contradictory, complicit and contingent negotiation of the local and global. The sexual subjectivities of Singapore lesbians problematise not just hegemonic Western queer constructions but also the postcolonial elites' naturalisation of non-normative sexualities in Singapore as Western afflictions. The sum of these dynamics requires a re-thinking of global same-sex subjectivities.

Queer? No way! I am not weird: labels and gendered lesbian lives

The term 'queer' originated from the coalitional identity politics of activist movements and academic circles in the United States, Australia and Europe. In Western sexual politics, 'queer' functions as an overarching, inclusive identity category meant to powerfully unite and mobilise all non-normative sexual and gender subjects who stand outside the fold of heteronormativity. Via dominant circuits of global cultural flows – gay rights politics, global media, popular culture and other circuits of queer cultural and knowledge production – the category 'queer' circulates centrifugally through these networks as a vector of 'foundational' Euro-American originated identity. Closely connected to these global circuits, activists in Singapore identify more with the term than other lesbian women. 'Queer', for instance, proliferates on the mission statements of local activist organisations, on their websites and events outreach collaterals. The appropriation of 'queer' is understandable given that English is the local lingua franca and activists could easily borrow and deploy terms and identifications already developed in the global gay ecumene to reach out to the community. However, in making sense of how global terms circulate within the local community, I was struck by how little individual lesbians identify with the identity category 'queer', and how they in fact understand it as a generic English term, emptied of its highly-charged politicised content. Even among the highly educated, globally connected middle-class respondents in my study, these women found it hard to connect to the term 'queer'. When I tried to ask Samantha whether she saw herself as a queer woman, she remarked to my bemusement:

> 'Queer'? No way! I am not weird. Why do I have to be the abnormal one compared to heterosexual society? I think people in the English-speaking world should know that queer holds negative connotations. All this negativity is self-imposed!

Ironically, the meaning this participant attached to the term was completely at odds with the global meaning of 'queer' as a coalitional, inclusive identity category. Not only did she question the universal use of the concept, she resisted and reversed its very usage, challenging its Western definitions and understandings instead. This respondent's reaction provides the first clue as to how local individual lesbians selectively respond to and identify with the global gay discourse, shaped as they are by their particular local-national context. Even though the women are always already connected to the global community through language access and the global embeddedness of the local cultural context, the usage of these linguistic terms does not signify for them global or Western identifications. They sought instead to re-interpret or re-define Western categories according to what made sense for them.

Most participants in this study seem to assume 'lesbian' as an identity category with more ease, consistent with *Sayoni*'s (2010a) survey of lesbians living in Singapore. Results from the survey indicate that only about seven per cent of its 530 respondents identify as 'queer' compared to 65 per cent as 'lesbians', with the rest identifying as 'bisexual', 'transgender' and others. Surveying whether same-sex-desiring women in Singapore identify as 'lesbian' (L), 'bisexual' (B) or 'transgender' (T) *Sayoni*'s measure is drawn from and based on the global 'LGBT' signifier. Like 'queer', 'LGBT' functions in global gay discourse as an inclusive, politicised identity category, appropriated by local activists in their reference to and mobilisation of the community and their cause.

Among the women I spoke to, 'lesbian' made more sense than 'queer' as the former, in the English vocabulary, means women who love women. Unlike same-sex-desiring women in Thailand who reject the label 'lesbian' (Sinnott 2004, Jackson 2001), the women in Singapore found it acceptable compared with 'queer'. But their understanding of 'lesbian' does not amount to an awareness of its politicised function or its significance as one part of the universal representative 'LGBT' category. Unlike the homosexual community in Indonesia which generally takes up LGBT identities to 'secure a stake in the global LGBT community' (Blackwood 2010: 181), same-sex subjects in Singapore already see themselves as a part of the global community and identify with these labels with a certain sense of inevitability, and, if I might add, hesitance. My respondents appear uncertain and to some extent uncomfortable with using either term. Like 'queer', the word 'lesbian' only serves functionally as an English term describing their non-normative sexual lives. Neither of the labels 'lesbian' or 'queer' work well in Singapore. Neither term resonates strongly nor circulates in the women's everyday vernacular, though 'lesbian' is more widely adopted.

If there was an organising principle among local lesbians, this appears to be gendered labels. As Kartini (2001: 56) observes of these gendered labels, '[they] are such an essential element of lesbian life and identity in Singapore that without them, its lesbian community would be unrecognisable to its members'. In *Sayoni*'s biennial surveys (2006, 2008b, 2010a), lesbian respondents were asked if they identified with any labels, such as 'butch', 'femme', and 'andro'. These three represent the most common classifications in contemporary local lesbian life, and indeed, all of my respondents were familiar with these classifications, though they also pointed out a chronology in the emergence and circulation of gendered lesbian labels where certain older terms have fallen into disfavour.

Appearance of 'active' and 'passive'

The older Singaporean lesbians in my study, who are between the ages of mid-30s and above, used the labels 'active' and 'passive' in the 1980s. These are gender-marked, age-specific terms referring to younger women involved in a romantic relationship in which one partner is masculine and the other feminine. 'Active' refers to the boyish characteristics and behaviour of a masculine lesbian, while 'passive' refers to a young, feminine woman. Although both labels have fallen into almost complete disuse within the contemporary lesbian community, in the mid-1980s, these two categories circulated popularly within all-girls Catholic convent schools, as Drew, a respondent, recollects:

> It was my first day in secondary school during recess time.[3] This was in 1988. I was having my meal when two seniors in school, both a year older than I, came up to me to ask me whether I was 'active' or 'passive'. They were a very well-known lesbian couple in school. One was masculine, the other was feminine. I didn't know them and I didn't know what they were

looking for. I was at first very puzzled but they kept pressing me for an answer. Thinking that I was generally rather sporty, and that I enjoy all sorts of outdoor activities, I decided that if I had to choose between the two words, I would be 'active'. When I said 'active', they both looked at each other then said out loud, 'we knew it!' It was only later when I was discovering my sexual identity that I found out that the words meant a certain kind of masculine and feminine role lesbians play.

Alyssa, another respondent who also attended a convent school in the 1980s, different from the one Drew went to, provides a similar recollection of how she first came to hear of those terms:

Someone in school, I can't remember who, explained it like you are active because you are tomboyish. You go after the girls therefore active. And since the girls just sit back, they are passives ... but I disagree ... it's the passive girls who chased me!

Confronted with these labels for the first time, both respondents' reacted by drawing on general understandings of 'active' as a personality trait as opposed to 'passive', which do not pertain to gay life as such. Drew and Alyssa's accounts suggest that the ways in which school-going lesbians came to appropriate these labels appear almost accidental. After the unexpected initiation, the women discuss the way they began to notice and make sense of what it means to be 'active' and 'passive' from their observations of, and interactions with, lesbians in their schools. It is unclear how the two schoolmates of Drew or Alyssa's informant learn of these labels, though it is significant that these exchanges took place in the context of convent schools proffering colonial, Christian-centred education where Anglicised, aspirational, first-generation Singaporeans from middle class backgrounds sent their teenage daughters for schooling. School girls from these family backgrounds would have resources and language access to the global circulation of LGBT-identifying terms.

On a more intimate level, Alyssa's account provides a further insight into how local schoolgirls possessed a level of self-awareness and confidence about their sexual desires, and had no qualms about expressing their same-sex affections. 'Actives' enjoy great popularity among the girls, and their feminine admirers often lavish on them thoughtful gifts of stationery, name-emblazoned key chains, handmade bracelets, cards, flowers, and love letters. Masculine 'actives' relish the role of being 'chased' and at times reciprocate these offers of affection. 'The boyish-looking girls were like stars and celebrities in school', Judy told me:

They were like revered and the epitome of cool. Everyone knew who they were but their girlfriends were not so high profile. People knew of the passives because they were with the actives. I don't remember who were the passives in school, but if you ask me, I can tell you who are the actives, how they looked, which class they belonged to.

In Judy's account, young, school-going lesbians were identified in terms of their masculinity. 'Actives' enjoyed considerable recognition and attention while feminine 'passives' were defined only in relation to the 'active' partner. Early lesbian consciousness was thus defined by an imagination of a masculine-feminine pairing, involving, compulsorily, the masculine lesbian. Without the figure of the 'active', the feminine 'passive' is erased from a lesbian existence.

In the history of Western queer sexuality, the terms 'active' and 'passive' surfaced in studies of ancient European sexualities, such as in Roman and Greek cultures, as a dichotomy characterising the sexual roles and positions played in both hetero- sex and in homoerotic acts. More specifically, 'actives' are penetrators and 'passives' are those penetrated (Karras 2000) and these sexual roles are correlated to gender constructions of masculinity and femininity. In connection with these distant European movements, the gendered and sexual roles of 'active' and 'passive' found expression in the setting of all-girls missionary schools in Singapore, where the masculine 'actives' initiate sexual advances, even if they are not the first to express romantic interest, while feminine 'passives' though self-confident in their expression of affection, are typically the recipient of kisses and touches leading to mutual fondling and heavy petting not untypical of sexually explorative teenagers.

Despite the strong religious and conservative influence in Christian missionary schools, it is common knowledge among my respondents and the lesbian community that all-girl convent schools in Singapore are a locus for the generation of lesbian knowledge, consciousness and pairings. Feminine schoolgirls got together with masculine ones, and younger girls having crushes on senior students and female teachers were not uncommon, and in fact, frequently made known through informal school grapevines. But the budding of same-sex desires in these schools is tenaciously policed. Principals, discipline mistresses, teachers, counsellors, and even school caretakers and janitors monitor the girls' interaction at every level, suppressing and disciplining non-normative sexualities and genders through specific forms of surveillance and punishment. Special school rules, for instance, have been implemented to arrest the development of same-sex relationships. These include bag and body searches for love notes and gifts exchanged between students, reading personal diaries, confiscating letters between the girls, defining acceptable lengths of short hair to suppress the performance of masculinity, checking students' bodies for men's cologne, making girls wear wigs when their hair is cut too short, policing student movement in and around the school vicinity, shaming students perceived to be same-sex attracted at the school assembly, and summoning the parents of girls 'at risk' of lesbian behaviour. These school disciplinary measures experienced by my respondents made them feel anxious and angry over the policing of their sexuality. One reported engaging in self-harm when she was publicly shamed for being caught in a same-sex romance. 'It was very confusing for me,' said this respondent:

> I was a school prefect and was attracted to an 'active' who was charming and persistent, so I gave in. When our relationship was found out, my

parents were called in. I was stripped of my duties and that brought a lot of shame. The school didn't help me make sense of my sexual orientation; there was no education. It only felt like discrimination.

These anecdotal evidences of homosexual policing within the setting of convent schools in the 1980s from my informants corroborate with the findings of a 2012 survey conducted by the LGBT counselling group Oogachaga, which reports that school-based discrimination remains rampant in the Singaporean school system. The disciplinary and discriminatory measures undertaken by the school system did little to stem the proliferation of love and same-sex attraction between the girls. Being gay in convent schools, one informant tells me, is the 'normal thing':

> It is not only after I got out of school that I felt that you can still feel comfortable with the opposite sex. It was more like after I came out of school then I came out and asked myself 'am I really gay'? It is not the other way round where I am straight and I ask myself if I am gay.

These narratives speak to a lack of sexuality education on same-sex love in the school system, and to the general inadequacy of sexuality education for Singaporean students. Like other state mechanisms, the education system takes a negative stance towards homosexuality, or is otherwise silent on the topic. Individual schools can supplement the government's sexuality education syllabus with programmes offered by external providers. The women's organisation, AWARE, for example, was offering its Comprehensive Sexuality Education programme in some schools until 2009, when a group of Christian conservative women made a great furore over how the AWARE instructors' guide contained neutral, and not negative language, when approaching the topic of homosexuality. The MOE's (Ministry of Education) response was to temporarily ban all schools from engaging external vendors. Vetting processes were put in place to ensure that all lesson material fell in line with the government's sexuality education framework reflecting 'mainstream views and values of Singapore society, where the social norm consists of the married heterosexual family unit' (MOE Press Release statement taken from *TheOnlineCitizen.com* 2009). When the ban was subsequently lifted and external organisations invited to submit applications to teach sexuality education, at least four out of the six organisations chosen by the MOE were linked to pro-family Christian organisations (*Straits Times* 2010c), including those with global, anti-gay affiliations, such as Focus on the Family (FOF). It is not transparent how individual schools select their sexuality education providers. Nor is it clear how the lesson material, meant to comply with the government's sexuality education framework, is delivered. But an open letter by a school student that went viral on social media made known how sexist and gender stereotypes were being proffered in FOF's sexuality education programme. 'No means yes?' and 'yes means no?' 'If she says this, she really means that' were some of the incredulously naïve and offensive things found in

FOF's 'It's (UN)Complicated' sexuality education workshop, which was subsequently withdrawn by the Education Ministry without explanation (*Straits Times* 2014).

If heterosexist and gendered images are allowed to inhabit and condition young people's imagination of sexual relationships, and objective treatments of homosexuality banned from discussion, how do these impoverished conceptualisations of sexualities and genders implicate the masculine-feminine pairings of lesbian love? What are the conditions that incubate opposite-attracting, gendered lesbian relationships that resist interpellation into dominant queer feminist ideology of gender-equal women who love women? Bound in an ostensible gender binary, what is the quality of lesbian relationships, beyond the young, schoolgirl pairing of 'actives' and 'passives'? Following the sexual lives of Singaporean lesbians will shed light on these questions.

Consolidation of 'butch' and 'femme' categories

The categories 'butch' and 'femme' came into circulation prior to the 1990s, and were adopted in the local vernacular of the lesbian community replacing the use of 'active' and 'passive'. In my respondents' understanding, butches are defined by outward, rather extreme, mannishness. Generally, they take on the behaviour of men, dress only in men's clothing, wear their hair shaven, visit male public toilets and sexually penetrate their partners through fingering and sex toys, but do not accept and receive sexual penetration because it is associated with being effeminate. Of all these masculine practices, breast binding appears to be the quintessential differentiating factor between 'butches' and 'actives'. Drew shared this story:

> ... this was in the 1980s and I was hanging out with the group of senior girls, a number of whom are actives with their girlfriends. Although I did not have a girlfriend the group saw me as an active since I was tomboyish. At a chalet during the school holidays, one active went into the bathroom and started binding her breasts with bandages and safety pins. When she came out of the bathroom everyone in the chalet exclaimed at her flat chest and started to examine how she had bound her breast. I remember she wrapped layer after layer of bandages around her chest, starting from the lower torso up to under the armpits, then fastened down at the side with safety pins. After that I remember the girls began using the term 'butch' calling these butches 'he' and 'him'. When I hung out with them at McDonalds, Burger King and Milano's Pizza, these butches used men's toilets.

Besides bandages, duct tape, elastic bands, clear wraps and other make-do contraptions were the materials butches used to bind their breasts. Today, breast binders come in professionally manufactured spandex and Velcro-adjustable versions. These are commercially available in a range of styles, from tank tops to singlets, sports bras to swimsuit binders. Where oversized shirts were a means to hide cumbersome and unsightly bandages, new breast binding technologies have introduced versatility into butch dressing. Available in an assortment of sizes, styles and colours to suit various body shapes and breast sizes, chest binders are sold as fashion merchandise in online shops and at bazaar stalls by lesbian entrepreneurs.

Just as breast binders are openly purveyed, so do butches don their chest contraptions in an open parade. Along the city's most fashionable streets, bosom-binding lesbians strut chest out and proud, flaunting a tight torso in a sleeveless tee or slim-fitting top. Butch expressions could be understood as a process of 'doing' (Goffman 1971) or a kind of 'performativity' (Butler 1990, 1993) that produce an identity through the continuous iteration or repetitive performance of walking, talking and dressing in ways that, in this case, consolidate an impression of being butch. 'Performing butch' in Singapore, or what Yue (2007: 156) calls, 'doing butch', occurs not just on the streets but also in local clubs and lesbian bars. 'Doing butch' in Singapore, I suggest, finds its ultimate expression in the local *Butch Hunt* competition where butches 'strut their stuff', so to speak, to the *de rigueur* of a pageant competition.

Touted by the largest regional gay news portal as 'one of the most unique events in Asia's lesbian scene' (*Fridae.com* 2005b), the *Butch Hunt* contest is both a pageantry and paean to a young set of butch lesbians, most of them in their twenties. It is organised biannually by *Club Herstory*, a lesbian-owned events management company. Each contest features about 10 to 15 butch finalists who catwalk, sing, dance, act and field questions on dating, sex and romance. As many as 1,600 people thronged the city's most well-known dance club, Zouk, for the inaugural 2001 *Butch Hunt* competition. The shows grew to be big extravaganzas. The spectacle of mannish lesbians bursting on stage firing mock machine guns, strutting on the runway in leather pants and jackets wearing tattoos on their arms, and appearing debonair in starched shirts and suits certainly make for a great deal of entertainment. But drawing in the crowd is not the only reason for the organisers to hold the *Butch Hunt* competition:

> *Butch Hunt* was started to create awareness of our community, to establish acceptance for us ... *Butch Hunt* showcases what Butches are capable of. It is for them to show that they are talented. They are not 'gremlins' like they are sometimes called.
> (Organiser from *Herstory*, quote taken from *Fridae.com* 2005b)

Butch Hunt in Singapore is organised as part of the social reproduction of lesbian identities in the local community. 'On pageant nights', described Gea, well known for her participation in lesbian activism, 'the sheer amount of lesbian visibility creates a palpable sense of excitement. One can almost sense a proud, unspoken declaration among the women who attend – a declaration along the lines of, 'I'm lesbian and proud of it!' (*Fridae.com* 2006b). By celebrating and empowering its most visible constituents, which takes the most 'homophobic flak by virtue of its visibility' (*Fridae.com* 2005b), a sense of community is built around the butch category. The celebration of butch identities in increasingly glamorised *Butch Hunt* competitions signal how butches are very much cherished in the local community's imagination of itself, even if this sometimes involve some teasing and scoffing at over-the-top butch posturing and their unabashed visibility. Said one respondent facetiously:

> Butches are so out and so open now. There is no restriction with them. You go to Orchard Road, you see them holding hands with their girlfriends. A lot of them will cut their hair very short. In Singapore they are so obvious ... And their names are all so manly! Terence *lah*, Shane *lah*, Chuck *lah* ... it can be too much, a bit unattractive *lah*!

These frequent jests never amount to an outright rejection of the local butch community. In the Singaporean context, butches are regarded as an integral, quotidian part of the local lesbian landscape, marking it to be quite distinct from the politics of lesbian identities in the region.

Research on masculine lesbian identities in Southeast Asia reveal that the *T*s in Taiwan (Chao 2000), *tom*s in Thailand (Sinnott 2004) and *tombois* in Indonesia (Murray 1999, Blackwood 2010) are regarded as abject debasements of feminist ideals of gender and sexual equality, disparaged for their 'backward' anti-woman subject positions, exoticised for their body-mutilating, breast-binding antics, and exiled to low or working class lesbian bar scenes. According to Blackwood (2010), Indonesia's well-known lesbian feminist, Gayatri, claims that masculine *tombois* are not like lesbians of the middle and upper-middle classes, and across the region in Taiwan, lesbian feminist intellectuals encountered by Chao (2000) find the performativity of *T*s an unacceptable and uncritical imitation of masculinity. Interpellated by a global queer discourse of modernity that assumes a woman-loving-woman model of lesbian identity, *tombois* and *T*s subjects exist only in the ghettoes of 'backward' working class bar cultures and outside the educated, middle-class imagined worlds of lesbianism.

Needless to say, this global queer discourse flowed through Singapore, and by the early 2000s, lesbian activists began to espouse gender equality and an ideology of 'women who love women', reflected as I have discussed, in the title of Singapore's only lesbian documentary. I have highlighted how the female protagonists in the local lesbian documentary, all of whom closely connected to activist networks, decried lesbian masculinity and defended their femininity in spite of their masculine appearance, suggesting therefore that a similar discourse have taken root in Singapore as it did in other Southeast Asian lesbian contexts. However, butch identities in Singapore continue to take front and centre stage in the local lesbian community. Whether performing their identities in excess at *Butch Hunt* competitions, or strolling chest out and proud with their girlfriends on public streets, the modernist fantasy of being unbound by gender unravels as soon as attention is paid to the phenomenon of socially and upwardly mobile, fashionable and 'modern' butch lesbians in Singapore.

Attention must also be paid to femmes, the prized accessory of butch performativity. In terms of appearance, femmes are indistinguishable from 'normal' heterosexual women. A typical femme in Singapore wears 'lipstick, makeup all the time, (her) dressing is very feminine, the way she talks, the way she behaves … it's in the small things, like the type of slippers she chooses, or like, how she wears her hair, and how she takes effort in picking out the appropriate bra for the appropriate dress, that sort of thing', as Devan (2010: 29) records of an insider's description. On the alternate year when the *Butch Hunt* competition takes a backseat, femmes saunter onto stage in an equivalent pageant called *Femme Quest*. The contest is organised by the same lesbian events management company, features about 10 young women mostly in their twenties, who are judged for their feminine poise, manners and comportment. Some contestants sport short and sassy hairstyles looking fresh-faced and vibrant. Others wear long tresses looking dainty and dignified. Since its inception in 2002, a year after the launch of *Butch Hunt*, *Femme Quest* has proven to be just as popular. Described as 'one of the biggest lesbian pageants in the region' (*Fridae.com* 2006b) *Femme Quest*, like its *Butch Hunt* predecessor, is a major crowd puller. Watching the stiletto-heeled and bikini-clad women sashay down the catwalk to loud cheers and wolf whistles at the 2010 *Femme Quest* competition, I cannot help but observe that the bodies on parade are not identifiably 'femme'. Unlike butch identities, femmes are not enacted into being at the level of dress and performativity. The women's looks and dressing do not place them into the marked category of lesbian. There is no way to tell femmes from heterosexual women. Where the difference is apparent is not on stage but on the sidelines, among the masculine lesbians cheering on their girlfriends and objects of affection. In the context of *Femme Quest*, femme identities only began to make sense when we take into account the entire spectacle.

Femmes come into their lesbian identities only through their relationships with butches. If femmes were to express lesbian identity, the butch partner then in fact becomes a key accessory. Femmes are also indistinguishable by their sexual desires. Primarily attracted to masculine lesbians, femmes claim they have been, and might in the future be, in a relationship with a man. This makes them just like 'normal' women, femmes say. Chantel, who was in a relationship with a masculine lesbian at the time of our interview, began with the caveat that she might not necessarily qualify as a respondent for my study on Singaporean lesbians:

> Actually I don't know if I should take part in your study because seriously until today I am still asking myself if I am gay. Even though I am now in a relationship with a girl, I think about getting married, starting a family and having children if this relationship is over. I have been with a guy before and who knows I might end up with a guy next. So am I still qualified to be your respondent?

Her relationship did come to an end. Chantel went on to be with another woman and continues to resist a lesbian identity. My respondents tell me that femmes like Chantel are called 'straight' girls, making a direct reference to their concurrent heterosexuality. 'Straight' girls float in and out of a homosexual lifestyle and are viewed with some suspicion by the community mainly because they are perceived as merely experimenting with lesbian love, have low investments in their same-sex relationships, and therefore destined to be heartbreakers. 'In the end, these girls will leave you for a man', an informant said warningly. The local similarities to regional femme sexualities are noteworthy: in Thailand, all feminine Thai women, including heterosexuals, are seen as potential *dee*s (Sinnott 2007); in Indonesia, femme *lesbi*s regard their relationships with *tombois* as heterosexual relationships (Blackwood 2010); and in Taiwan, *Po*s are characterised by their 'seduce and abandon' dalliances with *T*s (Chao 2000). Although the transnational dynamics of these contexts are dissimilar – marked by different global, cultural and national interpenetrations – these accounts collectively underscore that femmes share the category of normative heterosexual women and cling to unstable lesbian identities. In these non-Western accounts, being femme is not articulated as a fixed and enduring same-sex orientation in the same way as it has been suggested of white lesbians in the United States (see Munt 1998; King 2002). Rather, femme identities in the regional context are contingent on their relationships with their masculine partners.

When an informant unexpectedly confides in me that her current six-year relationship has reached something of a plateau, and she neither knows how to take it further or walk away from it, I asked her if she would consider being in another lesbian relationship if she were to break up with her partner. Her answer was a flat 'no'. It is easier to be with a guy and lead a typical married life, she tells me. Her decision is not unique as another femme said this to me:

> On the back of my mind when I started this relationship I really thought it was an interim. Often I will have these thoughts at the back of my mind. I often think that I am 33, 34 years old, I will give myself this experience just for a while. I can still *tahan*[4] for one or two years, and it won't be too late to have kids. At the back of my mind actually I have another reality and I just want to think that maybe I will have a chance of a proper family and proper marriage and have kids. There are things butches cannot offer: the institution of marriage and kids. You can't stop yourself from your emotions, from falling in love, from being in this relationship with someone you love but at the same time I think that maybe there is still a chance of having a proper family.

Bisexuality is the label given to these two informants in Western queer categorising. The women refer to their attraction to both men and women in their narratives but would only reluctantly acknowledge their bisexuality. Notions of proper family factor saliently in the women's heterosexual desires, while their same-sex desires are seen as sudden and impermanent. In the long term, a heterosexual relationship represents a more uncomplicated alternative. Falling into heterosexual love is to fall in line with state ideologies and socio-cultural expectations of marriage and motherhood for the women. Yet, there was never any sense that the women treated their same-sex relationships lightly. Committed in their current lesbian relationships, these femmes assume steadfast yet conditional same-sex love for their masculine partners.

Problematising gendered identities

Butch and femme identities flourished in the lesbian bar cultures of major US cities following World War II in the 1940s and 1950s (Miller 2006). Archived photographs from those eras show butches dressed in starched shirts, suit coats and Oxford shoes in the 1940s, and a subsequent generation of butches in rugged working class jeans, t-shirts and sweaters in the 1950s, revealing a distinct masculinity reminiscent of the dressing style on display in contemporary Singapore's *Butch Hunt* competitions. The goal then was not to pass as men but to demonstrate their lesbian identities and subvert cultural moirés as an act of resistance (Kennedy and Davis 1993). Initially seen as the innovators of lesbian activism, butch identities were by the 1960s and 1970s denounced by the second-wave feminist movement as antagonistic to women's ideals, a mimicry of heterosexuality and an 'embarrassing legacy of an oppressive past' (Nestle 1992: 296; Stein 1997). Following this, Faderman (1992) notes a shift away from gendered labels in America and Western Europe in the 1970s, and it was only in the 1980s that butch identities experienced a resurgence in the US and the UK (Ardill and O'Sullivan 1990).

Nevertheless, Western butch and femme identities continue to be read by feminists as foundationally located in shame. Munt (1998) for instance theorises the corporeality of sexual shame experienced by the butch, writing of how shame has its genesis in the body, breasts, genitals and sexual behaviour of butches, as well as in her 'failed copy' (1998: 5) of maleness. 'Shame is the foundational moment in lesbian identity, and I am arguing butch/femme identity', asserts Munt (1998: 7). This negative vector of identification contrasts sharply to how the butch/femme category was for an earlier generation positioned as pride symbols in the West, and confirms the continuous retreat from gendered labels in contemporary queer communities.

Noting also the demise of butch/femme labels within the Singapore lesbian community, Devan (2010: 41) writes that while the 'shift away from gendered labels in the US and Western Europe occurred in the 1970s, this shift has occurred in Asia only in the past few years'. In leaving unclear the conceptualisation of local same-sex identities in relation to the West, her account suggests a certain evolutionary lag and congruence between a Western past and those of contemporary Asian lesbian cultures. Butch and femme identities that gained circulation in Singapore in the 1980s – evidenced in Drew and Alyssa's early encounters with the term – coincided with the resurgence of these labels in the West in the same period. The subsequent retreat from butch/femme categories in Singapore was, if not simultaneous, surely similar to the West. But to explain the emergence and shifting identifications of local butch and femmes only as a replay of a Western past, or as a result of present feminist discourse and practices in the West, is to miss the nuances and specificities of local lesbian lives, the women's individual yearnings and desires, and their agency and struggle to define their same-sex subjectivities in the shifting sands of social and economic transformation in postcolonial Singapore. Butches and femmes did not just craft their subjectivities in relation to 'older' lesbian practices in the West. Local *Butch Hunt* and *Femme Quest* competitions, borrowing Yue's (2007) insight, are products of a burgeoning creative and culture industry cultivated by the postcolonial state as part of its efforts to re-make Singapore's economy in the wake of the 1997 Asian financial crisis. The performativity of lesbian identities in Singapore takes place in the city's trendiest clubs – and not in the ghettoes of working class lesbian bars – patronised by financially comfortable middle-class women who swipe credit cards at the bar, generously buying each other expensive cocktails over-laden with state alcohol tax. It is in these consumption practices that same-sex identities and practices flourish in contemporary Singapore.

While Munt (1998) locates butch performativity in a cultural politics of shame, Yue (2007) argues that the bold and brazen cultural practices of breast binding performed on the streets and on the stage in Singapore signifies not shame but 'a new agency, making it a source of empowerment and engagement' (2007: 157). This empowerment of local butch lesbians, however, never translates into a politicised stance of resistance and irreverence as it did in the West. Performing butch is not a source of political mobilisation, but a personal project of self-identification that never adds up into a coherent, unified identity project. This account from Foo, an older butch lesbian, is indicative:

> You can't go to the ladies. You have to go to the gents. Or you have to go to the handicapped toilet. That is one inconvenience. You go to the ladies they will stare at you. The toilet lady, the aunty outside will tell you, you are in the wrong toilet. You go to the guys' toilet you have to wait for a cubicle. My friends ask me if you use some kind of an apparatus. I said no as per normal. So unless I want to do it in the open, I'll need to use the apparatus. When I go to the guys' toilet I pass on easily. Everywhere I go, people perceive me to be a guy. I am used to it. In the beginning my girlfriend tried to correct them I said just leave it because as a butch person you dress up like a guy. The general perception is that I am a guy. So I just leave it. I am ok with it. It doesn't matter what pronouns others use or me, whatever works for them. I am fine with it. I am not disturbed by questions like 'why you call me a her?' If others use the male or female pronoun on me I am not bothered. Really totally not bothered.

Foo, who used to go by the pronoun 'he', no longer adopts a strict masculine identity for personal and pragmatic reasons. Foo's account is reminiscent of Anna's experience at her workplace, where gendered norms and expectations at work meant she had to present as female 'in order to get by'. In the experience of these respondents, the performativity of wearing one's hair short, putting on men's clothes and using men's toilets does not amount to an incremental consolidation of a gender identity as theorised by Butler (1990, 1993). Apart from Anna, two other lesbian women I met in the course of my research also experienced shifts in their gender orientations, moving from a highly masculinised identity to take on distinct feminine roles in a complete gender role reversal and transformation. Now in a lesbian relationship with masculine women, these women considered 'butchy' before are now seen as femmes among their friends who sometimes still marvel at the transformation. 'It was like ... wow how did that happen? She used to wear baggy jeans and bind her breasts, now she is so ladylike, always in dresses, carrying handbags!' A kind of agency, borne partially of performativity, partially of pragmatism and partially of personal taste, has transformed dominant notions of what being lesbian means.

The persistence of gendered relations and the ascension of 'andro'

Masculine identities and gendered lesbian relations are by no means swept away by the vortex of the feminist movement. To begin with, global feminism has never been a particularly strong force in postcolonial Singapore, where the reach of feminist discourses circulate within the delimited civil society space organisations such as AWARE operate in. Singaporean civil society has historically been a state-dominated, state-defined sphere (Rodan 1996; Koh and Ooi 2004) based on the Hegelian conception that civil society is a product of the state (Chong 2006). The NGOs that populate it, including AWARE, are ones politically aligned with state agendas, capable of mobilising 'national interest' or dominant ideology, as opposed to competing for political legitimacy and championing for alternative and marginal interests more characteristic of a conventional civil society in liberal democracies. Civil society in Singapore thus takes the form of a 'civic society' (Yeo 1991) wherein conservative and conflict-shy NGOs emphasise 'civic' responsibility rather than advance notions of citizen rights and freedoms (Chua 2000). For AWARE, engaged in this depoliticised 'civic' sphere, its feminist practices have been observed to be generally limited (Lyons 2000) and exclude the contentious issue of non-normative sexualities. Apart from the AWARE saga discussed earlier, which no doubt brought to the fore the twin issues of feminism and lesbianism, the two scarcely overlap in the local context.

Most of my informants possess some knowledge of the politics, tactics and ideologies of feminist movements, including the global queer feminist discourse of gender-equal lesbian relationships, but they are not partial to the ideas. Masculine-feminine pairings continue to be the dominant mode of local lesbian relationships. Consequently, local imaginations and understandings of lesbian relationships continue to be very gendered. Even though the women shy away from viewing themselves in terms of strict categories, gender continues to be an important organising principle in the women's social and personal relationships. Gendered identities are either ascribed by others in the community or worked out between the women in their relationships. For example, Shannon told me that others perceive her to be 'a butch by default' of her appearance but she did not see herself as one. Kang was clear that she would only be attracted to a femme. 'But that does not make me a butch', she clarified. Despite the disavowals of gendered labels, the women very quickly assume masculine and feminine roles in their relationships. Kit, who appears to be more feminine than her partner, Siew, felt it was her 'right' to be pampered with material gifts of clothes, handbags and shoes from her masculine partner. 'That's the benefit of being a girl! A girly-girl! I don't know why you want to be a butch', Kit said out loud looking at Siew, 'you lose all the power!' I looked at Siew, hopeful for a rebuttal. These were two university-educated professionals familiar with feminist language and popular notions of girl power. But all I got from Siew was a shrug and an acquiescence, 'I think I am traditional that way. Between us, I believe it is my job to provide for us as a couple.' Also eager to attribute gender roles, Constance and Theresa shared that one of the first things they did at the start of their relationship was to work out 'who would be butch and who would be femme. I mean someone has to step up and wear the pants right? And it ain't going to be me!' Constance declared. The two women could arguably fit into the queer feminist model of a gender-equal couple. One a gym instructor, the other a physical education teacher, it was hard to tell who would be the more feminine or masculine one. Constance and Theresa enjoyed an egalitarian relationship in almost all other aspects: both are financially independent, both play their part in the division of household chores, and their sexual relationship was based on mutual pleasure giving. Quizzically, Constance volunteered herself into a femme role for no ostensible reason, but the assumption of gender roles seemed to make sense for the couple. A kind of compulsory gendered relationship exists among the women I interviewed. But in Kang's disavowal of a 'butch' identity, Chantel's delight in her femininity, Constance's enthusiasm in embracing a feminine role and the benign manner with which masculine gender assignments were received by Siew and Theresa, what consistently marked these narratives for me was, rather contradictorily, an ambivalence with masculinity.

Somewhere between the early and mid-2000s, the term 'androgynous', or 'andro' for short, began circulating popularly in the local lesbian community to describe those who do not fit into clear masculine and feminine roles. It is a sort of a gender middle ground, a category for indeterminate masculinity and femininity. In the local context, however, 'andro falls more on the masculine side', an informant tells me. As with butch and femme labels, so too has the emergence of 'andro' been seized, packaged and commoditised into yet another competition held by *Two Queens Asia*, another lesbian events management company. Since 2007, over ten finalists take to the runway each year to compete for the title *So You Think You're Andro?* The contestants sport trendy short locks or longish *bishounen* hair, all possessing looks best described as pretty boys. Being 'andro' is a celebration of ambivalence and contradiction; it is not an identity status that can be affixed with the specific act of breast binding, for instance.

Androgyny has become the desired and most comfortable mode of gender identification taken up by most of my masculine respondents. Like Kang and Shannon eschewing mannish butch identities earlier, the women disassociate themselves from highly masculinised practices and labels. Yet, they continue to dress in a masculine manner, rarely make claims to their femininity and are at ease with their female bodies and womanhood. 'I love my breasts!' Theresa tells me 'and I wear these (masculine female Oxford) shirts because they fit me, I like the way I look this way, and I don't feel relaxed in girls clothes. People mistake me for a guy and that is upsetting and tiresome. I don't like men, why would I want to be a man?'

The partners of these masculine women also display a preference for less masculine traits. 'Butches and their "man-ness"', Maggie tells me, 'is nothing but a wall between themselves and their girlfriends but andros are without those "I am a guy" thingy'. The opinions of femmes range from simply that 'hard butches are passé' to more complex articulations such as this one from Samantha:

> It is easier to bring her out. It attracts a lot of stares. People call her 'sir'. I prefer that there is less attention on her. And if I want a man I would have gone for a man. I don't want a woman to dress up like a man. I don't want to date a transgender. And I think that she has a beautiful body and I don't want her to hide behind ugly man's clothes that are not made to fit a woman's body. I think primarily I want to be able to be with someone who is able to be comfortable in her own skin no matter what she wears. And to not be able to accept her own gender identity and to conceal it under men's clothes is quite troubling for me to accept and reconcile with.

Samantha's refusal to date a transgender and her flippant reference to the term, may sound offensive to trans masculine sensibilities. Hers is a narrative defensive of her lesbian identity, which involves the rejection of maleness embodied by transmen. In a sense then, she acknowledges and affirms the gender identification of transmen as male. But in being defensive, Samantha's narrative reveals the operation and reception of a dominant lesbian feminist discourse insisting on a woman-loving-woman model of gender egalitarianism that rejects all forms of maleness. The undermining of the 'other' gender, namely, men, also made Samantha seem like she was beholden to a kind of radical quasi-feminism. I tried to probe further but it was never really clear the extent to which her sexual and gender subjectivities were interpellations of global feminism. Desiring a less masculine partner was seen to be empowering, and Samantha concedes her attraction to androgynous women who embody both masculinity and femininity. Androgyny appears to offer a resolution for this ambivalence of adhering to dominant notions of women-only feminism and a still-palpable commitment to masculine and feminine role-taking in their same-sex relationships. Androgyny as an identity has allowed local lesbians to negotiate the contradictory space that has emerged from the community's general disassociation from, yet desire for, masculinity, reflecting both a resistance to, and an orientation towards, masculine lesbians.

'Modern' Western pairings demonstrate distinct processes: a movement towards a preference for the same, including androgynous sameness but never the kind of masculine-feminine dichotomous gender pairing, as evidenced in these discussions taken from an international online forum (Yahoo! 2010). As 'Soliel 9' posts:

> So, I'm a lesbian and have noticed that both in Europe and the states, androgynous lesbians seem only to date and to be attracted to one another. I am not pushing for femme-butch dichotomies, but am just wondering why I never see an androgynous girl with a long-haired one. I'm founding this upon about a year of observation in lesbian bars and clubs. Why is this? It seems to be a kind of cultural phenomenon ... or has it always been the case?

'Rebel' replied:

> Part of it might be because feminine girls (in my experience) have a penchant for only liking other feminine girls (obviously this isn't the case ALL the time, but it seems to be the case often enough). Having a preference is fine, but oftentimes these feminine girls are extremely vocal about their preference and take their disdain for androgynous and butch girls to cruel levels, comparing butch/andro girls to men and saying that they are gross, etc. Perhaps because of this tendency, butch/andro girls feel more confident approaching each other than approaching feminine girls?

Among my respondents in Singapore, even where both partners appear androgynous, as in the case of Constance and Theresa who were quick to organise their masculine and feminine roles in their relationship, or in the case of Judy longing for the more masculine version of Anna, a heterogenderal preference persists. When I asked Maggie if she could imagine two feminine lesbians together, she immediately conjured the image of the 'lipstick' lesbian of Western queer discourse and in a moment of reinterpretation, she quipped, 'I am sure even lipstick lesbians have got active roles!'

What is the origin of this impulse and imperative to organise one's social and personal relations along gendered role distinctions, and insisting in particular on the centrality of masculinity, even if it is a kind of feminised masculinity played out as androgyny in local lesbian relationships? This imperative, I argue, does not stem from a certain primordial localism or class location as has been positioned of *tombois* and *lesbi*, *toms* and *dees*, *T*s and *Po*s in other studies of queer

Asian sexualities. Neither do they represent the vestiges of an oppressive lesbian past as experienced in the West. For 'modern', middle-class lesbian couples, their complex subjectivities are drawn, on the one hand, from contemporary global queer feminist discourse, as the women's narratives reveal. On the other hand, the women's subjectivities are also shaped by the gendered nationalist ideology of the modern postcolonial state, which constructs Singaporean women 'by/in a phallogocentric ideology' (Tan 2009: 44). In this construction, women are expected to trade their role as 'not-men for that of like-men' (Deutscher 2002: 11) in order for them to be taken seriously in the public sphere (Tan 2009: 45). Lesbians, along with other women in postcolonial Singapore, negotiate ideological formulations of womanhood forged by a patriarchal developmentalist state, which holds the expectation that women, 'like men', are equally responsible for the survival and economic development of the postcolonial nation. Access to high levels of education and employment meant Singaporean women could, in theory, participate with equal vigour in the political and economic sphere of the nation. Yet, as 'not men', their role in the defence of the nation is seen primarily in terms of the reproduction of the nation. Thus, women must remain in the realm of the feminine, never threatening to emasculate the patriarchal state and all its pre-existing structures and assumptions through sexual and gender transgressions. As Tan (2009: 45) observed of Singaporean patriarchy:[5]

> ... in politics and the workplace, women ... must negotiate an ambivalent space between behaving like a man in order to be taken seriously and masquerading as feminine to avoid provoking the castration of anxieties of their male peers.

Even in senior positions women 'have had to provide an unthreatening reassurance of their femininity as defined by patriarchy'. Tan's (2009) observation is remarkably prescient of Anna's work experience in the military, where, if we recall her narrative at the start of the chapter, women are confined to rules of acceptable female behaviour, and these rules alter depending on seniority. As women moved up the ranks, the greater pressure it was for women to masquerade as 'not-man for that of like-man'. The first explanation for the persistence of masculine identifications in female same-sex relationships might thus lie in the particular phallogocentric culture of Singapore. Phallogocentrism, as feminists theorise, is centred on masculinity as a singular model that defines and constructs all other subjectivities, in particular the feminine. The binary is persistent and insidious, operating in such a way that 'man is the Universal, while woman is contingent, particular and deficient' (Hansen 2000: 202). The ways in which masculine identity is central in local lesbian relationships and feminine women are hailed into a lesbian existence only through a masculine/feminine, butch/femme dichotomy could be understood within a phallogocentric framing. A second, more common, explanation is to take the dichotomies as mimicry of heterosexual gender roles. Given that heterosexuality has been so naturalised in postcolonial Singaporean life, where, if we recall the earlier discussion, state policies, discourses, and institutions operate on entrenched heteronormative logics in its drive towards 'modernity', development and the reproduction of the nation, it does not take much to imagine how the set of heterosexual relations can be internalised and expressed in the lived experiences of everyday life in Singapore. But both explanations need to be qualified. It would be a mistake to understand butch and femme sensibilities entirely on these terms. Neither phallogocentrism nor heterosexual mimicry can capture the nuances and complexity of female same-sex love. For instance, my masculine respondents are often attentive towards their feminine partners. Nowhere is this more axiomatic than in butch/femme sexual relationships, where butches are the 'givers' and emphasise the sexual pleasures of their partners far more than their own physical pleasure. Furthermore, unlike the economic power asymmetry of patriarchal or heterosexist relations, the femmes either had equal economic power or earned more than their masculine partners who faced employment discrimination because of their non-normative gender appearance. Lesbian relationships are thus affected by the same gendered dynamics of Singaporean postcolonial 'modernity', but the women's sexual and gender non-normativity led them to navigate these gendered forces in specific ways.

'Coming out' in the city-state

In a tightly populated country where land is scarce and property-ownership expensive, lesbian and gay Singaporeans often share close quarters with their families. Up to 85 per cent of Singapore's resident population live in state-subsidised Housing and Development Board (HDB) flats, a provision materially and ideologically tied to the aims of population management and its heteronormative logic. Consequently, HDB policy (2008b) privileges the nuclear, heterosexual family and certainly not the individual gay Singaporean. For example, married couples, fiancés and fiancées, widowers or divorcees and their children, and orphans and siblings – all configured fundamentally around heteronormativity – qualify as a proper family nucleus to purchase from a wide selection of newly-built HDB apartments. By contrast, unmarried single citizens, the category into which LGBT citizens fall into, are only allowed to purchase subsidised new flats restricted by size, or buy more expensive market-determined re-sold flats, on the further condition that single applicants are above 35 years of age or living with their parents. As a consequence of the state's restrictive housing policy, the majority of queer women I spoke to live in public housing apartments with their parents and organise their lives within the structures of the heteronormative family.

'One thing about Singapore', Foo said to me, 'is that if your parents cannot accept you as a lesbian you will long to have your own place'. Foo continued:

> That is when they have their freedom to do what they want. That is why the lesbians here their first priority is to get a house. They are out there they are free already. That forms some sort of your identity.

Unlike Western cultural norms of young people moving out of familial homes as they reach adulthood, the rite of passage to adulthood in Singapore is through marriage. Unmarried persons are expected to live with their parents, and opting to move out before marriage is to transgress local cultural norms of filial obligation and what family means. When unmarried adults broach the topic of moving out, it is usually met with parental disapproval and inquisition: 'What is wrong with staying with us? We let you have your own freedom.' 'Can you survive on your own? Who is going to do your laundry?' 'Can you afford rent on your own?' 'You haven't gotten married, why do you want to stay on your own?' 'Next time, when you get married, then you can get your own place with your husband.' These responses given to my informants are shaped materially and ideologically by the reality of unaffordable housing in Singapore and the state's wide-reaching public housing policy that makes heterosexual marriage and the formation of a nuclear family a foundational qualification for state-subsidised housing. In the absence of a cultural trajectory of leaving familial homes to establish new lives and new sexual identities, sexual minorities find their own ways to assert and live out their sexual selfhoods within the family home. Several of my respondents live in their partner's parents' home or bring their partners back to live with their own family. None reported any particular difficulties with this living arrangement, although most harbour the ambition of moving out in order to lead their lives 'more fully'. As Das, who identifies as masculine, said to me:

> My parents don't mind me bringing my girlfriend back. To them, she is my friend and we share my room. Sometimes my mother looks unhappy but she doesn't say anything. Of course they know we share one single bed, but sometimes I go out and sleep on the couch so they don't get suspicious. When (my mother) is around, I also make sure that we spend more time in the living room. Not very nice also if we spend all day in the room. After a few months, they got used to her. Now when we have family gatherings, even with my uncles and aunties, it is normal for us to go together. It is quite obvious to my entire family that I am not straight, but nobody wants to talk about it.

Das' narrative reveals the intricate ways in which she navigated her family home while living out her sexual selfhood. Intrigued by her contradictory experiences of being in and out of the closet around family – avoiding intimate displays with her partner at home and attending family events as a 'normal' couple – I asked what if it all came out. 'Maybe they will chase me out'? Das replied. 'I don't know. If housing becomes easier in Singapore, I guess a lot more gay people would come out', Das ruminated. Midway through our conversation, Das stood up as her girlfriend, Lysa, approached our table. As Lysa took her seat next to Das, immaculately dressed in feminine clothes, it struck me that Das' parents could not have averted their eyes from the obvious, even stereotypical, fact of their couple-hood.

Conditioned by the material reality of living in Singapore, the Singaporean lesbian treads in and out of the closet of the family, one that is also constructed around state ideology linking family values to national identity and loyalty. Characteristic of postcolonial societies, the family in Singapore is constituted as a metonym of the nation and the basis of national development. Unsurprisingly then, the domestic unit has been a central object of social regulation (Salaff 1988) and the continual subject of state rhetoric, as Tan (2007b) analysed of National Day Rally speeches. Within the moral economy of the state's national development programme and its ideological construction of the Singaporean family, a particular heteronormative model of the family is valorised as homosexuality is demonised. In the words of a government minister, 'If more Singaporeans end up embracing this sexual orientation openly, the foundation of the strong family, which is the core building block of Singapore … would be weakened' (Lim Swee Say quoted in *Straits Times*, 6 June 2000).

Research has shown how the heteronormative family is for the Asian queer subject an 'impossible hideout' (Davies, 2010a), a site where queer Asian women have to exist within the structures of patriarchy and the family (Dasgupta 2009) and operate undetected within familial circles (Gopinath 2005). The Singaporean lesbian, even as she pragmatically navigates within the heteronormative family, is not like her Indonesian female counterpart who sometimes marries heterosexually to appease her family, pursues same-sex relationships clandestinely or defers her same-sex desires indefinitely (Blackwood 2008; Davies 2010b). Neither is she like the individualised Western gay subject, bound as she is by familial obligation, cultural norms, state governance, and the costs of living in Singapore, to live within the family. Yet, the so-called closet she is locked in is not quite the same as that of her Western counterpart. In it, she operates not quite so invisibly, and acceptance within the family, though tacit, appears largely to be taken for granted.

Queering the logic of 'coming out' to oneself

In dominant Western construction, 'coming out' is expressed in widening 'concentric spheres of decreasing familiarity' (Boellstorff 2005: 34): first to oneself, then to the family, then colleagues and so on until one is eventually 'out' in all spheres of life and achieves a unified sense of self. In this conceptualisation, coming out is a systematic and linear process of realising one's sexual identity. Applying this Western logic to Singaporean lesbian subject positions is to estrange the women from their sense of sexual selfhood. Although they understand 'coming out', it is never something the women consciously set out to achieve in order to realise their sexual identities. In the context of the all-girls convent school, Ashley told me, 'liking girls is already a norm'. There was 'never a point', Aaliyah told me, 'of not accepting that I was gay, being from a convent school and everything.' For these women, their same-sex desires and identity were always already assumed, which made coming out a trivial aspect of their sexual selfhoods. Asking the women to recall the moment of coming out and realisation of their sexualities frequently drew a blank:

> My first crush was at 13 years old. There was no moment when I knew. Maybe I was in an all-girls school. I was a more boyish, athletic type and the girls were interested. A lot of girls ... I won the admiration of the girls. I guess at 13 I realised I had no boyfriend and my first relationship was with a girl, which happened without me thinking too much about it.

Evelyn Blackwood notes that same-sex-desiring women in Indonesia fall by chance into a lesbian world through an 'external event', experiencing their desires as 'something that happened' to them through their relationships (Blackwood 2010: 135). This seemed to hold at least partially true for my respondents. However, the women I interviewed, connected closely to global queer circuits as they were, also possess the language and framework to process their lesbian consciousness and desires defined in dominant terms. They did not just fall suddenly into lesbianism but were well aware of their sexual proclivities. They spoke in the language of agency and choice:

> I had some friends who were not straight. From them I discovered this orientation that there is a possibility that beyond girls and guys there can be girl-girl or guy-guy. From there I know that there is this sort of liking. From there then I decided that I could choose whether I am straight or not straight.

The notion of being gay was never alien to the women. 'It's not that I had to figure out whether I was gay. I had to figure out whether I was straight! It was the other way round', Ashley related:

> In secondary school, they kept telling you 'it's wrong, it's wrong'. I heard them but it didn't and couldn't change how I felt. When I graduated and moved on to the poly(technic) where there were boys. That was the time I started figuring out – whether it was caused by my environment or what. I did go through the phase of trying to be straight.

The women eschewed a model of coming out but went about ascertaining and resolving their sexual identities in various ways. In Ashley's case, she socialised with the opposite sex in an attempt to work through her sexual identity. Despite the objections she faced, her same-sex identity was an enduring one born out of an individual resolve that did not require external validation. In the case of another respondent, Xing, she travelled to Perth on her own, visiting gay bars just 'to make sure I am not straight before having a relationship with a girl'. She added:

> I stepped into a gay club without knowing what is going to happen. I saw gay guys – those huge ones and hairy – sitting closely and kissing and all that and I didn't find that gross. I found that quite easy to accept. So I found out that there should be something wrong with me lah!

There was something incongruous about Xing proactively establishing her same-sex identity and then concluding that there was 'something wrong' with her when she realised her acceptance of homosexual behaviour. Yet her response is also intelligible in a local-cultural context where dominant, negative portrayal and conditioning of homosexuality in official discourse and popular media as we saw earlier can seep insidiously into the language of even same-sex-desiring subjects. In this, we might see Xing as representing the longstanding tendencies of colonial and postcolonial governmentality to debase same-sex sexualities. As the words rolled off her tongue, the irony became apparent and Xing quickly explained:

> Meaning to say that ... ey how come I can accept this kind of not-straight orientation? Is it because I am one of them? Because usually people who are straight they see two guys kissing they will go ew ... that is a freak and all that. But I don't. I could accept it very well. So I find that my orientation is ... I am closer to the fact that I am a lesbian ... I should ascertain I am not straight before I have a girlfriend. If not I will be making a U-turn and I don't want to waste time, including the time of the girl.

Xing went to some interesting lengths to arrive at her same-sex identity and contemplated her sexual orientation with great seriousness. It was an introspective process, and the resolution of the women's same-sex identities involved a kind of moral justification. In Maggie's case, it was 'like decide and accept and I did. Being gay wasn't hard, being indecisive is harder, isn't it'? She carried on to say:

> Can you imagine me being gay at one time and straight after, then gay and back again. It's a serious crime to hurt so many people including yourself.

If coming out is part of a Western confessional tradition, the idea of 'truthfulness' is in equal parts carried through these respondents' narratives. If one comes out to be 'truthful' to oneself and others so as to arrive at one's sexual identity, then, similarly, lesbians in Singapore do not deny their sexual selves. My respondents are upfront with their sexual identities, configuring and presenting it to themselves and others in terms of a pragmatic and moral imperative that does not 'waste the time' of the women they date or commit the 'serious crime' of hurting others out of indecisions over their sexual orientation. For the women, it seemed more like a personal affair that had to be sorted out privately rather than an identity that had to be asserted publicly and claimed in all social spheres.

Queering the logic of 'coming out' at home

Unlike the Western formularised logic of coming out systematically in all spheres, the women I spoke to were out only in discrete spheres – to certain people, in certain places, at certain times. But quite consistently, the women were not out within the closer sphere of the family even though they bring their partners to the family home and the fact of their sexual and gender non-normativity is evident. Foo shared:

> I am obvious, I guess, because of my dressing. My dressing is like a guy. In Singapore if you dress like a guy you are a lesbian. It's as simple as that. Our family members will make it harder. Friends and colleagues are okay. My family suspects but they are more conservative. As long as they don't see it they will not ask you. As long as I don't say anything they won't ask. The confrontation was only one time. They ask me one question: are you lesbian? I said no. That was it. That was like about 20 over years ago. Ever since then they never asked me again.

Alluding to her 'conservative Singaporean family', a trope manufactured in nationalist state discourse, Foo demonstrated little desire to make her sexual orientation known at home. The decision to stay silent about her sexual orientation at home is commonly interpreted as a version of the US 'don't ask, don't tell' policy.[6] But this dominant frame of reference does not capture how the women reveal their sexual identities through significant acts – bringing their partners home, living together, travelling with family members – and in the little actions –'starting my sentences with "Lysa says", "Lysa will be there", "Lysa this and Lysa that", said my respondent, 'After a while, (my parents) will surely put it together and go "oh …"'

Yet, when confronted with the question by family, the women would not divulge. My respondents tell me it is hard to reach for a positive language to explain homosexuality to their parents:

> All they have are negative associations and prejudice. It is the action that counts. They see us being together. They see us forming a bond. It is more natural than sitting down and talking about it. So awkward and I think I am scared, even though I think they will accept.

The fear, however, is not just perceived. Serious threats have been made against several respondents. Stella's mother, for instance, threatened to disown her. Chantel's mother said she would send her daughter to the psychiatrist should she be lesbian, and we shall soon follow the two stories of Celeste and Aaliyah whose coming out led to dire consequences for the two women. Coming out, as dominant discourse goes, resolves the issues of concealment and deception that mark the lives of gays and lesbians. The act represents an important step towards realising 'authentic' same-sex identities. When so idealised, what is concealed is the reality that coming out may in fact be more oppressive than staying in the closet. It undermines the serious consequences faced by homosexuals in Singapore when they find themselves out to the family, as the accounts of Celeste and Aaliyah show.

Interlude: narratives of Celeste and Aaliyah

Celeste is a Chinese Singaporean in her mid-twenties. Recently graduated from university, she works as a researcher in the public health sector. At the time of our interview, she was living with her girlfriend. They share a bedroom in the condominium apartment of her girlfriend's parents who regard Celeste as a very good friend of their daughter's. Her girlfriend's parents have never asked about their daughter's relationship with Celeste, although in Celeste's opinion, it would be naïve to think they did not already know. 'We have been living under the same roof for two years!' Celeste said to me.

Two years ago, Celeste had to move out of her parents' home after she had come out to her mother. Celeste said she could not pinpoint the exact moment of her coming out. Asserting her lesbian identity at home was a long and tiring process that took place over a number of years. Her mother, Celeste described, was passive-aggressive throughout Celeste's struggle to come out. 'She was very good at compartmentalising', Celeste recalled, 'but she also kept wanting to address the issue.' Celeste elaborated:

> My mum was able to compartmentalise. But that doesn't mean she was okay with it. She kind of said 'this is this and that is that. I am proud of you in all these ways. You are perfect except that you are gay.' I was the outlet. My mum kept talking to me. Every time I was with her, whenever I was around, she would find a chance to talk about it. I had to run away and now that I ran away, of course, I couldn't be the perfect daughter that she wanted.

While studying at university, Celeste chose to stay at the campus hostel so she could avoid the incessant questioning. Eventually she moved back after graduation. When Celeste's mother fell ill with diabetes, Celeste became the main caregiver, a role she quickly assumed as a daughter. However, with caregiving responsibilities, it meant Celeste's interaction with her mother became even more intense:

> Because of that I was exposed to it every single day. After like four months, I collapsed. She knew I collapsed because I was displaying behaviour that was totally unlike me, that she's never seen in me all my life. I couldn't even see her without trembling. It was physiological. I couldn't even look at her without trembling. I think it finally sunk in because I have always been very strong. I am usually the strongest in the family. I am the optimist. They are always filled with anxiety, filled with terrible fright, they think it is the end of the world, they are not going to find jobs, so I was this little bubble that kind of burst and she couldn't reconcile, she didn't believe me. I went through several months convincing her what I was going through.

Finally, the tension at home reached tipping point. Celeste moved out to live with her girlfriend. 'Psychologically', she said, 'I was driven to the edge':

> I was undergoing trauma. It was so bad that I had to see counselling. And it was accompanied by physiological responses. It was very bad. Think I could have taken drugs if I wanted to. But I didn't want to.

Celeste located the source of her anxiety and trauma in her one-on-one interaction with her mother. The only way she could maintain her relationship with her mother was through her father and sister, both of whom were 'cool' with her homosexuality:

> My sister was very cool. My dad was amazingly cool. But he was the last I came out to. I came out to him because I didn't want him to blame my mother. I explained very clearly to him in a letter why I went off and out of the house. I told him that at no time he was to blame my mum. So that is the only reason why I came out to him. So he could support her while I was gone. My dad told me it was okay, he said, 'very common what'. He told me over the phone after I wrote the letter to him. He took one week and when he called me back he was really cool. And when he called me he told me he will always be proud of me. So that was really moving. I think for my dad, what is important for him is that I finished school and get a job. I guessed I kind of satisfied that one bit of it.

Celeste avoided going home and would only meet her mother at a safe distance, outside of the family home and only when her father and sister were also present. When her father and sister are around, Celeste explained, her mother would never bring up the issue of her sexual orientation. After a few family outings, Celeste felt she was more ready to meet her mother alone, and perhaps work at their relationship. But 'separate from the house', Celeste said to me, 'the house was a source of trauma. That was where I lost it all'.

Several thousand miles away, Aaliyah is sitting across from me in a Sydney café. She moved a long way from her family 'to be lesbian', she told me matter-of-factly. Aaliyah is in her early thirties, a Muslim and of Arabic descent. She grew up in Singapore living for the most part with her parents. I first met Aaliyah in Singapore. At the discreet location where we met, she appeared in sunglasses and asked to sit away from the main road of the corner café. She cannot be spotted in Singapore, she said to me. 'I am supposed to be on a business trip out of the country.' Fast-forward a year later, Aaliyah is now living in Sydney with her 38-year-old Singaporean partner, Alyssa, who made the transnational move to join Aaliyah. Aaliyah is a highly valued employee of a multinational company in the media industry. She is currently on a four-year work visa in Australia, and was able to organise for Alyssa to be here for the same period through a joint partner visa.

Aaliyah described her relationship with her family as 'fucking close', that is, she said, 'until the shit hit the fan'. She never openly came out to her family but constantly brought home her girlfriends and other gay friends. She said:

My parents were very nice people until they realised. It was just like one after another. They kept seeing my girlfriends around the house. My girlfriends were always a large part of my life. I brought them home openly. Then my parents stopped seeing my ex- and they met my current girlfriend. I didn't bring her home a lot. She did meet the family a couple of times. They invited her over for dinners. It was the constant appearance of gay people around me – that's how my parents found out. There were a lot of dykes and no boys.

Nobody told them. They just observed the life I was living that they didn't quite appreciate. One day I was at work and my brother said 'I need to talk to you now' and then it blew out of proportion. My girlfriend was waiting for me downstairs and I said 'go home, I will call you later'. At that point everything fell apart. My brother was told to confront me. I don't think my parents dared to confront me. During the confrontation I said I could possibly be gay. That already threw him off. I don't think I could have said outright I am gay.

The point that everything fell apart for Aaliyah was her brother's confrontation. Her family had known about her lesbian inclinations, and in recent months, Aaliyah sensed their increasing displeasure. When confronted by her brother, she knew she could not come out. Aaliyah had suggested she might 'possibly be gay' but it was never directly stated.

Yet, soon after, Aaliyah found herself under complete surveillance. 'It came to a point where I was kind of like locked up under house arrest', Aaliyah said. She was allowed to go to work but would be picked up and escorted wherever she went. Her social life was restricted to gatherings with people known to her family and supervised under the watch of her brother and his friends. Kept away from her own friends, she felt immense distress. Beyond physical surveillance, Aaliyah was also subject to substantial emotional pressure. Her parents began urging her to get married on the heterosexist logic that it was a gentler way to correct her homosexuality, as Aaliyah's account reveals:

When they kind of realised that taking my friends away from me were affecting me this much, it came down to 'you want to know this guy, this guy wants to get to know you'. My parents tried to match make me with some random guy from the Arab society. I was like 'right ...' Now it started getting pressuring at that point.

Before that my family wasn't like that. As Muslim as we are and as Arab as we are, my parents were never that square. It kind of shocked me when they treated me the way they did. I was thirty and I was being treated like twelve. My parents were calling me every single hour. It was becoming rather dramatic. I didn't expect them to take it to that extent.

The intense surveillance and pressure went on for six months, during which Aaliyah mustered her wherewithal to plot her way out. She turned to her company for support, requesting for a long-term overseas work posting:

> For about six months after my parents found out, there was a whole big plan with my company to basically get me out of the country ... It's kind of strange the way my whole company got together. It was easy. It has to do a lot with the fact that my bosses are not Asians. My bosses were my friends before my colleagues. So they were helpful and said 'get her out of the country before she gets forced into marriage!'

This was a major life decision involving an international move, not just for herself but also for her partner. The decision had to be made quickly but there were many plans to be made and questions to be answered. Where would they live? How much money would it need to uproot from Singapore and set up in the new country? What kinds of economic opportunities and laws in the new country would allow Aaliyah to establish her new life with Alyssa? The women settled on Australia. It was near enough, yet away, from family in Singapore. It would accommodate their couplehood with its relatively more supportive attitudes towards same-sex relationships. It was decided that Aaliyah would make her escape quickly and Alyssa would follow after as soon as she could. Alyssa traded the job she loved in Singapore, packed her bags and belongings, and left friends and family behind for a life with Aaliyah. For someone who has neither lived nor worked overseas, it was for Alyssa a time of great uncertainty.

Now working and living in Sydney, Aaliyah told me she goes back to visit her family at least once a year, particularly during religious festivals on the Muslim calendar. Her relationship with her family, perhaps no longer close, is at least cordial. At family gatherings a few times a year, they all skirt the issue of Aaliyah's homosexuality but are well aware that she has chosen to move away to lead her own life. To a certain extent, Aaliyah told me, she could sense her family's relief that she had taken charge to resolve her problems with the family by moving out of the country.

Aaliyah is content with how things have worked out with her family. What she felt she had gained from the dramatic episode was that she had held up on her end as a responsible daughter and sister to her parents and brother. 'I was always the one', she said, 'who had a job and was independent and despite all that happened, there would always be respect for my parents, respect for my brother'. In that regard, she would never want to assert or address the issue of her sexual orientation with her family:

> There is never a time I am going to go and sit my parents down and say, 'Okay everybody hold on to something. I am going to make an announcement'. It is never going to be like that. I don't think it is necessary, you know. The whole thing about 'coming out' so that you are true to yourself? Whether I come out or not I am always going to be true to myself. I know I am gay and I don't think I need to announce it.
>
> I think it is a good point to not come out to your parents especially when you're with someone. If you are thinking of coming out you should

do it while you are single. If not your parents will go, 'it is her fault'. If I did want to come out I will come out when I was not seeing anybody.

A common wish, held by Aaliyah and other respondents, is for good relationships with their families. Accepting or acknowledging their same-sex relationships, even in an unspoken way, would make it more practical for such an outcome. What lesbian daughters desire is not an 'out and proud' gay self, but one embedded within an extended family life beyond, even if this involved a complex management of familial relations around their couplehood. The women's relationships with their family recalls the case of Chinese gay men in Kong's (2010) study, in which Kong described similar practices of staying in the closet and playing the role of filial sons who demonstrate a 'relational self' embedded in the biopolitics of the family (2010: 107).

The act of 'coming out' in dominant discourses is premised on an exclusive and singular sexual and social identity, and demands that one's sexual identity must be reconciled, even if not all at once, at least slowly and systematically in all spheres of social life in order to achieve 'authentic' and legitimate sexual citizenship. The act is taken as both a signifier of personal liberation and political resistance against the hegemony of heterosexuality expressed so powerfully in the institution of the family. Not coming out and staying in the closet, particularly within the family, is constituted within this discourse as a negative and 'inauthentic' way of being lesbian. Based on the experience of my respondents, it appears, however, that their liberation, sense of self and peace of mind, contrary to how these are represented in dominant 'coming out' discourse, are not achieved in the act of coming out, but in the careful and creative ways in which they negotiate their same-sex identities in relation to familial heteronormativity. The women draw on their resources, near and far, to develop new ways of living out their sexual selfhoods. Though tacit, their tactics nonetheless re-configure ways of being lesbian within the family without confrontation. Closet practices in this sense should not only be seen as repressive and limiting, fashioning a self-loathing homosexual. Rather, closet practices might also be liberating and productive, fashioning confident and contented gay selves within a protected space that permits these individuals to navigate pathways between their relational worlds.

Queering 'coming out' with the logic of nationalist narrative: Yuen's response

One salient element in my respondents' narratives on 'coming out' is a discernibly nationalist one, involving the tropes of productivity, meritocracy and self-sufficiency. Deploying these notions no doubt reflects the privilege of the middle-class, socially-mobile women who demonstrate how global gay discourses on what being lesbian means intersect with local nationalist discourses to produce complex and contradictory, yet clear and logical, assertion of their sexual identities. Yuen, who has been in a long-term lesbian relationship, said:

> Being surrounded by people who accept you and who accept your relationship, like my partner's parents and her friends, makes a lot of difference. It begins to give me courage that it is okay to be in this relationship, to enjoy it now and not be ashamed about it.

Having said that, Yuen then expressed very little affiliation with the global gay discourse on sexual identity and rights, which I found surprising for someone who had lived three years overseas in a metropolitan city:

> To me it's really something that is very personal and very private. I don't need to tell everyone that I am gay. I don't need to assert my sexual identity to the whole word. I don't want people to know as well. I think that it is irrelevant. I think that who I am and how I contribute to society is sufficient. I don't have to project that and tell the whole world that I am gay. I don't want to force it upon everyone. I don't think it is important. I still can contribute to the economy of the society, I can still contribute to the community, I can still be a functional person. I don't want to fight for gay rights or participate in certain demonstrations to force everyone to accept it. It's none of their business to tell me what is right and what is wrong in my private life. I can do what I want!

Although insisting on the right to a private life, Yuen's desire to play a part in the national community, contributing as a functional and productive person to society and the economy, are infused with the postcolonial state's nationalist rhetoric of communitarianism and national survival. If Singapore is to survive, as the rhetoric goes, every citizen must pull in the same direction of public spiritedness, discipline and self-motivation to make a living (Chua 1995: 15), all the sort of qualities that Yuen speaks of in defining her sexual subjectivity. Yuen carried on to say:

> I feel that my rights are not deprived. I am not deprived of the education I want to pursue. I am not deprived of the resources I want to have. If I want a car, a big house, a certain status, I go out and get it, and I get it! I am not being deprived of that because I am gay.

Yuen's comments are, on one level, illustrative of how the state's meritocratic ideology is a deeply ingrained one, keeping alive the 'Singapore Dream of social improvement for oneself, one's family, and the society as whole' (Brown *et al.* 2001: 257). On another level, Yuen's narrative barely conceals how the neoliberal capitalist state has been successful in creating queers as creatures of capitalism. Freed to pursue their individual lives but with their rights, in effect, cast out by the state's insistence to preserve the heteronormative nation so as to produce the next generation of citizens, 'modern' queer Singaporeans exemplify the internal contradictions of the nation. This model of internal contradiction is sometimes taken to its logical limits, evident when queer

Singaporeans unwittingly valorise the heterosexual nuclear family and participate in the construction of homosexuality as a social ill. 'For this relationship, it's good to just protect my parents from it,' Yuen said to me:

> It's not that I think being gay is shameful. It is deviant, out of the social norms. It could be my own thinking. It could be my own belief. But I don't think they can take this deviant act. I just want to protect them. All they need to know is this daughter is taking care of herself, who is striving, who is doing well professionally and in all aspects of her life. That is all they need to know.

On the one hand, Yuen does not locate her sexual subjectivity in shame. On the other hand, she saw a need to 'protect' her parents from the 'deviance' of her sexual orientation and the disruption of the traditional family. These contradictory and contingent attitudes mark what it means to be lesbian in Singapore. Hegemonic concepts of homosexuality, particularly that of coming out, are, in these local instances, clearly reconfigured through state discourse and cultural interpretations of what it means to be queer in Singapore. In a previous chapter, we saw how as homosexuals tip toe out of the closet, these homosexual lives have been 'edited out' (Leong 2005: 163) in state-controlled mainstream media serving a nationalist project of public morality. Likewise my respondents choose to lead their sexual lives in privacy, out of public view and away from their families. Yet, this desire for privacy does not equate easily with invisibility, for the women consciously and creatively live out their same-sex identities within the family, transforming familial heteronormative values in an everyday, taken-for-granted manner by performing and slipping in and out their multiple roles as 'responsible adult', 'filial daughter', and 'homosexual self'. In the performance of these multiple roles, local lesbian women are not so much 'edited out' as they live between the lines of heteronormativity and their non-normative female sexualities.

A queer turn

As I reflected on my informants' sexual subjectivities, wondering how much they spoke for queer women in Singapore, my attention was drawn to a particular Facebook furore. An activist had posted the comments of a Singaporean actress, whose sexual orientation is well-known in the lesbian circle but better known to the general public as the heterosexual wife of Phua Chu Kang, the boss of a construction company who embodies a dominant masculine stereotype and is the namesake of a popular family sitcom. 'My take on *Pink Dot*', the actress was quoted as saying, 'will probably offend a lot of people. I feel that it's just for the young gay boys and girls to have fun. They don't even know the message behind the unity'. Her message seemed to be that the playful, recreation-oriented interests of young Singaporean gays and lesbians do not represent a unified gay cause, which, presumably, must pursue an antagonistic social or political resistance characteristic of global queer politics. Then she went on to say how being gay is contingent, 'As a gay person, you have to earn respect. You must be of use to your society first, before being gay' (Koh 2010). Her latter views were considered by many lesbians and gay men as an affront to the local gay community, as evidenced by the number of outraged online comments the activist's post elicited. 'I really don't agree that anyone need to earn their right to be gay', read one comment. The actress' views and the reverberations it caused, nonetheless, demonstrates that queer knowledge circulates unevenly on transnational lesbian bodies despite the seemingly totalising global subject positions they represent, or are made to represent by the postcolonial state through its yoking of homosexuality with Westernisation in an Asia/West binary.

The ethnographic data supports the conclusion that lesbian subjectivities, rather than being thoroughly Westernised, are instead also forged through the ideological discourses of the postcolonial state, which produces complex, contingent and contradictory negotiations of what it means to be lesbian in Singapore. This finding is well-supported in Yue's concurrent work, which demonstrates how lesbian consumption practices in Singapore's global media hub create a 'local lesbian identity without assimilating into the liberal Western discourse of sexual rights and emancipation' (2011: 250). Any easy naturalisation of gay subject positions as 'global' or 'Western' as opposed to 'conservative' or 'Asian', are in this regard, invalid.

Embodying the nationalistic impulses of the nation, queer women in Singapore appear, above all, pragmatic about their sexual subjectivities. In their negotiation of the everyday, they take in stride the challenges of their same-sex desires and work out how they might lead their lives as lesbian women even within the most heteronormative domain of the Singaporean family. However, such pragmatism, as Yue (2007) argued elsewhere, cannot be reduced to a 'whatever works' attitude or be merely understood as a response to social crisis and problems. Instead, as the women go about 'doing gay' (Yue 2007), visibly within the family and out in society, they consciously and creatively de-stabilise asymmetrical knowledge productions of what it means to be lesbian. Drawing from both global and local cultural resources, queer women in Singapore embody a particular hybridising and transnational sexual subjectivity that enables them to re-claim and re-assert their sexual selfhoods as forms of 'reverse discourses' in a Foucauldian sense. Singaporean lesbian practices may very well be the realistic undercurrent of social liberalism in non-Western contexts. As Yue (2007) argues similarly, therein lies the potential of pragmatism as a form of creative democracy.[7] The women's everyday experience and experiment of 'doing gay' is the invisible and not so invisible constitution of democratic social action. Therefore in Singapore, we have this peculiar phenomenon of globally conscious lesbian and gay citizens who appear politically apathetic and quite content to lead their individual lives. Yet, it is they, and not the parties, parades and politics of the out, global gay subject, who make Singapore the queer Mecca it really is.

Notes

1 For a comprehensive and in-depth analysis of 'agency', see Emirbayer and Mische (1998).
2 Archer (1988) for instance makes a strong theoretical critique against the conflation of agency and structure in such a conceptualisation.
3 Secondary school education in Singapore is for students between the ages 14 and 16.
4 *Tahan* is Malay for 'wait out'.
5 In his piece titled 'Who is Afraid of Catherine Lim? The State in Patriarchal Singapore', Tan (2009) insightfully analyses the gendered nature of the relationship between the state and two of Singapore's most prominent women in the public sphere, the local writer Catherine Lim, and the politician Lim Hwee Hwa.
6 'Don't ask, don't tell' (DADT) was a military policy instituted under the Clinton Administration in 1993, prohibiting military personnel from discriminating against closeted homosexual or bisexual service members or applicants while barring openly gay, lesbian, or bisexual persons from military service. DADT was repealed during Barack Obama's presidency in 2011.
7 Yue relies on Cornel West's (1989) philosophy of pragmatism to expound her argument in relation to queer cultural productions in Singapore. For the full theoretical treatise, see Yue (2007: 155–158).

7 Recollections, remarks and re-making the relations

A postcolonial politics of difference

I began this book with the conviction that global hegemonic codes not only shape middle-class Singaporean lesbian's narratives on sexuality and gender, but also help sustain the seemingly self-evident nature of progressive queer ideologies such as 'liberation' and 'coming out'. I advanced the idea that what forms the contours of lesbian selfhood in the globalised, hyper-capitalist city-state of Singapore, is the women's embeddedness in, access to, and reception of international queer circuits and discourses. Cosmopolitan, educated and English-speaking middle-class lesbians in Singapore carry with them a certain imagined way of being gay, and the expectation is for them to express a self-consciousness and sexual identity that do not trouble these taken-for-granted categories.

These ideas and the imagination of what it means to be homosexual are embodied by the global gay, a universalising figure delineated in part by Altman (1996a, 1996b, 1997). Being a 'modern' global gay or lesbian is to be in a same-sex relationship with another person of the same gender, it is to engage in homoeroticism, it is to place one's sexuality as an anterior aspect of one's identity, and for this sexual identity to be recognised in public around which a community can be built and mobilised for a collective good. I have argued that these images of the global gay are essentially based on an Anglo-American model of same-sex sexuality imbued with Western assumptions of identity as singular, stable and unified. As sexual identities globalise and become visible around the world, the Anglo-American model of being gay has risen dominantly on the global gay horizon, naturalised as the climax, or core, of all 'modern' homosexualities around which same-sex identities should converge and look 'just like'. Therefore, as we saw in the discussion and review of the Singaporean documentary, *Women Who Love Women*, in Chapter 1, it became virtually irresistible to interpret the sexual subjectivities of those contemporary same-sex loving lesbians as yet another instantiation of the 'modern', universal global gay. Same-sex subjectivities in Singapore, I contend, have been queer-ed in a dominant Anglo-American way.

Seen as another exemplar of the global gay identity, Singaporean same-sex subjects hardly fit into, and are certainly under-featured, in the Asian global queer literature problematising the idea of a homogenising Western queer.

While other studies of non-Western sexualities, such as the Asian queer literature, have generally turned to excavating the many forms of local cultural differences in the hopes of 'helping to dissolve the idea of a single universal lesbian or gay identity' (Weeks 2007: 219), my approach is to resist producing yet more evidence of Singaporean non-normative sexualities as different in some intrinsic, essential manner. In any case, specifying the difference of the 'modern', 'globalised' character of same-sex identities in Singapore, as I have argued in Chapter 2, is both futile and impossible given that the country and its citizens are 'foundationally' are borne along circuits of global capital.

What I have excavated instead are the deeper rubrics and logics conditioning studies of queer globalisation. Through an elementary framework, I illustrated the inherent assumptions and attendant binaries in the workings of developmentalist and cartographic frames which continue to bind analyses of the non-Western queer in perpetual convergence to, and comparison with, the dominant global gay. My point in drawing out the temporal and spatial links is to re-imagine the study of global sexual identities in ways that transcend the conceptual borders inherent in the global gay domain. For what gets locked in within these conceptual frames is a one-sided conception of global gay relations: the non-Western queer is seen to exist only in a static past to the West or as a derivative of an 'original' Western model of gay identity. Consequently, the agency and authenticity of non-Western sexual identities is denied. Such understandings are both unfruitful and unconvincing in 'fundamentally' delineating what is different or particular about non-Western same-sex sexualities, and in specifying the multiple ways of being gay.

The politics of difference is important for at least two reasons. First, it is a postcolonial politics of difference that calls for a revaluation of colonised people's agency, and in the context of this work, the colonised non-Western same-sex identities in the global gay domain. Second, it calls for the clearing of pedagogic and research space for non-Eurocentric analyses. It is through the questioning of the omission of Singaporean lesbians from an Asian queer scholarship challenging the colonising imperialism of the Western queer that I have been able to re-think the dominant sexual globalisation thesis and its mire in Eurocentric definitions.

Moving beyond teleological or cartographic conceptions of global sexual flows within the global gay domain, I placed Singaporean lesbian subjectivities within a broad postcolonial framework that explicitly subverts the fixed binaries of traditional/modern, 'past versus present', and the local/global, 'us against them'. In particular, I re-theorised the processes of hybridisation and transnational sexualities for a view of global gay relations as creative interplays between Western and non-Western queers. In this postcolonial approach, 'modern' Western sexual culture is recognised as a powerful cultural system historically endowed with economic power and institutional hegemony to intrude into other cultures by way of material processes via capitalism and mass media technologies, for instance. But the West is not taken as a superior cultural system. In the postcolonial turn, hybrid meanings and transnational sexualities are formed as non-Western queers transform and transfigure these power-laden queer constructions, resulting in the transformation and production of both the Western and non-Western sexual identity, each mutually constituting and mutually sustained by the other. The result is neither cultural imperialism of one bounded system over another, nor of opposition pitting one against the other, but the stimulus of overlapping and creative interplay at the contact zone of multidimensional cultural encounters (Hannerz 1992: 265).

In this subversion of binary oppositions, the postcolonial politics of difference fuses with poststructuralism. But it is never a kind of anti-structuralism. I have made this explicit by insisting on the material dimension of the postcolonial, taking into account the particular historicity of the postcolonial nation, the state, economy, society and bodies that inhabit the nation. Thus, the postcolonial model of cultural difference deployed in this work is combined with the material questions of Singapore's history, contact and change to understand the making of sexual identities and meanings in the postcolonial nation state. It is this point, when the interplays and movements of hybridising and transnational sexualities are traced in conjunction with these historical and material processes, that new distinct sexual subjectivities and sites of power are produced.

Figure 2.2 makes visible the processes by which sexualities and sexual cultures 'are never unitary in themselves, nor simply dualistic in relation of Self to Other' (Bhabha 1999: 207). It illustrates the production of partial, fluid and dynamic sexualities always in the making. This conceptualisation of sexuality also takes into account changing political and historical processes that shape the culture of the colonised, which is a further challenge to essentialist understandings of the Other as determined by fixed cultural characteristics.

This is the main theoretical framework through which the specificity of global same-sex identities can be comprehended. I have used the case of globalised Singaporean lesbians to illustrate this. Initially misunderstood and left out for its mundane mimicry of the global gay, what emerges through the prism of postcolonial theory is the menace of 'modern' Singaporean same-sex subjectivities, which in their very mimicry, directly draw attention to the anxious standoff between the colonising Western queer and the colonised non-Western same-sex subject, and their mutual constitution. The ethnographic findings show that even as Singaporean queer activists and lesbian women inadvertently tap into the global discourse on gay rights, desires and freedoms to form their same-sex subjectivities, these de-localised conceptions are re-configured in a particular postcolonial context, producing specific sexual identities and practices. From a postcolonial perspective, the women's identities and practices represent hybridising and transnational sexual forms that intrude and disrupt dominant ideas of the global gay. In the politics of local queer activists, the reverse implantation of the *Pink Dot* movement in the US is perhaps the clearest illustration of this process. Among non-activist lesbians, their hybridising and transnational sexual forms, as we saw, can be complex, contradictory and contingent. For instance, the women I interviewed see themselves as gay and yet not gay; they volunteer for my study on lesbians in Singapore, then wonder if they qualify as a respondent; the women do not see a need to assume a unitary, stable sexual and gender identity; their identity constructions at times entail the disciplinary and regulatory effects of state discourse on homosexuality. The women recognise the desirable effects of coming out but do not desire it; they sometimes conceal their sexual identities but always go to great lengths to establish and live out their sexual selfhoods. My findings reveal that Singaporean lesbians go against the grain of what it means to be lesbian in global feminist writing, which as Katie King (2002: 42) highlights, is 'lifelong, stable after "coming out", autonomous of heterosexuality, sex-centred, politically feminist, not situational, and exclusive of marriage.' In the narratives of my respondents, every single one of these global lesbian identifications has been re-interpreted and transformed by the Singaporean lesbian.

These contradictory sexual subjectivities cannot be reduced by a utopian teleology to the status of being 'less legitimate', 'less liberal' or 'less lesbian'. From a postcolonial perspective, as Bhabha (1989: 67) insists:

> ... the only place in the world to speak from was at a point whereby contradictions, antagonism, the hybridities of cultural influence, the boundaries ... were not sublated into some utopian sense of liberation ... the place to speak from was through those incommensurable contradictions within which people survive, are politically active, and change.

The contrary and complex ways in which Singaporean lesbians live their sexual lives are far from just being bad copies of any 'original'. Rather they can be read as subversions from within, demonstrating the ambivalence and instability of the colonising, imperial power defining what it means to be lesbian. Along with Bhabha (1994), we can argue that postcolonial processes may very well be the most potent position of resistance in the global gay domain.

Poststructuralism, state-sexuality relations and local resistance

Despite my initial objection to poststructuralist notions of anti-structuralism, the value of the poststructuralist link to postcolonial theory is that it enables a productive leverage on a Foucauldian power-resistance paradigm, from which I have drawn on and deployed the notions of bio-power and governmentality to account for how same-sex identities and sexual subjectivities in Singapore have been shaped and formed, not just by global hegemonic codes, but also by the hegemonic state. We saw in Chapter 3 the heavy-handed ways in which the PAP disciplined non-normative sexualities through the policing, portrayal and pronouncements of homosexuality as always already anti-nationalist and a Western 'disease'.

Operative within Foucault's (1978) power-resistance paradigm is a conception of power as capillary and productive, dispersed within a matrix of governmentality in which a set of state structures – its institutions, agencies and relations – function as 'dense transfer points for relations of power' (Foucault 1978: 103). On the one hand, this Foucauldian framework accounts for the pervasiveness of power over sexualities as it multiplies and consolidates over various nodal points. On the other hand, the view of power dispersed across multiple transfer points allows for the possibility of 'gaps' and 'contradictions' between these very nodes. Through this theoretical lens, it is possible to grasp, as was attempted in Chapters 3 and 4, clear evidence of the contradictory positions and policies of postcolonial elites towards homosexuality.

It is this latter aspect of Foucault's (1978) framework that fits neatly into contemporary feminist sexuality and queer theory writings calling for analyses to 'sexualise' (Puri 2008) or 'queer' (Duggan 1994) state-sexuality relations. Key to these conceptions is the notion that the state should no longer be seen as a unitary, monolithic entity acting singularly on sexuality, but one disaggregated into its related set of structures, institutions, agencies and authorities. The danger of leaving the state 'unqueered' and unravelled in an overarching, immutable form is that we tend to easily fall back on the assumption of the state as an all-powerful, all-pervasive force, especially and ironically when we critique its dominance and discipline of non-normative sexualities. Disaggregating the state is therefore a way to interrogate state power without inadvertently reproducing its power. When so disaggregated, the dissonance and fractures of power become visible, and it is through these fissures that forms of a 'reverse discourse' (Foucault 1978: 101) and resistance rise to the fore. Therefore, we can argue alongside Foucault (1978) and critical sexuality scholars (Duggan 1994; Uberoi 1996; Puri 1999, 2008; Dwyer 2000), that sexuality enters the system of governmentality not just as a site of repression, but also as a site of resistance. Power and repression engender politics and resistance, which reared strongly in the two local mobilisations against the discriminating male sodomy law of Section 377A, and over the issue of lesbianism in AWARE. There is thus a politics of sexuality not reducible to a binary polarising of power against resistance. This brings us to the realisation that the powers of the state and queer resistance are hybrid forms each producing, limiting, sustaining and suppressing each other dynamically in a field of power relations continually interconnected. In this regard, the re-formulated state-sexuality relationship is well aligned with the broad postcolonial framework expounded in this book.

This re-theorisation of state-sexuality relations is the secondary theoretical framework or 'subplot' of this work, which I have argued is pivotal role in helping us recognise how queer activists and lesbian leaders in Singapore have engaged individual state agents and agencies to assert the legitimacy of their same-sex identities, and to resist what is an ostensibly repressive political, economic, legal, and cultural postcolonial regime. My discussion of *Pink Dot* in Chapter 5 illustrated some instances of resistance, and two examples can be quickly highlighted here. One, responding to the discourse of postcolonial elites who constructed homosexuality as a 'frivolous lifestyle' not accepted by the 'conservative heartlanders', and hence anti-nationalist, the activists adopted as *Pink Dot*'s central theme the very nationalist rhetoric of 'family values' and 'multiculturalism', transforming received ideas of homosexuality. Two, responding to the negative portrayals of homosexuality in the state-affiliated media, the activists singled out the media as their prime object of engagement and won it over through the spectacle of *Pink Dot*. Positive media coverage of the event in the local mainstream media and international news carriers transformed the negative representations of same-sex sexualities in the public sphere. Engaging various elements of the homophobic state enabled activists to press for political claims.

Alongside public activist discourse espousing sexual equality, recognition and liberalism, as we saw when the local community mobilised over the repeal of Section 377A and the tussle in AWARE, I have also argued in the last chapter that the private and pragmatic ways in which non-activist lesbians carry out their sexual lives also constitute a form of resistance and intervention. Whether it was Das who lived with her partner in the family home for years invisibly and not so invisibly as a couple; Celeste who dealt with her mother's passive-aggressiveness over her sexual orientation to the point of trauma; Aaliyah who, in her own words, 'stayed true' to both who she was and her family by moving out of the country to resolve their issues over her homosexuality; or Yuen who was not ashamed of being gay but would never declare her same-sex identity to her family, what is compelling in the narratives of each of these individual respondents is how they choose to construct their sexual selfhoods in complex and contingent ways that made sense for them, and how they see themselves as agents of change. Through an interplay between their sexual agency and desire, and the social structures of the state, the local community, and the family they find themselves in, the women adopt tactics to negotiate – through resistance, re-definitions and accommodation – a range of possibilities for their non-normative sexual and gender selves. Certainly their lesbian identities do not take a stable and singular form in the same way prescribed by global queer and feminist discourse. Instead the women forge a sexual category always in a relationality with their multiple roles as daughter, worker, woman and citizen. Consistently, the women transform and re-fashion in their everyday practical ways, an unspoken but visible sexual identity in the conservative 'heartland' of Singaporean families. In so doing, they have created new cultural meanings of what it means to be gay, tangibly for themselves and for those around them.

I have suggested, using the example of Singaporean lesbians, that these transformations in the private sphere may very well be the realistic undercurrent of queer liberalism in non-Western contexts. Caught up in the transnational flow of global queer culture, Singaporean lesbians desire to combat social discrimination and fight for their rights. They are also aware of the liberatory claims and achievements of the West. However, in contradistinction to the very public politics and parading of same-sex identities in Anglo-American sexual cultures, Singaporean lesbians go about in private and pragmatic ways to assert their sexual identities and desires. Rather than see these practices as weaknesses or less than liberating gestures on the part of Singaporean lesbian cultures, I contend along with postcolonial theorisations, that, if these practices are understood as part and parcel of hybridisation processes and transnational sexual forms returning to thoroughly penetrate and re-define what are 'modern', 'liberated' and 'legitimate' global sexual identities, then we will be able to grasp how inequalities may be challenged through forms that do not just appear in public activism and movements, but in the private everyday lives of gay individuals and lesbians. We will also be able to grasp that there are multiple ways of being gay in the global ecumene.

This is the point where theoretical work links up with the real-life question of political representation. When the local lesbian activist ties a 'modern', 'changing' Singapore to a teleological, puristic notion of gayness, and insists dogmatically on the universal virtue of coming out drawn from a Western liberation project, what she has refused or failed to see is that all sexual cultures are hybrid and transnational to begin with, and there is no superior cultural system producing 'original' and 'authentic' queer lives. It is in these hybridising and transnational spaces that Singaporean queer life thrives. However, in denying the coevalness of these complex and contradictory manifestations, and insisting that global sexual identities must achieve their place in a utopian teleology emblematic of Euro-American lesbian and gay movement, LGBT activism ironically erases the very identities that it claims to represent and fight for. Dominated by a Stonewall-diffusion fantasy, the queer cultural elite or CMELs in Singapore have at times eagerly adopted, appropriated and aligned themselves with what they perceive as powerful global gay symbols and discourses, projecting a collective fantasy on Singaporean 'modern' sexual identities. This process of producing a 'modern', 'global' identity is perhaps best described as a form of domestic colonialism, enacted through the imperial silencing of 'other' queer sexualities, and denying the power and agency of the postcolonial sexual subject to construct legitimate sexual identities and relations. In denial of its own hybridity, and in refusing to recognise the validity of ambivalent sexualities sown in the contradictory and co-constitutive hybridising and transnational zones, the fantasy projected by Singaporean queer activists ironically enters into a rapprochement with state agents who, in the name of puristic notions of nationalism and Singaporean-ness, seize and denounce homosexuality as a purely Western construction, alien to Singaporeans. The polemics of puristic gayness and puristic nationalism gloss over the variety of lives buried under the ideological conventions of politically hegemonic structures in the global and the local domain, whether in Singapore or elsewhere.

Final notes

In this book, I have, hopefully, re-claimed the possibilities of Singaporean lesbian lives by presenting the ethnographic evidence and narratives of local queer women. My findings reveal compelling evidence of how 'modern' middle-class lesbians in Singapore draw on both global discourses and local nationalist rhetoric to construct their sexual identities, and how the women live out their sexual selfhoods within the postcolonial context of Singapore. The lives and narratives of these middle-class lesbian women, as we have seen, problematised the larger questions of how fictions of their sexuality and gender have been constructed and normalised. They also provided important insights into how the women contend with and undermine the normalising disciplinary effects in their lives.

By interrogating the empirical evidence and narratives of Singaporean lesbian women through an engagement with postcolonial theory and feminist sexuality studies, I have re-queered or re-read the 'modern' and thoroughly globalised same-sex sexualities of Singaporean women as a kind of subterranean, unrecognised form of resistance and, therefore, a legitimate part of the historiography of non-Western sexualities challenging imperialising and colonising Eurocentric versions of what it means to be gay or lesbian. What fundamentally questions the imperialist and colonialist notions are the very changing, adaptive, contradictory and discrepant politics and cultures of hybridising and transnational sexualities, such as those we find among Singaporean lesbians. These transformative processes are certainly not the exclusive privilege or particular experience of Singaporean lesbians, but those of queer individuals around the world, including Westerners, who, on the margins of metropolitan centres, also destabilise the putative hegemony of the 'global gay' by their multiple sexualities, desires and practices.

Through postcolonial understandings, I have used the case of Singaporean lesbians to offer a more productive way of challenging the hegemony of universalising Western assumptions, premised not on static and unproductive binaries but in a dynamic, mutually-constituting relationality between the Western and non-Western queer. This approach contributes to a 'fundamental' shift in our understanding of the asymmetric relationship between the Western and non-Western queer, and provides an important contribution to the debate on the globalisation of gay identities. It offers a way of challenging the global gay discourse based not just on oppositional identities and practices but on non-oppositional, mutually-constituting positions created in the interplay of hybridising and transnational sexualities. The distinction of the postcolonial politics of *difference* therefore lies in its notion of non-oppositional difference. This insight invites research on sexual cultures and identities not automatically or 'naturally' perceived as 'traditional' or 'indigenous', such as 'modern' non-Western sexualities. View through a postcolonial lens, it is solidarity politics and not a politics of cultural difference and appropriation that might now link queer groups internationally. All are contemporary, legitimate sexual citizens of the present and not just derivatives or borrowed forms of an original. Furthermore, as I have argued, the search for 'traditional' or 'indigenous' tends to end up reinforcing essentialist understandings and dichotomous thinking. As these novel hybridising and transnational sexual identities emerge and come into view, as they have in this study of Singaporean lesbians, what falls to the side are the temporal and spatial assumptions and binaries, which have been the particular malady in studies of global sexual identities. What this does is to 'foundationally' dismantle the Eurocentric grids that have so quickly colonised our sexual imaginations and queer knowledge production.

Methodological appendix

Methodological prerequisite: terms of discussion

Following sociological research convention that meanings of concepts must be precise, and taking Butler's heed that it is a 'methodological prerequisite' (1990: 5) to lay out all postulations behind social categories, this section qualifies and contextualises the main terms of discussions used in the book.

Although this study looks at Singaporean lesbian lives, the inquiry is not about the personhood of these women per se, but their subject positions. 'Subject positions' underscore the fact that 'lesbian' is not just an identity; it is a social category always in the making and always located in multiple domains. 'Subject positions' are produced within the Foucauldian truism of 'systems of power', which are at once disabling and enabling for the sexual subject. As Foucault described in the first volume of *The History of Sexuality* (Foucault 1978), the 'personage' of the homosexual was an invention of multiple power sites: where before there were only condemnable 'acts', people who practised those acts were later assigned a psychology, a set of emotions, a medical condition, a particular kind of childhood, an illegality and so on, to become the 'homosexual' subject. It is therefore these very systems of power that not only constrain the homosexual subject but also create, in its power matrix, the very conditions allowing the proliferation of the category 'homosexual' across its multiple sites. Therefore, I use 'subject positions' and 'subjectivities' to attend to the shifting, elastic identity-category of 'Singaporean lesbians' and the complexity of their sexual selfhoods.

Where I use the word 'identity', it is in the sense of an 'identity-positionality', a term I borrow from Bacchetta (2002: 954) to mean:

> ... a self-elaborated political stance that is positioned within time-space-specific conditions, that is impermanent, unfixed in its relation to a shifting symbolic-material context traversed by multiple global flows.

'Identity-positionalities' point to a more dynamic and transformative process of self-positioning as subjects take up, engage and rework socially-constituted subject positions. These terms – of subject positions, subjectivities and identity positionalities – address the unfixed, multiple processes by which lesbian selves are produced and negotiated, and highlight the total social fact of the category 'lesbian'. Although it is by now a touchstone of contemporary cultural studies and social theory that identities are never unified but are changing, fragmented and multiply constructed, such iterations remain important in a field where the notion of a lesbian or gay 'identity' – evidenced in the LGBT movement in the 1980s and 1990s in the US, for instance – has meant one stable or unchanging sense of self (Blackwood 2010; Jagose 1997).

I use the terms 'West' and 'Western' to refer to 'Europe' and 'US-America', or more specifically to 'Western Europe' and 'North America'. But these are not geographical constructs. They are temporal and spatial concepts shaped by the history of colonialism and modernity, encapsulating the power and knowledge of the West as distinct from 'the rest'. It is used in the same sense as Akhil Gupta's (1998: 36) 'speaking of "the West"', which refers to:

> ... the effects of hegemonic representations of the Western self rather than its subjugated traditions. Therefore I do not use the term to refer simply to a geographic space but to a particular historical conjugation of place, power, and knowledge.

I also borrow from Boellstorff's (2005) reference of Stuart Hall (1992: 59) who sees the 'West' as a 'very common and influential discourse, helping to shape the public perception and attitudes down to the present.' In this study, Western discourses of homosexuality are the dominant forms 'precisely the ones that would seem most capable of globalising, and intentionally does not account for the great diversity in sexual and gendered regimes' (Boellstorff 2005: 9).

While this book is primarily a sociological enquiry of same-sex identities, it has also drawn from overlapping multidisciplinary fields including queer theory, postcolonial theory, sexuality studies, critical feminist scholarship, queer geography, globalisation studies, and anthropology. As such, I alternate between various interdisciplinary terms when referring to the West. 'Global north' or 'Anglo-American' are commonly used in queer geography and sexuality studies; 'Euro-American' or 'Anglo-US' in anthropological studies; and the 'imperialist' in postcolonial scholarship, for instance. These are all various iterations of the 'West' and 'Western', which I use in capital form throughout this book to denote their hegemonic status as ideas and practices, as well as Eurocentric bias.

I use the terms 'Western' and 'non-Western' because there is no precedence for not doing so. They are drawn from and frame the terms of the wider debate in global queer studies which I have engaged. In speaking of the 'Western queer', I do not presume any internal coherence to the term 'Western'. The French, for instance, struggle against the idea of a singular Americanisation of gay identities (Provencher 2007: 5–7). The model of the white, cosmopolitan global gay model is most significantly challenged on the basis of class and race from within the West (Binnie 2004). Haylett (2001), for instance, has shown how the white working class and black sexual dissidents in the United Kingdom

(UK) were unable or unwilling to conform to the strictures and norms of a global gay identity and culture. Thus, Hayes (2001) correctly argues that many of the statements applied to non-Western contexts and polities, cultures around the limits of a modern, Western approach to gay subjectivity and identity are also applicable to the West.

It is therefore useful to think of the 'West' and 'Western queers' not as a specific and identifiable space and social group but as 'ideology'. In such an ideological formulation, the 'West' is a normative term. It denotes progress and liberalism, the promise of freedom and of how things should be. Among my respondents, the 'West' is presumed to be synonymous with the United States or Europe, and also includes Australia. A common assumption among my informants, whenever I share that I am based in Sydney with my partner, is that I can live out my gay selfhood since I am in a Western country. One respondent remarked that I will never return to Singapore because 'it is easier to be gay in Sydney'. Insofar as being gay is imagined through the lens of Stonewall, Sydney's Mardi Gras and San Francisco, the West is constituted as a unified site of 'freedom' and 'choice' as opposed to the location of Singapore still cast in the shadow of an archaic sodomy law. In such a construction, the modern/tradition binary is reinvented in which the US and Europe are figured as the 'modern' endpoint to which all must aspire, while other parts of the world must cast off the mantel of their oppression and 'traditional' way of being in regard to sexuality. It is these putative categories of the West and non-West, the hegemonic assumptions and inherent Eurocentrism that this book challenges.

I use the term 'gay' sometimes as a shorthand form of referring to the local lesbian and gay community. I also use 'gay' to refer to my lesbian respondents because the women themselves frequently use 'I am gay' when referring to their sexual orientation. The terms 'gay' and 'lesbian' originated in North America and Western Europe. In the West, these are politicised terms charged with demands for human rights and protection guaranteed under international human rights treaties and conventions. English-speaking Singaporean lesbians recognise and respond to these global identifiers. There are no other cognates of 'lesbian' or other colloquial terms that mark same-sex-desiring women in Singapore. Therefore, I am able to use the term 'lesbian' in an unproblematic manner to refer to the women who love women in this study. But this certainly does not mean that lesbian Singaporeans completely subscribe to the tenets of the politicised term 'gay' or 'lesbian', which carry a Eurocentric notion of a singular sexual orientation that is a core and undeniable aspect of one's self. In other words, the identifier 'lesbian' (or 'gay') in Singapore does not share the exact same meanings and resonances as its Western origin. Yet this is precisely why the term is useful. It signifies, on the one hand, Singaporean lesbians' embeddedness in global discourses of sexuality, and on the other hand, their uneven subscription to these dominant ideas and to global LGBT membership.

I use the term 'queer', sometimes interchangeably with 'lesbian', as adjective and noun. I describe my respondents as 'queer' women and also view them as 'queers'. The term originated in US and Australian academic and activist circles, functioning as a collective oppositional site for all those who stand outside the folds of heteronormativity, yet find themselves estranged and alienated from mainstream LGBT discourses and ideologies (Blackwood 2010). 'Queer' disrupts the normalising discourses of LGBT identity politics. Taking these signifiers of 'queer' together, I use the term to refer to the transgressive sexual practices of Singaporean lesbians and their complex sexual subjectivities that go beyond normalising discourses of what it means to be lesbian or gay.

Methods of the study

I use qualitative methods of gathering data to facilitate an inside view. I employ ethnography as a central technique in an attempt to modestly mimic past ethnographic studies on sexual minorities (Blackwood 2010; Provencher 2007; Boellstorff 2005; Sinnott 2004 among others). During 2009 and 2010, I collected ethnographic data from in-depth interviews with 20 lesbians in Singapore. Of these, five are activists and the other 15 are non-activist lesbian women. Although 20 formal interviews were conducted, I was able to speak to well over 30 women at the various social gatherings I attended during the period of fieldwork. Table A1 lists the women mentioned in the book. It does not include those I interviewed or spoke to during participant observation not referred to in the book. All names have been replaced and job titles made general so as to preserve the anonymity of the participants. These interviewees were found through personal contacts and subsequently through a method of snowballing. In 2009, I attended *IndigNation*, the annual local pride event, where I met with several lesbian activists who, thorough their goodwill and interest in generating local LGBT scholarship, introduced and connected me to their personal network of friends. Although these women were friends of local activists, they were seldom, if at all, involved in activist circles. Through these women, I was introduced to other lesbians who were further removed from the circle of activists I met at the local pride event where I had begun my fieldwork for this study.

Standard protocols for research interviews were followed. At the beginning of each interview, I explained the nature of the study carefully, sought the women's consent formally, and emphasised research confidentiality. The interviews were conducted in public places at mutually agreed locations. My concern was whether the location was safe and conducive for interviewing and voice recording. My respondents' concern was mostly that of convenience. Often they nominated a place close to where they lived, worked or hung out with friends. I met most of the women during their lunch hour or after work in the evenings. Details of where I met my informants have been altered for confidentiality.

Interestingly, the rigour of ethics regulation prescribed by the academic research process, such as going through the participant information sheet and gaining signed consent from the respondents, did not matter much to the research participants. Some of the respondents I spoke to, particularly the activists, were either insistent that I use their real names or said it did not matter if I used pseudonyms. Most of the respondents were just eager to get on with the interview and enthusiastic to be part of the research. They showed no qualms about meeting me, a stranger, to talk about their sexual identities. They signed the consent forms without reservation and had few questions about their 'rights' as a participant. This made an interesting insight into Western standards of fieldwork regulation when applied in 'overseas' research settings. While the ethical procedures have been put in place to protect the respondents, ironically, those whose rights were being protected expressed, at times, slight impatience at having to go through the procedures. Perhaps this is a reflection of how the notion of 'rights', so important in an Australian 'Western' context, is unfamiliar in the Singaporean context. Or it could be a reflection of an openness towards homosexuality in contemporary Singapore. My research experience, for instance, contrasted starkly with Offord's (1999) study of the local LGBT community when interviews with gay men had to be conducted in stealth and 'it was even more difficult to obtain information from lesbians' (Offord 1999: 305). The women I spoke to were keen to meet, open about sharing their life stories, and showed little anxiety about meeting me, a stranger, for a study.

My interviews were open-ended and the questions I prepared served as a guide rather than as a closed list to tackle and accomplish. The interview questions were structured to probe in a somewhat biographical manner: when the respondents became aware of their sexual orientations, the means by which they understood and negotiated their sexual identities, desires and relationships, their ties with friends and family, their wider work and social networks, and their opinions of, and participation in, the local LGBT community. At each interview, the questions were adapted and re-ordered, keeping to the flow of the women's narratives and stories. Often the interview segued into a conversation and the women spoke freely of their experiences. All the interviews were conducted on a one-to-one basis, except on the one occasion a group interview arose spontaneously when a respondent I was about to meet in a few hours asked if her lesbian friends could join in the interview. Two friends found out that she would be spending her Saturday afternoon participating in my study and asked if they could join in. During the group interview, I asked questions from my interview guide and facilitated the interview in a focus group format allowing each participant equal opportunity to share their stories.

In addition to interviewing, I spent time with some of these informants, observing and participating in their informal social circles. I wanted to be immersed in the women's worlds. They generously invited me to gatherings at the pub, to a picnic in the park, and to mah-jong sessions at their homes where they spoke about their lives, loves and aspirations. Detailed and meticulous notes were taken at the end of each day after these interactions, and these were compared with my transcribed data from the interviews. The fieldwork interviews and notes constitute the primary empirical materials used in the study.

Secondary data material included archival newspaper articles, government documents and official speeches accessed and collated mainly through online resources provided by the University of Sydney. I scanned the archives for news stories relating to the LGBT community in postcolonial Singapore, starting

Table A1 Participant information at time of research

Aaliyah	34	Arab	O Level	Media consultant
Alyssa	36	Eurasian	Diploma	Retail manager
Anna	27	Chinese	Diploma	Civil defence officer
Celeste	26	Chinese	Postgraduate	Research psychologist
Chantel	28	Chinese	Bachelor	Business manager
Constance	35	Eurasian	Bachelor	Teacher
Das	36	Malay	O Level	Sales manager
Drew	40	Chinese	Diploma	Sales consultant
Eileena	39	Chinese	A Level	Self-employed
Foo	43	Chinese	A Level	Self-employed
Jean	36	Chinese	Postgraduate	Self-employed
Kit	40	Chinese	Bachelor	Banker
Maggie	42	Chinese	O Level	Training consultant
Theresa	35	Indian	Bachelor	Manager
Samantha	34	Chinese	Postgraduate	Banker
Shannon	29	Indian	O Level	Sales marketing trainer
Siew	34	Chinese	Diploma	Technical director
Xing	37	Chinese	O Level	Manager
Yuen	29	Chinese	Bachelor	Teacher

from the period of national independence in the mid-60s, through the short-lived merger with Malaysia ending in 1965, and then through contemporary postcolonial times. These news articles were sourced mainly from local mainstream newspapers, such as *The Straits Times* and *TODAY*, from international press such as the *BBC*, *Time* magazine and the *New York Times* and from the regional LGBT news portal, *Fridae.com*. Official ministerial speeches were mainly sourced from the government website (gov.sg), a portal providing public access to the collection of ministerial speeches and press releases in the last 30 years. These secondary data sources provide the material for the construction of the backdrop of state-sexuality relations and the socio-economic and historical development of postcolonial Singapore within which the lesbian subjects of this study negotiate, construct and understand their sexual identities. In order to access the subject positions of 'modern' local LGQ lives, it was important to first understand the particular postcolonial context of Singapore from where the women's same-sex subjectivities emerged. The analysis of the archival sources was therefore carried out both prior to and concurrently with my interviews.

My data analysis of the primary data involved the elementary practice of identifying salient themes from the women's narratives and marking out selected texts. The approach was a descriptive qualitative analysis privileging participant subjectivity and the 'voice' of my respondents. I colour-coded the transcribed interviews. Narratives with similar themes and stories were marked out in the same colour. These common experiences were written as descriptive passages or captured in a direct quote from a respondent. The themes and texts were then analysed not only in relation to the literature and debate on the globalisation of gay identities but also in relation to regional queer communities and the local historical, political and material circumstances of postcolonial Singapore.

My analysis of the secondary data involved a studied engagement with the archival information, using a discourse analytic lens focusing on the ideological function of state-led constructions of homosexuality. Focusing on relevant material, I construct the historical condition of postcolonial Singapore to uncover how same-sex identities have been shaped and produced in various social locations by dominant sites and discourses. Themes that occurred repeatedly over the archival sources were compared and analysed in relation to my respondents' narratives.

Taken together, the method of this study was to tack back and forth between local postcolonial LGQ lives, the region-wide context and the wider global gay domain, adopting a data triangulation approach that uses different sources of information to locate the subject positions of Singaporean lesbians. The analysis involved the meticulous task of connecting the particular to the general, the micro accounts of my respondents to macro material processes and cultural discourses, and the everyday realities and experiences of Singaporean lesbian subject to larger social, political and economic historical forces, making visible the intersecting factors that inform and organise the lives of postcolonial LGQ subjects.

Researcher's reflection

In adopting the qualitative epistemology and methods outlined above, I have, throughout the research process, been acutely aware of the poststructuralist critique of epistemic privilege. This concern is particularly pertinent for a study that takes issue with imperialist accounts and authority. In this final section, therefore, I wish to address this persistent methodological concern, offering reflections and a hopeful resolution based on my research experience.

The issue of 'epistemic privilege' stems from the nineteenth century formalisation of the social sciences as a discipline in the West when the field researcher was set up as the imperial knowing-self, imbued with experiential authority, and positioned as the objective voice of the field. This 'Ethnographic-Self', in Bhaskaran's (2004) terms, is historically the white, academically-trained expert arriving from the metropole to observe and interpret the ways and practices of 'other' natives out in the field. While the bifurcation of ethnographer/native, self/other and metropole/margin provides a mode of distancing which, arguably, enhances the objectivity of the researcher, poststructuralists question the production of an ethnographic authority premised on these epistemological assumptions and inequities. The objection is largely against the power invested in the field researcher's 'unquestioned claims to appear as the purveyor of truth in the text' (Geertz 1988: 32). Given the inherent power asymmetries, the field researcher operates from an irrefutable position of privilege. The very distance that, arguably, enabled detached objectivity also runs the risk of producing one-sided accounts, particularly when the researcher selectively mines data in the margins for a specific agenda originating in the West. Rendering subjects to the 'enlightening' intellectualism and mission of the researcher could, in this sense, be exploitative rather than emancipatory.

As an overseas-based researcher seeking training in a Western academic institution, and then returning with an armoury of theories developed in the metropolitan West to investigate the community of local lesbians, I am in part implicated by the problem of epistemic privilege and ethnographic authority. I feel a major compunction about presenting myself as an authority on the local community. The annual pride event where I had first begun to establish a network for my fieldwork was into its fourth run, but it was my first attendance. Prior to undertaking this research, I had spent years running away from anything related to my sexual identity. In the 1990s, I avoided taking undergraduate classes dealing with the topics of sexuality and gender at a time when my sexual orientation was still a secret. But even as I came out as a gay, young, working professional in the 2000s, I turned down invitations from my Chinese, middle-class, educated liberal friends to partake in what was then a very nascent local queer movement. For some reason, I have always felt a strange estrangement from my sexual selfhood, and never felt the sort of indignant feelings my friends held towards the discrimination against homosexuality in Singapore. Having been uninvolved and unaware of the community's activities, I was very much an outsider in this sense.

Lesbian and gay researchers often invoke their insider/outsider status as a way to mitigate the problem of representation. Observers have pointed out that as more and more self-identified lesbian and gay researchers begin to investigate their own communities, the old split between the subject/researcher collapses (Lewin and Leap 1996; Kong 2010). As has been asked in feminist fieldwork, what if the 'other' that the researcher is studying is simultaneously constructed, as partially, a 'self' (Abu-Lughod 1991)? The positive implication is that more accurate and 'authentic' understandings of gay men and lesbian women can be produced. I cannot claim such a positionality for when it came to the Singaporean lesbian community, I have never felt as an insider, and certainly cannot invoke this 'special' privilege. Nevertheless, it must be confessed that, similar to the experiences of other lesbian and gay researchers (see for example Williams 1996, Lang 1996 and Kong 2010), my default insider status, simply by virtue of my sexual orientation, certainly facilitated my research in ways I cannot measure. Revealing my sexual identity eased my entry into a community that quickly accepted me, and I was able to establish good rapport with my respondents.

Now returning to this very community I feel I had turned my back on for so long, I constantly worry about how to represent this world to which I have been given privileged access. How do I tell the 'truths' of this community? Might I inadvertently reinforce stereotypes that result in harmful consequences for the community? How will the community I need for support, have grown to respect, and feel an increasing affiliation with, respond to this research once I have uncovered its inner workings? The more I understand the dynamics of the community, the more I am able to make sense of my erstwhile unease. I recognised the larger-than-life global gay discourses circulating in local queer circuits, saw, for instance, how 'coming out' mattered to me in a profound manner, but developed an empathy towards those resisting and struggling to keep up to the 'promise' of being gay. In writing and involving in some form of 'cultural representation' (Hall 1997), how do I avoid giving power to dominant notions of what it means to be homosexual? An outsider perspective may afford objectivity, but as soon as the division between 'scholarship' and 'personal quest' is assailed, the question of ethnographic distance and the struggle for objectivity is put to question. Furthermore, the more cachet queer studies gain in the Western academic circuits I find myself participating in, presenting and writing about Singaporean lesbians to 'outsiders' becomes a more intense exercise as these questions weigh heavily on me. These questions are not just of representation, but ethical considerations to which no easy solutions can be offered. However, rather than allow these self-examinations to lead to paralysis, what is required, as many scholars have argued, is self-reflexivity. While the appeal for self-reflexivity on the part of the researcher seems an all-too-common, and at times, simple response, the solution is certainly not its dissolution. Self-reflexivity is a research imperative, but what is equally important, I argue, is continuous self-disclosure and discussion of our scholarly experience to add to the growing debate about the nature of the ethnographic enterprise.

References

Aarmo, Margrete. 1999. How Homosexuality Became 'Un-African': The Case of Zimbabwe. In *Female Desires: Same-sex Relations and Transgender Practices across Cultures*, edited by E. Blackwood and S.E. Wieringa. New York: Columbia University Press.

Abu-Lughod, Lila. 1991. Writing against Culture. In *Recapturing Anthropology: Working in the Present*, edited by R. Fox. Santa Fe: School of American Research Press.

Albrow, Martin. 1996. *The Global Age: State and Society Beyond Modernity*. Cambridge: Polity Press.

Alicia. 2007. Review by Alicia. *Women Who Love Women*. 25 August, accessed on 3 November 2011, http://womenwholovewomensingapore.blogspot.com/2007/08/review-by-nizhen-hsieh.html

Altman, Dennis. 1989. *Homosexuality, which Homosexuality?: International Conference on Gay and Lesbian Studies*. Amsterdam: Uitgeverij An Dekker/Schorer; London: GMP.

Altman, Dennis. 1996a. On Global Queering. *Australian Humanities Review*, accessed on 10 November 2010, www.australianhumanitiesreview.org/archive/Issue-July-1996/altman.html

Altman, Dennis. 1996b. Rupture or Continuity? The Internationalization of Gay Identities. *Social Text 48* 14(3): 77–94.

Altman, Dennis. 1997. Global Gaze/Global Gays. *GLQ: A Journal of Lesbian and Gay Studies* 3: 417–436.

Altman, Dennis. 2001. *Global Sex*. Chicago: University of Chicago Press.

Ammon, Richard. 2002. *The New Gay Singapore Part Three*, March, accessed 31 March 2007, www.globalgayz.com/the-new-gay-singapore-02-06/350/.

Anderson, Benedict. 1983. *Imagined Communities: Reflections on the Origin and Spread of Nationalism*. London: Verso.

Ang, Ien and John Stratton. 1995. The Singapore Way of Multiculturalism: Western Concepts/Asian Cultures. *Sojourn: Journal of Social Issues in Southeast Asia* 10(1): 65-89.

Appadurai, Arjun. 1996. *Modernity At Large: Cultural Dimensions of Globalization*. Minneapolis: University of Minnesota Press.

Archer, Margaret. 1988. *Culture and Agency: The Place of Culture in Social Theory*. Cambridge: Cambridge University Press.

Ardill, Susan and Sue O'Sullivan. 1990. Butch/Femme Obsessions. *Feminist Review* 34: 79–85.

Associated Press. 2003. Strict Singapore Will Permit Its Citizens to Leap for Joy. In *The New York Times*, July 13, accessed on 24 July 2012, www.nytimes.com/2003/07/13/international/asia/13SING.html.

Astraea Foundation. 2011. Meet a Grantee Partner: Queer Women of Color Media Arts Project, accessed on 13 February 2012, www.guidestar.org/ViewEdoc.aspx?eDocId=1714802&approved=True.

Au, Alex. 1997. *Gay Culture in Singapore*. Talk given at the Substation Singapore, 21 September.

Au, Alex. 2009. Soft Exterior, Hard Core. In *Impressions of the Goh Chok Tong Years in Singapore*, edited by B. Welsh, J. Chin, A. Mahizhnan and T.H. Tan. National University of Singapore: NUS Press.

Babb, Florence. 2003. Out in Nicaragua: Local and Transnational Desires after the Revolution. *Cultural Anthropology* 18(3): 304–328.

Bacchetta, Paola. 2002. Rescaling Transnational 'Queerdom': Lesbian and 'Lesbian' Identitary-Positionalities in Delhi in the 1980s. *Antipode* 34(5): 947–973.

Bangkok Declaration. 1993. *Report by the Secretariat, Bangkok NGO Declaration on Human Rights*, 19 April, accessed on 27 March 2012, www.internationalhumanrightslexicon.org/hrdoc/docs/bangkokNGO.pdf.

BBC News. 2000. Gay Marriage: In the Pink, 18 September, accessed on 10 August 2012, http://news.bbc.co.uk/2/hi/in_depth/uk/930296.stm.

BBC News. 2006. Singapore Censor Passes Brokeback, 15 February, accessed on 8 October 2011, http://news.bbc.co.uk/2/hi/entertainment/4716610.stm.

Bech, Henning. 1992. Report from a Rotten State: 'Marriage' and 'Homosexuality' in 'Denmark'. In *Modern Homosexualities: Fragments of Lesbian and Gay Experience*, edited by K. Plummer. London and New York: Routledge.

Bello, Walden. 1990. *Dragons in Distress: Asia's Miracle Economies in Crisis*, edited by W. Bello and S. Rosenfeld. San Francisco: Institute for Food and Development Policy.

Berlant, Lauren and Elizabeth Freeman. 1993. Queer Nationality. In *Fear of a Queer Planet: Queer Politics and Social Theory*, edited by M. Warner. Minneapolis: University of Minnesota Press.

Bernstein, Henry. 1971. Modernization Theory and the Sociological Study of Development. *Journal of Development Studies* 7(2): 141–160.

Berry, Chris. 1996. Chris Berry Responds to Dennis Altman. *Australian Humanities Review*, accessed on 10 November 2010, www.australianhumanitiesreview.org/emuse/Globalqueering/berry.html.

Berry, Chris, Fran Martin and Audrey Yue. 2003. *Mobile Cultures: New Media in Queer Asia*. Durham; London: Duke University Press.

Bhabha, Homi. 1989. Location, Intervention, Incommensurability: A Conversation with Homi Bhabha. *Emergences* 1(1): 63–88.

Bhabha, Homi. 1994. *The Location of Culture*. London and New York: Routledge.

Bhabha, Homi. 1999. Arrivals and Departures. In *Home, Exile, Homeland: Film, Media, and the Politics of Place*. New York: Routledge.

Bhambra, Gurminder. 2007. *Rethinking Modernity: Postcolonialism and the Sociological Imagination*. New York: Palgrave Macmillan.

Bhaskaran, Suparna. 2004. *Made in India: Decolonizations, Queer Sexualities, Trans/national Projects*. New York: Palgrave Macmillan.

Bhattacharjee, Anannya. 1992. The Habit of Ex-Nomination: Nation, Woman, and the Indian Immigrant Bourgeoisie. *Public Culture* 5(1): 19–44.

Binnie, Jon. 2004. *The Globalization of Sexuality*. London, California and New Delhi: SAGE Publications.

Blackwood, Evelyn. 1999. Tombois in West Sumatra: Constructing Masculinity and Erotic Desire. In *Female Desires: Same-sex Relations and Transgender Practices across*

Cultures, edited by E. Blackwood and S.E. Wieringa. New York: Columbia University Press.

Blackwood, Evelyn. 2002. Reading Sexuality across Cultures: Anthropology and Theories of Sexuality. In *Out in the Field: Reflections of Lesbian and Gay Anthropologists*. Urbana, IL: University of Illinois Press.

Blackwood, Evelyn. 2005. Gender Transgression in Colonial and Postcolonial Indonesia. *The Journal of Asian Studies* 64(4): 849–879.

Blackwood, Evelyn. 2008. Transnational Discourses and Circuits of Queer Knowledge in Indonesia. *GLQ: A Journal of Lesbian and Gay Studies* 14(4): 482–507.

Blackwood, Evelyn. 2010. *Falling into the Lesbi World: Desire and Difference in Indonesia*. Honolulu: University of Hawaii Press.

Blackwood, Evelyn and Saskia E. Wieringa, eds. 1999. *Female Desires: Same-sex Relations and Transgender Practices across Cultures*. New York: Columbia University Press.

Blackwood, Evelyn and Saskia E. Wieringa. 2007. Globalization, Sexuality, and Silences: Women's Sexualities and Masculinities in an Asian Context. In *Women's Sexualities and Masculinities in a Globalizing Asia*, edited by S.E. Wieringa, E. Blackwood and A. Bhaiya. New York: Palgrave Macmillan.

Blasius, Mark. 2001. An Ethos of Lesbian and Gay Existence. In *Sexual Identities, Queer Politics*, edited by M. Blasius. Princeton, NJ: Princeton University Press.

Boellstorff, Tom. 1999. The Perfect Path: Gay Men, Marriage, Indonesia. *GLQ: A Journal of Lesbian and Gay Studies* 5(4): 475–510.

Boellstorff, Tom. 2005. *The Gay Archipelago: Sexuality and Nation in Indonesia*. Princeton University Press: Princeton and Oxford.

Boellstorff, Tom. 2007a. Queer Studies in the House of Anthropology. *Annual Review of Anthropology* 36: 17–35.

Boellstorff, Tom. 2007b. *A Coincidence of Desires: Anthropology, Queer Studies, Indonesia*. Durham and London: Duke University Press.

Boellstorff, Tom. 2012. Some Notes on New Frontiers of Sexuality and Globalisation. In *Understanding Global Sexualities: New Frontiers*, edited by Peter Aggleton, Paul Boyce, Henrietta Moore, and Richard Parker. London: Routledge.

Bourdieu, Pierre. 1977. *Outline of a Theory of Practice*, translated by Richard Nice. Cambridge; New York: Cambridge University Press.

Bourdieu, Pierre. 1990. *The Logic of Practice*, translated by Richard Nice. Stanford, CA: Stanford University Press.

Bourdieu, Pierre. 2001. *Masculine Domination*, translated by Richard Nice. Cambridge, UK: Polity Press.

Brenkenridge, Carol and Arjun Appadurai. 1988. Editors' Comment. *Public Culture* 1(1): 1–4.

Brown, David. 1993. The Corporatist Management of Ethnicity in Contemporary Singapore. In *Singapore Changes Guard: Social, Political and Economic Directions in the 1990s*, edited by G. Rodan. New York: St. Martin's Press.

Brown, Phillip, Andy Green and Hugh Lauder. 2001. *High Skills: Globalization, Competitiveness, and Skill Formation*. Oxford and New York: Oxford University Press.

Bunzl, Matti. 2004. *Symptoms of Modernity: Jews and Queers in Late-Twentieth-Century Vienna*. Berkeley: University of California Press.

Butler. Judith. 1990. *Gender Trouble*. New York: Routledge.

Butler. Judith. 1993. *Bodies That Matter: On the Discursive Limits of 'Sex'*. New York: Routledge.

Carrillo, Héctor. Imagining Modernity: Sexuality, Policy, and Social Change in Mexico. *Sexuality Research and Social Policy* 5(3): 74–91.

Carver, Terrell and Véronique Mottier, eds. 1998. *Politics of Sexuality: Identity, Gender, Citizenship*. London, USA and Canada: Routledge.

Castells, Manuel. 1988. The Development of City-State in an Open Economy: The Singapore Experience. In *Berkeley Roundtable on the International Economy Working Paper No. 31*: University of California.

Césaire, Aimé. 1972. *Discourse on Colonialism*. New York: Monthly Review Press.

Chakrabarty, Dipesh. 2000. *Provincializing Europe: Postcolonial Thought and Historical Difference*. Princeton, NJ: Princeton University Press.

Chalmers, Sharon. 2002. *Emerging Lesbian Voices from Japan*. London and New York: Routledge-Curzon.

Chao, Antonia. 2000. Global Metaphors and Local Strategies in the Construction of Taiwan's Lesbian Identities. *Culture, Health and Sexuality* 2(4), Critical Regionalities: Gender and Sexual Diversity in South East and East Asia: 377–390.

Chatterjee, Partha. 1986. *Nationalist Thought and the Colonial World: A Derivative Discourse*. London: Zed Books.

Chatterjee, Partha. 1993. *The Nation and its Fragments: Colonial and Postcolonial histories*. Princeton, NJ: Princeton University Press.

Chiang, Howard and Ari Larissa Heinrich. 2014. *Queer Sinophone Cultures*. London and New York: Routledge.

Chin, James. 2009. Electoral Battles and Innovations: Recovering Lost Ground. In *Impressions of the Goh Chok Tong Years in Singapore*, edited by B. Welsh, J. Chin, A. Mahizhnan and T.H. Tan. National University of Singapore: NUS Press.

Chong, Terence. 2006. Embodying Society's Best: Hegel and the Singapore State. *Journal of Contemporary Asia* 36(3): 283–304.

Chong, Terence. 2011. Filling the Moral Void: The Christian Right in Singapore. *Journal of Contemporary Asia* 41(4): 566–583.

Chou, Wah-Shan. 2001. Homosexuality and the Cultural Politics of Tongzhi in Chinese Societies. In *Gay and Lesbian Asia: Culture, Identity, Community*, edited by G. Sullivan and P.A. Jackson. New York: The Haworth Press.

Chu, Wei-Cheng and Fran Martin. 2007. Editorial Introduction: Global Queer, Local Theories. *Inter-Asia Cultural Studies* 8(4): 483–484.

Chua, Beng-Huat. 1990. *Confucianisation in Modernising Singapore*. Paper presented at the conference on Beyond the Culture? October, Loccum, West Germany.

Chua, Beng-Huat. 1993. The Changing Shape of Civil Society in Singapore. *Commentary* (Singapore) 11(1): 9–14.

Chua, Beng-Huat. 1995. *Communitarian Ideology and Democracy in Singapore*. London and New York: Routledge.

Chua, Beng-Huat. 2000. The Relative Autonomies of the State and Civil Society. In *State-Society Relations in Singapore*, edited by G. Koh and O.G. Ling. Singapore: Institute of Policy Studies and Oxford University Press.

Chua, Beng-Huat. 2005. *Life is Not Complete Without Shopping: Consumption Culture in Singapore*. Singapore: Singapore University Press.

Chua, Beng-Huat. 2007. Singapore in 2007: High Wage Ministers and the Management of Gays and Elderly. *Asian Survey* 48(1): 55–61.

Chua, Lynette. 2003. Saying No: Sections 377 and 377A of the Penal Code. *Singapore Journal of Legal Studies* 2003: 209–261.

References

Chua, Lynette. 2014. *Mobilizing Gay Singapore: Rights and Resistance in an Authoritarian State*. Philadelphia, PA: Temple University Press.

Connell, Raewyn. 2007. The Northern Theory of Globalization. *Sociological Theory* 25(4): 369–385.

Connell, Raewyn. 2011. The Shores of the Southern Ocean: Steps Towards a World Sociology of Modernity, with Australian Examples. In *Worlds of Difference*, edited by S.A. Arjomand and E. Reis. Sage Studies in International Sociology.

Corboz, Julienne. 2009. Globalisation and Transnational Sexualities. *Australian Research Centre in Sex, Health and Society*, accessed on 12 April 2012, http://iasscs.org/sites/default/files/Globalisation%20and%20Transnational%20Sexualities.pdf.

Connors, Michael. 1995. *Disordering Democracy: Democratisation in Thailand*. Unpublished paper. Melbourne University.

Cruz-Malavé, Arnaldo and Martin F. Manalansan. 2002. *Queer Globalizations: Citizenship and the Afterlife of Colonialism*. New York: New York University Press.

D' Emilio, John. 1983. *Sexual Politics, Sexual Communities*. Chicago, IL: University of Chicago Press.

Dasgupta, Romit. 2009. The 'Queer' Family in Asia. *Gender Relations in the 21st Century Asian Family Inter-Asia Roundtable*, National University of Singapore. 1–30.

Davies, Sharyn. 2010a. Socio-Political Movements: Homosexuality and Queer Identity Movements, Southeast Asia. In *Encyclopedia of Women and Islamic Cultures*, edited by J. Saud. Leiden: Brill Academic Publishers.

Davies, Sharyn. 2010b. *Gender, Diversity in Indonesia: Sexuality, Islam, and Queer Selves*. London: Routledge-Curzon.

Deutscher, Penelope. 2002. *A Politics of Impossible Difference: The Later Work of Luce Irigaray*. Ithaca, NY: Cornell University Press.

Devan, Pamela. 2010. *Butch, Femme and Other Labels in the Singaporean Lesbian Community: Should We Escape the Heteronormative Gender Binary?* Unpublished academic exercise. Department of Sociology, Faculty of Arts and Social Sciences, National University of Singapore.

Dirlik, Arif. 1994. The Postcolonial Aura: Third World Criticism in the Age of Global Capitalism. *Critical Inquiry* 20: 328–356.

Drysdale, John. 1984. *Singapore, Struggle for Success*. North Sydney: George Allen & Unwin.

Duberman, Martin B. 1993. *Stonewall*. New York: Plume.

Duggan, Lisa. 1994. Queering the State. *Social Text* 39: 1–14.

During, Simon. 2000. Postcolonialism and Globalization: Towards a Historicization of their Inter-relation. *Cultural Studies* 14(3/4): 385–404.

Dwyer, Leslie. 2000. Spectacular Sexuality: Nationalism, Development and the Politics of Family Planning in Indonesia. In *Gender Ironies of Nationalism: Sexing the Nation*, edited by Tamar Mayer. London: Routledge.

Emirbayer, Mustafa and Ann Mische. 1998. What is Agency? *The American Journal of Sociology* 103(4): 962–1023.

Enloe, Cynthia. 1989. *Bananas, Beaches & Bases: Making Feminist Sense of International Politics*. London: Pandora.

Faderman, Lilian. 1981. *Surpassing the Love of Men*. New York: Morrow.

Faderman, Lilian. 1992. The Return of Butch and Femme: A Phenomenon to Lesbian Sexuality of the 1980s and 1990s. *Journal of the History of Sexuality* 2(4): 578–596.

Featherstone, Mike. 1990. Global Culture: An Introduction. *Theory, Culture & Society* 7(1): 1–14.

Featherstone, Mike. 1995. *Undoing Culture: Globalization, Postmodernism and Identity*. London: Sage.
Featherstone, Mike. 1998. The *Flaneur*, the City and Virtual Public Life. *Urban Studies* 15: 909–926.
Finlayson, Alan. 1998. Sexuality and Nationality: Gendered Discourses of Ireland. In *Politics of Sexuality: Identity, Gender, Citizenship*, edited by H. Keman and J.W. van Deth. London and New York: Routledge/ECPR Studies in European Political Science.
Florida, Richard. 2002. *The Rise of the Creative Class: And How it's Transforming Work, Leisure, Community and Everyday Life*. New York: Basic Books.
Foster, Robert. 1991. Making National Cultures in the Global Ecumene. *Annual Review of Anthropology* 20: 235–269.
Foucault, Michel. 1978. *The History of Sexuality*, Vol. 1. New York: Pantheon.
Foucault, Michel. 1982. The Subject and Power. *Critical Inquiry* 8(4): 777–795.
Fox, Richard. 1990. *Nationalist Ideologies and the Production of National Cultures*. Washington DC: American Anthropological Association.
Fridae.com. 2001a. *Drama Queen: Madeleine Lim*. 23 February, accessed on 15 February 2012, www.fridae.asia/newsfeatures/printable.php?articleid=925.
Fridae.com. 2001b. *Eileena Lee*. 7 March, accessed on 15 February 2012, www.fridae.asia/newsfeatures/2001/03/07/882.eileena-lee?n=sec.
Fridae.com. 2003. *Accept Gays as Fellow Human Beings: Singapore PM*. 18 August, accessed on 2 April 2016, www.fridae.asia/gay-news/2003/08/18/559.accept-gays-as-fellow-human-beings-singapore-pm.
Fridae.com. 2005a. *Singapore Health Minister's Comments on HIV Surge and Gay Parties Draw Criticism*. 10 March, accessed on 22 October 2011, www.fridae.asia/gay-news/printable.php?articleid=1386.
Fridae.com. 2005b. *Bring on the Hunt*. 10 July, accessed on 25 May, www.fridae.asia/newsfeatures/2005/07/10/1449.bring-on-the-hunt.
Fridae.com. 2006a. *Gay Couple Calls on Couples in Taiwan to Join Mass Wedding*. 26 April, accessed on 10 October 2011, www.fridae.asia/lifestyle/printable.php?articleid=1618.
Fridae.com. 2006b. *Razzle Dazzle 'em!* 7 July, accessed on 25 May, www.fridae.asia/newsfeatures/2006/07/07/1665.razzle-dazzle-em.
Fridae.com. 2007a. *Women Who Love Women: Conversations in Singapore*. 5 July, accessed on 3 November 2011, www.fridae.asia/newsfeatures/2007/07/05/1891.women-who-love-women-conversations-in-singapore.
Fridae.com. 2007b. *Singapore's Lee Kuan Yew Questions Gay Sex Law*. 23 April, accessed on 10 October 2011, www.fridae.asia/gay-news/printable.php?articleid=1833.
Fridae.com. 2007c. *Theology Professor Supports Repeal of Anti-gay Law*. 11 May, accessed on 13 October 2010, www.fridae.asia/newsfeatures/2007/05/11/1848.theology-professor-supports-%20repeal-of-anti-gay-law-in-singapore?n=sea&nm=377.
Fridae.com. 2007d. *Face to Face with Sir Ian McKellen*. 19 July, accessed on 13 October 2010, www.fridae.asia/newsfeatures/printable.php?articleid=1902.
Fridae.com. 2008. *Singapore Censors Fine Cable TV operator S$10,000 for Ad Featuring Lesbian Kiss*. 10 April, accessed on 16 March 2016, www.fridae.asia/gay-news/2008/04/10/2040.singapore-censors-fine-cable-tv-operator-s-10000-for-ad-featuring-lesbian-kiss.
Fuss, Diana. 1991. *Inside/Out: Lesbian Theories, Gay Theories*. New York: Routledge.
Gandhi, Leela. 1989. *Postcolonial Theory: A Critical Introduction*. Crows Nest: Allen & Unwin.

Garcia, Neil. 1996. *Philippine Gay Culture: The Last 30 Years, Binabae to Bakla, Silahis to MSM*. Manila: University of the Philippines Press.

Garcia, Neil. 2008. Villa, Montano, Perez: Postcoloniality and Gay Liberation in the Philippines. In *AsiaPacifiQueer: Rethinking Genders and Sexualities*, edited by F. Martin, P.A. Jackson, M. McLelland and A. Yue. Urbana and Chicago: University of Illinois Press.

Geertz, Clifford. 1988. *Works and Lives: The Anthropologist as Author*. Stanford, CA: Stanford University Press.

George, Cherian. 2001. *Singapore: The Air-Conditioned Nation; Essays on the Politics of Comfort and Control 1999–2000*. Singapore: Landmark Books.

Giddens, Anthony. 1976. *New Rules of Sociological Method: A Positive Critique of Interpretative Sociologies*. London: Hutchinson.

Giddens, Anthony. 1979. *Central Problems in Social Theory: Action, Structure and Contradiction in Social Analysis*. Berkeley, CA: University of California Press.

Giddens, Anthony. 1984. *The Constitution of Society: Outline of the Theory of Structuration*. Berkeley: University of California Press.

Goffman, Erving. 1971. *The Presentation of Self in Everyday Life*. Harmondsworth: Penguin.

Goh, Chok Tong. 1988. Speech by Mr Goh Chok, First Deputy Prime Minister and Minister for Defence at the PAP Youth Wing Charity Night, 28 October, accessed on 15 November 2011, www.nas.gov.sg/archivesonline/speeches/record-details/7157e523-115d-11e3-83d5-0050568939ad.

Goh, Chok Tong. 1997. *Singapore 21 – A New Vision for a New Era*. Speech by the prime minister in the debate on the president's address in Parliament, 5 June, accessed on 17 December 2011, http://vision.cer.uz/Data/lib/vision_texts/Singapore/SING_Singapore21_A_New_Vision_for_a_New_Era_EN_1997.pdf.

Goh, Chok Tong. 1998. Speech by the Prime Minister at the Official Opening of Republic Plaza, 8 January, accessed on 22 March 2012, www.nas.gov.sg/archivesonline/speeches/view-html?filename=1998011805.htm.

Goh, Chok Tong. 2000. *Globalisation – A Perspective from Singapore*. Speech by Prime Minister Goh Chok Tong at the annual dinner 2000 of the Economic Society of Singapore, 5 May, accessed on 22 March 2012, www.nas.gov.sg/archivesonline/speeches/view-html?filename=2000050506.htm.

Goh, Chok Tong. 2001. Speech at the National Day Rally. Singapore. 11 August.

Goh, Daniel. 2011. State Carnivals and the Subvention of Multiculturalism in Singapore. *The British Journal of Sociology* 62(1): 111–133.

Goh, Keng Swee. 1978. *Report on the Ministry of Education*. Singapore: Ministry of Education.

Gopalan, Mohan. 2007. A Heftier List of s.377A Cases. *Yawning Bread*. May, accessed on 18 August 2011, www.yawningbread.org/guest_2007/guw-136.htm.

Gopinath, Gayatri. 1997. Nostalgia, Desire, Diaspora: South Asian Sexualities in Motion. *Positions* 5(2): 467–489.

Gopinath, Gayatri. 2005. *Impossible Desires: Queer Diasporas and South Asian Public Cultures*. Durham, NC: Duke University Press.

Girling, John. 1988. Development and Democracy in Southeast Asia. *The Pacific Review* 1(4): 332–333.

Gramsci, Antonio. 1971. *Selections from the Prison Notebooks*. New York: Lawrence and Wishart.

Grewal, Inderpal and Caren Kaplan. 1994. Introduction: Transnational Feminist Practices and Questions of Postmodernity. In *Scattered Hegemonies: Postmodernity and Transnational Feminist Practices*, edited by I. Grewal and C. Kaplan. Minneapolis, MN: University of Minnesota Press.

Grewal, Inderpal and Caren Kaplan. 2001. Global Identities: Theorizing Transnational Studies of Sexuality. *GLQ: A Journal of Lesbian and Gay Studies* 7(4): 663–679.

Gross, Larry. 1993. *Contested Closets*. Minneapolis, MN: University of Minnesota Press.

Gunkel, Henriette. 2010. *The Cultural Politics of Female Sexuality in South Africa*. New York and London: Routledge.

Gupta, Akhil. 1998. *Postcolonial Developments: Agriculture in the Making of Modern India*. Durham, NC: Duke University Press.

Gupta, Akhil and James Ferguson. 1992. Beyond 'Culture': Space, Identity, and the Politics of Difference. *Cultural Anthropology* 7(1): 6–23.

Hall, Stuart. 1992. The West and the Rest: Discourse and Power. In *Formations of Modernity*, edited by S. Hall and B. Gieben. Cambridge: Polity, pp. 276–318.

Hall, Stuart. 1995. When was 'the Post-colonial'? Thinking at the Limit. In *The Postcolonial Question: Common Skies, Divided Horizons*, edited by I. Chambers and L. Curti. London and New York: Routledge.

Hall, Stuart. 1997. *Representation: Cultural Representations and Signifying Practices*, edited by S. Hall. London: SAGE Publications.

Hamer, Dean H., Stella Hu, Victoria L. Magnuson, Nan Hu and Angela M.L. Pattatucci. 1993. A Linkage Between DNA Markers on the X Chromosome and Male Sexual Orientation. *Science* 261(5119): 321–327.

Hannerz, Ulf. 1992. *Cultural Complexity: Studies in the Social Organisation of Meaning*. New York: Columbia University Press.

Hansen, Jennifer. 2000. Introduction to 'There are Two Sexes, Not One, Luce Irigaray'. In *French Feminism Reader*, edited by K. Oliver. Lanham, MC: Rowman & Littlefield.

Hayes, Jarrod. 2001. Queer Resistance to (Neo-)Colonialism in Algeria. In *Post-colonial Queer: Theoretical Interventions* edited by J.C. Hawley. Albany, NY: State University of New York Press, pp. 79–97.

Haylett, Chris. 2001. Illegitimate Subjects? Abject Whites, Neoliberal Modernisation and Middle-Class Multiculturalism. *Environment and Planning D: Society and Space* 19(3): 351–370.

Heng, Geraldine and Janadas Devan. 1992. State Fatherhood: The Politics of Nationalism, Sexuality and Race in Singapore. In *Nationalisms and Sexualities*, edited by edited by A. Parker, M. Russo, D. Sommer and P. Yaeger. New York: Routledge.

Heng, Russell. 2001. Tiptoe out of the Closet: The Before and After of the Increasingly Visible Gay Community in Singapore. In *Gay and Lesbian Asia: Culture, Identity, Community*, edited by G. Sullivan and P. Jackson. New York: Harrington Park Press.

Hill, Michael. 2000. 'Asian' Values as Reverse Orientalism: Singapore. *Asia Pacific Viewpoint* 41(2): 177–190.

Hong, Derek. 2009. Sermon to the Church of Our Saviour congregation, 25 April.

Housing and Development Board. 2008a. *Public Housing in Singapore: Residents' Profile, Housing, Satisfaction and Preferences: HDB Sample Household Survey 2008*. Singapore: Housing and Development Board.

Housing and Development Board. 2008b. *Eligibility to Buy New HDB Flat*, accessed on 6 July 2016, www.hdb.gov.sg/cs/infoweb/residential/buying-a-flat/resale/eligibility-schemes.

Hsieh, Nizhen. 2007. Review by Nizhen Hsieh. *Women Who Love Women*. 25 August, accessed on 3 November 2011, http://womenwholovewomensingapore.blogspot.com/2007/08/review-by-alicia_25.html.

Huang, Hans Tao-Ming. 2011. *Queer Politics and Sexuality Modernity in Taiwan*. Hong Kong: Hong Kong University Press.

Humphreys, Laud. 1972. *Out of the Closets: The Sociology of Homosexual Liberation*. Englewood Cliffs, NJ: Prentice-Hall.

Humphreys, Laud. 1979. Exodus and Identity: The Emerging Gay Culture. In *Gay Men*, edited by M. Levine. New York: Harper and Row.

Huntington, Samuel. 1997. After Twenty Years: The Future of the Third Wave. *Journal of Democracy* 8(4): 3–12.

International Monetary Fund. 2009. *World Economic and Financial Surveys*, accessed on 25 July 2010, www.imf.org/external/pubs/ft/weo/2009/02/weodata/groups.htm#ae.

Jackson, Peter A. 1995. *Dear Uncle Go: Male Homosexuality in Thailand*. Bangkok: Bua Luang Books.

Jackson, Peter A. 1997a. Kathoey – Gay – Man: The Historical Emergence of Gay Male Identity in Thailand. In *Sites of Desire, Economies of Pleasure: Sexualities in Asia and the Pacific*, edited by L. Manderson and M. Jolly. Chicago: University of Chicago Press.

Jackson, Peter A. 1997b. Thai Research on Male Homosexuality and Transgenderism and the Cultural Limits of Foucauldian Analysis. *Journal of the History of Sexuality* 8(1): 52–85.

Jackson, Peter A. 1999. An American Death in Bangkok: The Murder of Darrell Berrigan and the Hybrid Origins of Gay Identity in 1960s Thailand. *GLQ: A Journal of Lesbian and Gay Studies* 5(3): 361–411.

Jackson, Peter A. 2001. Pre-Gay, Post-Queer: Thai Perspectives on Proliferating Gender/Sex Diversity in Asia. *Journal of Homosexuality* 40(3/4): 1–25.

Jackson, Peter A. 2003. Performative Genders, Perverse Desires: A Bio-History of Thailand's Same-Sex and Transgender Cultures. *Intersections: Gender and Sexuality in the Asia and the Pacific* 9: 1–52.

Jackson, Peter A., ed. 2011. *Queer Bangkok: Twenty-First-Century Markets, Media, and Rights*. Hong Kong: Hong Kong University Press.

Jagose, Annamarie. 1997. *Queer Theory: An Introduction*. New York: New York University Press.

Jay, Karla and Allen Young, eds. 1992 [1972]. *Out of the Closets*. New York: New York University Press.

Johnson, Mark, Peter Jackson and Gilbert Herdt. 2000. Critical Regionalities and the Study of Gender and Sexual Diversity in South East and East Asia. *Culture, Health and Sexuality* 2(4): 361–375.

Jolly, Margaret and Lenore Manderson, eds. 1995. *Sites of Desire Economies of Pleasure: Sexualities in Asia and the Pacific*. Chicago and London: University of Chicago Press.

Joseph, Nathan and Nicholas Alex. 1972. The Uniform: A Sociological Perspective. *American Journal of Sociology* 77(4): 719–730.

Kam, Lucetta. 2008. Recognition through Mis-recognition: Masculine Women in Hong Kong. In *AsiaPacifiQueer: Rethinking Genders and Sexualities*, edited by F. Martin, P.A. Jackson, M. McLelland and A. Yue. Urbana and Chicago: University of Illinois Press.

Kang, Wen Qing. 2009. *Obsession: Male Same-sex Relations in China, 1900–1950*. Hong Kong: Hong Kong University Press.

Kant, Immanuel. 1956. *Critique of Practical Reason*, translated by Lewis White Beck. Indianapolis, IN: Bobbs-Merrill.

Kant, Immanuel. 1965. *Critique of Pure Reason*, translated by Norman Kemp Smith. New York: St. Martins.

Karras, Ruth. 2000. Active/Passive, Acts/Passions: Greek and Roman Sexualities. *The American Historical Review* 105(4): 1250–1265.

Kartini, Abdul Rahman. 2001. *The Lesbian Community in Singapore*. Unpublished academic exercise. Department of Sociology, Faculty of Arts and Social Sciences, National University of Singapore.

Katz, Jonathan. 1983. *Gay/Lesbian Almanac*. New York: Harper and Row.

Kearney, Michael. 1995. The Local and the Global: The Anthropology of Globalization and Transnationalism. *Annual Review of Anthropology* 24: 547–565.

Kennedy, Elizabeth and Madeline Davis. 1993. *Boots of Leather, Slippers of Gold: The History of a Lesbian Community*. New York: Penguin Books.

Khor, Diana, and Saori Kamano, eds. 2006. *Lesbians in East Asia: Diversity, Identities and Resistance*. Binghamton, NY: Harrington Park Press.

Kim, Hyun Sook, Jyoti Puri and H.J. Kim-Puri. 2005. Conceptualizing Gender-Sexuality-State-Nation: An Introduction. *Gender and Society* 19(2): 137–159.

King, Katie. 2002. There Are No Lesbians Here: Lesbianisms, Feminisms, and Global Gay Formations. In *Queer Globalizations: Citizenship and the Afterlife of Colonialism*, edited by A. Cruz-Malavé and M.F. Manalansan. New York: New York University Press.

Kinsman, Gary. 1996. *Regulation of Desire: Sexuality in Canada*. Canada: Policy Alternatives of Montreal.

Koh, Dan. 2010. CEO of Fly Entertainment, Irene Ang. *I-S Magazine Online*. 12 August, accessed on 21 August 2010, http://is.asia-city.com/movies/article/ceo-fly-entertainnment-irene-ang.

Koh, Gillian and Ooi Giok Ling. 2004. Relationship between State and Civil Society in Singapore: Clarifying the Concepts, Assessing the Ground. In *Civil Society in Southeast Asia*, edited by H.G. Lee. Singapore: ISEAS.

Koh, Tai Ann. 1989. Culture and the Arts. In *Management of Success*, edited by K.S. Sandhu and P. Wheatley. Boulder: Westview Press.

Kong, Travis. 2010. *Chinese Male Homosexualities: Memba, Tongzhi and Golden Boy*. Abingdon, Oxon and New York: Routledge.

Lang, Sabine. 1996. Travelling Woman: Conducting a Fieldwork Project on Gender Variance and Homosexuality among North American Indians. In *Out in the Field: Reflections of Lesbian and Gay Anthropologists*, edited by E. Lewin and W. Leap. Urbana, IL: University of Illinois Press.

Latif, Asad-Ul Iqbal. 2009. Re-imagining the Nation: Goh Chok Tong's Singapore. In *Impressions of the Goh Chok Tong Years in Singapore*, edited by B. Welsh, J. Chin, A. Mahizhnan and T.H. Tan. National University of Singapore: NUS Press.

Lee, Benjamin and Edward LiPuma. 2002. Cultures of Circulation: The Imaginations of Modernity. *Public Culture* 14(1): 191–213.

Lee, Hsien Loong. 2007. Speech to Parliament on reading of Penal Code (Amendment) Bill, 22 October.

Lee, Kuan Yew. 2007. *The Singapore Story: Memoirs of Lee Kuan Yew*. Singapore: Prentice Hall.

Lee, Kuan Yew. 2011. *Lee Kuan Yew: Hard Truths to Keep Singapore Going*. Singapore: Straits Times Press.

Leong, Wai Teng. 1997. Sociolegal Control of Homosexuality: A Multi-nation Comparison. In *Sociolegal Control of Homosexuality*, edited by D. West and R. Green. New York: Plenum Press.

Leong, Wai Teng. 2005. The 'Straight' Times: News and Sexual Citizenship in Singapore. In *Journalism and Democracy in Asia*, edited by A. Romano and M. Bromley. London: Routledge.
Lester, Paul Martin, ed. 1996. *Images that Injure: Pictorial Stereotypes in the Media*. Westport: Praeger.
Leung, Helen. 2008. *Undercurrents: Queer Culture and Postcolonial Hong Kong*. Vancouver: UBC Press.
Leupp, Gary. 1995. *Male Colors: The Construction of Homosexuality in Tokugawa Japan*. Berkeley, CA: University of California Press.
LeVay, Simon. 1991. A Difference in Hypothalamic Structure between Heterosexual and Homosexual Men. *Science* 253(5023): 1034–1037.
Lewin, Ellen and William Leap, eds. 1996. Introduction. In *Out in the Field: Reflections of Lesbian and Gay Anthropologists*, edited by E. Lewin and W. Leap. Urbana, IL: University of Illinois Press.
Leyl, Sharanjit. 2009. Singapore Gays in First Public Rally. *BBC News*, 17 May.
Lim, Kean Fan. 2004. Where Love Dares (Not) Speak Its Name: The Expression of Homosexuality in Singapore. *Urban Studies* 41(9): 1759–1788.
Lim, Swee Say. 2000. Letter – All Can be Part of Singapore 21. *The Straits Times*, 6 June.
Lipset, Seymour M. 1960. Economic Development and Democracy. In *Political Man: The Social Bases of Politics*. Garden City, NY: Doubleday.
Loomba, Ania. 1998. *Colonialism/Postcolonialism*. London and New York: Routledge.
Lowe, Lisa and David Lloyd, eds. 1997. *The Politics of Culture in the Shadow of Capital*. Durham, NC: Duke University Press.
Lyons, Lenore. 2000. The Limits of Feminist Political Intervention in Singapore. *Journal of Contemporary Asia* 30(1): 67–83.
Macan-Markar, Marwaan. 2007. RIGHTS-SINGAPORE: Gay Events Banned for 'Political' Overtones. *Inter Press Service News Agency*, 8 August, accessed on 22 September 2011, www.ipsnews.net/2007/08/rights-singapore-gay-events-banned-for-political-overtones/.
Mah, Philip. 2000. Letter – No Proof Society can be Tolerant of Gays. *The Straits Times*, 16 June.
Manalansan, Martin F. 1997. In the Shadows of Stonewall: Examining Gay Transnational Politics and the Diasporic Dilemma. In *The Politics of Culture in the Shadow of Capital*, edited by L. Lowe and D. Lloyd. Durham, NC: Duke University Press.
Manalansan, Martin F. 2003. *Global Divas: Filipino Gay Men in the Diaspora*. Durham and London: Duke University Press.
Manderson, Lenore and Margaret Jolly, eds. 1997. *Sites of Desire, Economies of Pleasure: Sexualities in Asia and the Pacific*. University of Chicago Press, Chicago and London.
Markowe, Laura. 1996. *Redefining the Self: Coming out as Lesbian*. Cambridge, UK: Polity Press.
Marshall, Gordon. 1994. *The Concise Oxford Dictionary of Sociology*. Oxford and New York: Oxford University Press.
Marte, Rodelyn. 2006. *L Talk: Eileena Lee on the Challenges of GLBT Activism in Singapore*, accessed on 6 July 2016, www.isiswomen.org/index.php?option=com_content&view=article&id=268:l-talk-eileena-lee-on-the-challenges-of-glbt-activism-in-singapore&catid=66&Itemid=452.
Martin, Fran. 1996. Fran Martin Responds to Dennis Altman. *Australian Humanities Review*, accessed on 10 November 2010, www.australianhumanitiesreview.org/emuse/Globalqueering/martin.html.

Martin, Fran, Peter A. Jackson, Mark McLelland and Audrey Yue, eds. 2008. *AsiaPacifi Queer: Rethinking Genders and Sexualities*. Urbana and Chicago: University of Illinois Press.

Massad, Joseph. 2002. Re-orienting Desire: The Gay International and the Arab World. *Public Culture* 14(2): 361–385.

Mattelart, Armand. 1983. *Transnationals and the Third World: The Struggle for Culture*, translated by D. Buxton. South Hadley, MA: Bergin and Garvey Publishers.

Mauzy, Diane K and Robert S. Milne. 2002. *Singapore Politics Under the People's Action Party*. London, USA and Canada: Routledge.

McKellen, Ian. 2007. *Ian McKellen Supports Indignation*, video, YouTube uploaded by kwongheng, 27 July, accessed on 13 October 2010, www.youtube.com/watch?v=abcQulpjxDM.

McLelland, Mark. 2000. Is There a Japanese 'Gay Identity'? *Culture, Health & Sexuality* 2(4): 459–472.

MDA. 2003. Press Release: 'MediaWorksFined for Breach of Programme Code'.

MDA. 2011. *Mission & Core Values*. Singapore: Media Development Authority, accessed on 22 September 2011, www.mda.gov.sg/AboutMDA/MissionVisionCoreValues/Pages/MissionVisionCoreValues.aspx.

Miller, Neil. 2006. *Out of the Past: Gay and Lesbian History from 1869 to the Present*. New York: Alyson Books.

Morris, Rosalind C. 1994. Three Sexes and Four Sexualities: Redressing the Discourses on Gender and Sexuality in Thailand. *Positions* 2(1): 15–43.

Morton, Donald. 2001. Global (Sexual) Politics, Class Struggle, and the Queer Left. In *Postcolonial, Queer: Theoretical Intersections*, edited by J. Hawley. Albany, NY: State University of New York Press.

Mosse, George Lachmann. 1985. *Nationalism and Sexuality: Respectability and Abnormal Sexuality in Modern Europe*. New York: Howard Fertig.

Munt, Sally. 1998. Introduction. In *Butch/Femme: Inside Lesbian Gender*, edited by S.R. Munt and C. Smyth. London, Washington: Cassell.

Murray, Alison. 1999. Let Them Take Ecstasy: Class and Jakarta Lesbians. In *Female Desires: Same-sex Relations and Transgender Practices across Cultures*, edited by E. Blackwood and S.E. Wieringa. New York: Columbia University Press.

Mutalib, Hussin. 2009. Constructing a 'Constructive' Opposition. In *Impressions of the Goh Chok Tong Years in Singapore*, edited by B. Welsh, J. Chin, A. Mahizhnan and T.H. Tan. National University of Singapore: NUS Press.

Nestle, Joan. 1992. Butch-Fem Relationships: Sexual Courage in the 1950's. In *Lesbianism*, edited by W.R. Dynes and S. Donaldson. New York: Garland Publications.

Nettl, John Peter. 1967. *Political Mobilization: A Sociological Analysis of Methods and Concepts*. London: Faber.

New Paper. 2008. '*Hong Lim Green' to Turn Somewhat Pink*, 26 September. Singapore: Singapore Press Holdings.

New Paper. 2009. *Emotions Overflow as Women Exchange Bards*, 25 April. Singapore: Singapore Press Holdings.

New Paper. 2010. *Man Gropes Cop in Cemetery*, 11 June. Singapore: Singapore Press Holdings.

New York Times. 2009. Singapore's Gay Community Holds First-Ever Rally, 16 May.

Offord, Baden. 1999. The Burden of (Homo)sexual Identity in Singapore. *Social Semiotics* 9(3): 301–316.

Ortmann, Mathias. 2008. SIFF Review by Mathias Ortmann. *Women Who Love Women*. 7 April, accessed on 3 November 2011, http://womenwholovewomensingapore.blogspot.com/2008/05/siff-review-by-mathias-ortmann.html.
Oswin, Natalie. 2006. Decentering Queer Globalization: Diffusion and the Global Gay. *Environment and Planning D: Society and Space* 24: 777–790.
Oswin, Natalie. 2010. Sexual Tensions in Modernizing Singapore: The Postcolonial and the Intimate. *Environment and Planning D: Society and Space* 28: 128–141.
Oswin, Natalie. 2014. Queer Time in Global City Singapore: Neoliberal Futures and the 'Freedom to Love'. *Sexualities* 17(4): 412–443.
Parker, Andrew, Mary Russo, Doris Sommer and Patricia Yaeger. 1992. *Nationalisms and Sexualities*. New York: Routledge.
Patton, Cindy. 1993. Tremble, Hetero Swine! In *Fear of a Queer Planet: Queer Politics and Social Theory*, edited by M. Warner. Minneapolis, MN: University of Minnesota Press.
Peebles, Gavin and Peter Wilson. 1996. *The Singapore Economy*. Cheltenham; Brookfield, US: Edward Elgar.
Peizhi. 2007. Review by Peizhi. *Women Who Love Women*. 23 September, accessed on 3 November 2011, http://womenwholovewomensingapore.blogspot.com/2007/09/review-by-peizhi.html.
People Like Us. 2003. *History of the Gay Movement: Phoney Liberalisation and the Banned Forum*, accessed 6 July 2016, https://plusg.wordpress.com/2003/08/08/history-of-the-gay-movement-phoney-liberalisation-and-the-banned-forum/.
Pieterse, Jan Nederveen. 1994. Globalisation as Hybridisation. *International Sociology* 9(2): 161–184.
Pinkdotsg. 2009a. *Pink Dot Loves Singapore!* Video, YouTube, May 16, accessed on 16 January 2012, www.youtube.com/watch?v=Z9gDazG4cC0&feature=player_embedded.
Pinkdotsg. 2009b. *Pink Dot FAQ*, May 5, accessed on 16 January 2012, http://pinkdot.sg/about-pink-dot/faq-general/.
Pinkdotsg. 2010. *Pink Dot 2010 – From the Heart*. Video, YouTube, May 15 accessed on 12 December 2010, www.youtube.com/watch?v=IKLhpkIrmc4&feature=player_embedded#!.
Pinkdotsg. 2011a. *Channel News Asia's Coverage of Pink Dot 2011*. Video, YouTube, June 18, accessed on 17 January 2012, www.youtube.com/watch?v=fDFdjwkPEfA.
Pinkdotsg. 2011b. *PINKDOT 2011: SUPPORT THE FREEDOM TO LOVE – 18 JUNE 2011*. Video, YouTube, May 13, accessed on 18 January 2012, www.youtube.com/watch?v=FrIB5Ojbqns&feature=player_embedded.
Plummer, Ken, ed. 1992. *Modern Homosexualities: Fragments of Lesbian and Gay Experience*. London and New York: Routledge.
Plummer, Ken, ed. 2001. The Square of Intimate Citizenship: Some Preliminary Proposals. *Citizenship Studies* 5(3): 237–253.
Plummer, Ken, ed. 2010. Hybridic Sexualities and the Search for Global Intimate Citizenship. In *Chinese Male Homosexualities: Memba, Tongzhi and Golden Boy*, edited by T. Kong. Abingdon, Oxon and New York: Routledge.
Poore, Grace. 2011. *Amazing Responses by CEDAW to Address LGBT Discrimination in Singapore*, 27 July, accessed on 18 October 2011, http://iglhrc.wordpress.com/2011/07/27/amazing-responses-by-cedaw-to-address-lgbt-discrimination-in-singapore/.
Povinelli, Elizabeth A. and George Chauncey. 1999. Thinking Sexuality Transnationally. *GLQ: A Journal of Lesbian and Gay Studies* 5(4): 439–450.

Provencher, Denis. 2007. *Queer French: Globalization, Language, and Sexual Citizenship in France*. England and USA: Ashgate Publishing.

Puar, Jasbir. 2007. *Terrorist Assemblages: Homonationalism in Queer Times*. Durham, NC: Duke University Press.

Puri, Jyoti. 1999. *Woman, Body, Desire in Post-colonial India: Narratives of Gender and Sexuality*. New York: Routledge.

Puri, Jyoti. 2004. *Encountering Nationalism*. Malden, MA: Blackwell Publishing.

Puri, Jyoti. 2008. Sexualizing the State: Sodomy, Civil Liberties, and the Indian Penal Code. In *Contesting Nation: Gendered Violence in South Asia. Notes on the Post Colonial Present*, edited by A. Chatterji and L. Chowdhury. Zubaan Books.

Quah, Sharon. 2015. *Perspectives on Marital Dissolution: Divorce Biographies in Singapore*. Singapore: Springer.

Repeal377A. 2007. *Repeal 377A Singapore*. Video, 11 October, accessed on 13 October 2010, www.youtube.com/watch?v=mTGrzte9ZjQ.

Rhoads, Robert. 1994. *Coming out in College: The Struggle for a Queer Identity*. Westport, USA: Greenwood Publishing Group.

Rich, Adrienne. 1980. Compulsory Heterosexuality and Lesbian Existence. *Signs* 5(4), Women: Sex and Sexuality: 631–660.

Robertson, Roland. 1992. *Globalisation: Social Theory and Global Culture*. London: Sage.

Rodan, Gary. 1989. *The Political Economy of Singapore's Industrialization: National, State and International Capital*. New York: St. Martin's Press.

Rodan, Gary. 1996. State–Society Relations and Political Opposition in Singapore. In *Political Oppositions in Industralising Asia*, edited by G. Rodan. London: Routledge.

Rodan, Gary. 2009. Goh's Consensus Politics of Authoritarian Rule. In *Impressions of the Goh Chok Tong Years in Singapore*, edited by B Welsh, J. Chin, A. Mahizhnan and T.H. Tan. National University of Singapore: NUS Press.

Rofel, Lisa. 1999. Qualities of Desire: Imagining Gay Identities in China. *GLQ: A Journal of Lesbian and Gay Studies* 5(4): 451–474.

Rofel, Lisa. 2007. *Desiring China: Experiments in Neoliberalism, Sexuality, and Public Culture*. Durham and London: Duke University Press.

Sa'at, Alfian. 2007. *Happy Endings: Asian Boys Vol. 3*. Singapore: W!LDRICE.

Sadasivan, Balaji. 2005. Speech in Parliament. Singapore. 9 March.

Said, Edward. 1978. *Orientalism*. London: Routledge.

Said, Edward. 1979. Zionism from the Standpoint of its Victims. *Social Text* 1: 7–58.

Salaff, Janet. 1988. *State and Family in Singapore: Restructuring a Developing Society*. Ithaca: Cornell University Press.

Sanders, Douglas. 2007a. *377 and the Unnatural Afterlife of British Colonialism*. August. Chulalongkorn University, Mahidol University, accessed on 17 August 2011, http://signelwiki003.pbworks.com/w/file/fetch/36066434/douglas_sanders_377_unnatural_afterlife.pdf.

Sanders, Douglas. 2007b. Momentum for Change. *Fridae.com*. 4 August, accessed on 18 August 2011, www.fridae.asia/newsfeatures/printable.php?articleid=1918.

Sayoni. 2006. *Sayoni Queer Women Survey 2006 Report: For Queer Women Living in Singapore*. January, accessed on 18 March, www.sayoni.com/glbt-resources/downloads?task=viewcategory&catid=3.

Sayoni. 2007. *A Brief History of the Rainbow Flag*. 5 January, accessed on 18 March, www.sayoni.com/articles/activism/2031-a-brief-history-of-the-rainbow-flag.

Sayoni. 2008a. *TV Station Fined S$15,000 for Showing 'Normal' Gay Family (Singapore)*. 26 April, accessed on 16 March 2016, www.sayoni.com/lgbt-rights/2077-tv-station-fined-s15000-for-showing-normal-gay-family-singapore.

Sayoni. 2008b. *Sayoni Queer Women Survey 2008 Report: For Queer Women Living in Singapore*. November, accessed on 18 March 2011, www.sayoni.com/glbt-resources/downloads?task=viewcategory&catid=3.

Sayoni. 2010a. *Sayoni Queer Women Survey 2010 Report: For Queer Women Living in Singapore*. March, accessed on 18 March 2011, www.sayoni.com/glbt-resources/downloads?task=viewcategory&catid=3.

Sayoni. 2010b. *What If I'm Gay?* 20 August, accessed on 18 March 2011, www.sayoni.com/glbt-resources/downloads?task=view.download&catid=4&cid=4.

Sayoni. 2011. *Report on Discrimination against Women in Singapore based on Sexual Orientation and Gender Identity*. 20 June, accessed on 8 September 2011, http://iglhrc.files.wordpress.com/2011/07/sayoni-singapore-cedaw-shadow-report-2011.pdf.

Schein, Louisa. 1999. Of Cargo and Satellites: Imagined Cosmopolitanism. *Postcolonial Studies* 2: 345–375.

Schneider, Jeffrey. 1997. The Pleasure of the Uniform: Masculinity, Transvestism, and Militarism in Heinrich Mann's Der Untertan and Magnus Hirshfeld's Die Transvestiten. *Germanic Review* 72(3): 183–200.

Sedgwick, Eve. 1990. *Epistemology of the Closet*. Berkeley and Los Angeles, California: University of California Press.

Seidman, Steven. 2004. Are We All in the Closet? In *Matters of Culture: Cultural Sociology in Practice*, edited by R. Friedland and J. Mohr. Cambridge: UK: Cambridge University Press.

Shimizu, Akiko. 2008. Let Us Talk About 'Queer' (But In Which Language?). *Social Science Japan Journal* II(2): 357–360.

Shohat, Ella. 2001. Area Studies, Transnationalism, and the Feminist Production of Knowledge. *Signs: Journal of Women in Culture and Society* 26(4): 1269–1272.

Siew, Kum Hong. 2007. Speech on the Penal Code (Amendment) Bill: 22 October 2007, accessed on 3 September 2015, http://siewkumhong.blogspot.com.au/2007/10/speech-on-penal-code-amendment-bill-22.html.

SiGNeL. 2008. *Hong Lim Green*, 29 September, accessed on 12 January 2012, http://groups.yahoo.com/group/signel/message/20930.

Signorile, Michelangelo. 1993. *Queer in America*. New York: Random House.

Signorile, Michelangelo. 1995. *Outing Yourself*. New York: Simon and Schuster.

Silvio, Teri. 2008. Lesbianism and Taiwanese Localism in the Silent Thrush. In *AsiaPacifiQueer: Rethinking Genders and Sexualities*, edited by F. Martin, P.A. Jackson, M. McLelland and A. Yue. Urbana and Chicago: University of Illinois Press.

Singapore Parliament. 1991. White Paper on shared values. Singapore: [s.n.], pp. 1–2.

Sinnott, Megan. 2004. *Toms and Dees: Transgender Identity and Female Same-sex Relationships in Thailand*. Honolulu: University of Hawaii Press.

Sinnott, Megan. 2007. Gender Subjectivity: Dees and Toms in Thailand. In *Women's Sexualities and Masculinities in a Globalizing Asia*, edited by S.E. Wieringa, E. Blackwood and A. Bhaiya. New York: Palgrave Macmillan.

Sinnott, Megan. 2010. Borders, Diaspora, and Regional Connections: Trends in Asian 'Queer' Studies. *Journal of Asian Studies* 69(1): 17–31.

Smith-Rosenberg, Carroll. 1985. The Female World of Love and Ritual. In *Disorderly Conduct*. New York: Oxford University Press.

Spivak, Gayatri C. 1988. Can the Subaltern Speak? In *Marxism and the Interpretation of Culture*, edited by C. Nelson and L. Grossberg. Basingstoke, UK: Macmillan Education.

Spurlin, William J. 2001. Broadening Postcolonial Studies/Decolonizing Queer Studies: Emerging 'Queer' Identities and Cultures in Southern Africa. In *Postcolonial, Queer: Theoretical Intersections*, edited by J. Hawley. Albany, NY: State University of New York Press.

Stein, Arlene. 1997. *Sex and Sensibility: Stories of a Lesbian Generation*. Berkeley, CA: University of California Press.

Stoler, Laura A. 1995. Sexual Affronts and Racial Frontiers: European Identities and the Cultural Politics of Exclusion in Colonial Southeast Asia. In *Tensions of Empire: Colonial Cultures in a Bourgeois World*, edited by F. Cooper and A. Stoler. Berkeley, Los Angeles, California: University of California Press.

Straits Times. 2007a. *Man Gets Jail, Cane for Molesting 2 Boys in his Flat*, 26 April. Singapore: Singapore Press Holdings.

Straits Times. 2007b. *377A Debate and the Rewriting of Pluralism*, 27 October. Singapore: Singapore Press Holdings.

Straits Times. 2008a. *Love Ladies*, April 6. Singapore: Singapore Press Holdings.

Straits Times. 2008b. *Indian Gays Hold Rare March for Their Rights*, 25 April. Singapore: Singapore Press Holdings.

Straits Times. 2008c. *Surge in HIV Cases among Gay Men*, 7 December. Singapore: Singapore Press Holdings.

Straits Times. 2008d. *First Gay Protest at Speakers' Corner?* 25 November. Singapore: Singapore Press Holdings.

Straits Times. 2009a. *Europe Opens up to Gay Politicians*, 14 October. Singapore: Singapore Press Holdings.

Straits Times. 2009b. *Delhi Ruling a Victory for Gays*, 5 July. Singapore: Singapore Press Holdings.

Straits Times. 2009c. *Delhi Court Legalizes Homosexual Acts*, 3 July. Singapore: Singapore Press Holdings.

Straits Times. 2009d. *Group's Agenda 'Took a Gay Turn'*, 24 April. Singapore: Singapore Press Holdings.

Straits Times. 2009e. *Nothing 'Sneaky' about Elections*, 26 April. Singapore: Singapore Press Holdings.

Straits Times. 2009f. *Old Guard Members Counter Allegations of a Pro-gay Stance*, 25 April. Singapore: Singapore Press Holdings.

Straits Times. 2009g. *Too Diversified or Too Focused? Which is it?* 25 April. Singapore: Singapore Press Holdings.

Straits Times. 2009h. *Should Faith-driven Groups Take over Secular Organizations?* 2 May. Singapore: Singapore Press Holdings.

Straits Times. 2010a. *Man Fined $3K for Oral Sex*, 10 November. Singapore: Singapore Press Holdings.

Straits Times. 2010b. *Drugs Turn Gay Sex Romp into Fatal Affair*, 22 June. Singapore: Singapore Press Holdings.

Straits Times. 2010c. *Ministry Pick Groups to Teach Sexuality Education*, 29 April. Singapore: Singapore Press Holdings.

Straits Times. 2011a. *The Lesbian-themed The Kids Are All Right*, 16 February. Singapore: Singapore Press Holdings.

Straits Times. 2011b. *Same Theme, Different Takes*, 23 February. Singapore: Singapore Press Holdings.

Straits Times. 2011c. *Woman Committed Obscene Acts with Girl*, 17 March. Singapore: Singapore Press Holdings.
Straits Times. 2011d. *Pink Dot Event Draws 10,000 This Year*, 19 June. Singapore: Singapore Press Holdings.
Straits Times. 2014. *Relationship Workshop: Controversial Course to End by December*, 9 October. Singapore: Singapore Press Holdings.
Taipei Times. 2004. Socially-conservative Singapore Bans Popular Gay-oriented Taiwanese Film, Reuters News, 23 July, accessed on 25 June 2016, www.taipeitimes.com/News/taiwan/archives/2004/07/23/2003180053.
Tamale, Sylvia, ed. 2011. *African Sexualities: A Reader*. Cape Town, Dakar, Nairobi and Oxford: Pambazuka Press.
Tan, Alvin. 2006. Nation Retrospective 2001–2003. *Fridae.com*. 19 October, accessed on 11 August 2010, www.fridae.com/newsfeatures/2006/10/19/1724.nation-retrospective-2001-2003?n=sec.
Tan, Beng Hui. 1999. Women's Sexuality and the Discourse on Asian Values: Cross-Dressing in Malaysia. In *Female Desires: Same-sex Relations and Transgender Practices across Cultures*, edited by E. Blackwood and S.E. Wieringa. New York: Columbia University Press.
Tan, Chong Kee. 2001. Transcending Sexual Nationalism and Colonialism. In *Postcolonial, Queer: Theoretical Intersections*, edited by J. Hawley. Albany, NY: State University of New York Press.
Tan, Joel. 2007. When Saying 'Traditional, Conservative Society' Doesn't Cut it Anymore. *The Online Citizen*. 19 September, accessed on 12 October 2010, www.theonlinecitizen.com/2007/09/when-saying-traditional-conservative-society-doesnt-cut-it-anymore/.
Tan, Kenneth P., ed. 2007a. *Renaissance Singapore? Economy Culture and Politics*. Singapore: NUS Press.
Tan, Kenneth P., ed. 2007b. Singapore's National Day Rally Speech: A Site of Ideological Negotiation. *Journal of Contemporary Asia* 37(3): 292–308.
Tan, Kenneth P., ed. 2009. Who's Afraid of Catherine Lim? The State in Patriarchal Singapore. *Asian Studies Review* 33: 43–62.
Tan, Kenneth P. and Gary Jack Jin Lee. 2007. Imagining the Gay Community in Singapore. *Critical Asian Studies* 39(2): 179–204.
Tan, Mervyn. 2008. Review by Mervyn Tan. *Women Who Love Women*. 7 April, accessed on 3 November 2011, http://womenwholovewomensingapore.blogspot.com/2008/04/review-by-mervyn-tan.html.
Tang, Shawna. 2011. Re-examining 'Transnationality' through Singapore Lesbian Identities. *The Australian Sociological Association Conference*, Newcastle, NSW, Australia.
Tang, Shawna. 2012. Transnational Lesbian Identities: Lessons from Singapore? In *Queer Singapore: Illiberal Citizenship and Mediated Cultures*, edited by A. Yue and J. Zubillaga-Pow. Hong Kong: Hong Kong University Press.
Time magazine. 2003. *The Lion in Winter*. 30 June.
The Economist. 1996. *Gay Marriage. Let Them Wed*. January.
TheOnlineCitizen.com. 2009. MOE Statement on Sexuality Education Programme (Updated: AWARE's response). 6 May, accessed on 6 July 2016, www.theonlinecitizen.com/2009/05/moe-statement-on-sexuality-education-programme/.
The Star Online. 2008. *Giving People Space to Let off Steam*, 23 August, accessed on 30 June 2016, www.thestar.com.my/opinion/letters/2008/08/23/giving-people-space-to-let-off-steam/.

The Times. 2001. Glad to Vote Gay – Cover story. 19 June.
TODAY. 2007. *Silly Stuff that Hurts the Image,* 11 October. Singapore: MediaCorp.
TODAY. 2009. *In Singapore: Surveying the Responses to the AWARE Daga,* 23 April. Singapore: MediaCorp.
TODAY. 2011. *To Love and be Loved Alan Seah, Pink Dot,* 9 August. Singapore: MediaCorp.
Tong, Carmen. 2008. Being a Young Tomboy in Hong Kong: The Life and Identity Construction of Lesbian Schoolgirls. In *AsiaPacifiQueer: Rethinking Genders and Sexualities,* edited by F. Martin, P.A. Jackson, M. McLelland and A. Yue. Urbana and Chicago: University of Illinois Press.
Turnbull, Constance M., 1989. *A History of Singapore 1819–1988.* Singapore: Oxford University Press.
Uberoi, Patricia. ed. 1996. *Social Reform, Sexuality and the State.* New Delhi: Sage Publications.
Weeks, Jeffrey. 1977. *Coming Out: Homosexual Politics in Britain from the Nineteenth Century to the Present.* London: Quartet.
Weeks, Jeffrey. 2007. *The World We Have Won: The Remaking of Erotic and Intimate Life.* London and New York: Routledge.
Welker, James and Lucetta Kam, eds. 2006. Introduction: Of Queer Import(s): Sexualities, Genders and Rights in Asia. In *Intersections: Gender, History and Culture in the Asian Context* 14.
Welsh, Bridget, James Chin, Arun Mahizhnan and Tan Tarn How, eds. 2009. *Impressions of the Goh Chok Tong Years in Singapore.* National University of Singapore: NUS Press.
Wei, Sze. 2008. Review by Sze Wei. *Women Who Love Women.* 18 January, accessed on 3 November 2011, http://womenwholovewomensingapore.blogspot.com/2008/01/review-by-sze-wei.html.
Werbner, Pnina. 1999. Global Pathways: Working Class Cosmopolitans and the Creation of Transnational Ethnic Worlds. *Social Anthropology* 7(1): 17–35.
West, Cornel. 1989. *The American Evasion of Philosophy: A Genealogy of Pragmatism.* Madison, Wisconsin: University of Wisconsin Press.
Weston, Kath. 1993. Lesbian/Gay Studies in the House of Anthropology. *Annual Review of Anthropology* 22: 344.
Whisman, Vera. 1996. *Queer by Choice: Lesbians, Gay Men, and the Politics of Identity.* New York: Routledge.
Wieringa, Saskia E. 2007. Silence, Sin, and the System: Women's Same-Sex Practices in Japan. In *Women's Sexualities and Masculinities in a Globalizing Asia,* edited by S.E. Wieringa, E. Blackwood and A. Bhaiya. New York: Palgrave Macmillan.
Wieringa, Saskia E., Evelyn Blackwood and Abha Bhaiya, eds. 2007. *Women's Sexualities and Masculinities in a Globalizing Asia.* New York: Palgrave Macmillan.
Wikipedia contributors. 2010. Singapore Gay Personalities. *Wikipedia, The Free Encyclopedia,* accessed on 12 August 2010, www.sgwiki.com/wiki/Singapore_gay_personalities.
Wikipedia contributors. 2011. Pink Dot SG. *Wikipedia, The Free Encyclopedia,* accessed on 12 January 2012, http://en.wikipedia.org/wiki/Pink_Dot_SG.
Williams, Walter. 1996. Being Gay and Doing Fieldwork. In *Out in the Field: Reflections of Lesbian and Gay Anthropologists,* edited by E. Lewin and W. Leap. Urbana, IL: University of Illinois Press.
Wilson, Ara. 2006. Queering Asia. *Intersections: Gender, History and Culture in the Asian Context,* Issue 14. November, accessed on 1 June 2010, http://intersections.anu.edu.au/issue14/wilson.html.

Women Who Love Women (WWLW). 2006. *Women Who Love Women: Conversations in Singapore*, video, accessed on 6 July 2016, http://v.youku.com/v_show/id_XMzk3MjIxOTU2.html.
Women Who Love Women (WWLW). 2007. *About the Documentary*. July, accessed on 2 November 2011. http://womenwholovewomensingapore.blogspot.com/.
Wong, Day. 2007. Rethinking the Coming Home Alternative: Hybridization and Coming out Politics in Hong Kong's Anti-homophobia Parades. *Inter-Asia Cultural Studies* 8(4): 600–616.
Worthington, Ross. 2003. *Governance in Singapore*. London and New York: Routledge.
Yahoo! 2010. *Androgynous Lesbians ... What's the Deal?*, accessed on 20 May 2012, http://answers.yahoo.com/question/index?qid=20090701184251AAbl4e7.
Yao, Souchou. 2007. *Singapore: The State and the Culture of Excess*. New York: Routledge.
Yau, Ching, ed. 2010. *As Normal As Possible: Negotiating Sexuality and Gender in Mainland China and Hong Kong*. Hong Kong: Hong Kong University Press.
Yawning Bread. 2000. Radio Journalists Ask the Gay Question. December, accessed on 10 October 2015, www.yawningbread.org/arch_2000/yax-216.htm.
Yawning Bread. 2003. Gay Civil Servants, and What Next? December, accessed on 10 October 2015, www.yawningbread.org/arch_2003/yax-319.htm.
Yawning Bread. 2005. *Towards an Open and Inclusive Society*. February, accessed on 29 June 2016, www.yawningbread.org/apdx_2005/imp-183.htm.
Yawning Bread. 2006. *Cable TV Fined over Lesbian Sex*. October, accessed on 14 March 2016, www.yawningbread.org/arch_2006/yax-669.htm.
Yawning Bread. 2007a. *Why Section 377A is Redundant*. May, accessed on 18 August 2011, www.yawningbread.org/arch_2007/yax-749.htm.
Yawning Bread. 2007b. *'Eventually,' said Lee Kuan Yew*. April 24, accessed on 19 August 2011, www.yawningbread.org/apdx_2007/imp-347.htm.
Yawning Bread. 2011a. *In Singapore, Some Thoughts are not All Right*. 17 February, accessed on 12 September 2011, http://yawningbread.wordpress.com/2011/02/17/in-singapore-some-thoughts-are-not-all-right/.
Yawning Bread. 2011b. *Pink Accused of Failing the Smell Test*. June 22, accessed on 11 April 2012, https://yawningbread.wordpress.com/2011/06/22/pink-accused-of-failing-the-smell-test/.
Yeo, George. 1991. *Civic Society – Between the Family and the State*, Inaugural National University of Singapore Society Lecture, World Trade Centre Auditorium, Singapore, 20 June.
Yue, Audrey. 2007. Creative Queer Singapore: The Illiberal Pragmatics of Cultural Production. *Gay & Lesbian Issues and Psychology Review* 3(3): 149–160.
Yue, Audrey. 2011. Doing Cultural Citizenship in the Global Media Hub: Illiberal Pragmatics and Lesbian Consumption Practices in Singapore. In *Circuits of Visibility: Gender and Transnational Media Cultures*, edited by R. Hegde. New York: New York University Press.
Yue, Audrey and J. Zubillaga-Pow, eds. 2012. *Queer Singapore: Illiberal Citizenship and Mediated Cultures*. Hong Kong: Hong Kong University Press.
Zizek, Slavoj. 1989. *The Sublime Object of Ideology*. London and New York: Verso.

Index

Altman, D. 4–6, 21–34, 43, 162, 179–80
'andro' 131, 152–5
androgynous 22, 46, 153–5
ASEAN SOGIE (Sexual Orientation, Gender Identity and Expression) Caucus 114–15
AsiaPacifiQueer (APQ) 7–8, 11
AWARE 19, 21n3, 78, 85–8, 90, 134, 142, 166–7
anti-nationalist 19, 165–6
antinomy 27
area studies 8–9, 32
artefact 3, 6, 12, 63, 108, 116
asymmetric 9, 15–16, 21–4, 40, 45, 47, 160, 169
asymmetry 10, 29, 34, 44, 147
authenticity 1, 12, 17, 22, 28, 30, 33–4, 36, 40, 118, 163

Bhabha, H. 39, 41–2, 44–6, 164–5
binary 9–10, 33–4, 36–7, 41–2, 45, 50, 55, 60–1, 66, 75, 78, 90, 98, 122, 135, 146, 160, 164, 166, 172
binaries 9, 16–18, 21–3, 30–1, 34–5, 38, 40, 42–3, 45, 47, 51, 78, 97, 118, 121, 163, 169
binary opposition 60, 164
Blackwood, E. 5, 8, 10–12, 14, 18, 48, 52–3, 126, 128, 131, 137, 139, 149–50, 171, 173
Boellstorff, T. 5, 7, 11, 16, 18, 23, 30–1, 36, 41–4, 48–9, 52–3, 149, 171, 173
butch 11–12, 124–6, 131, 135–47
butch-femme 2, 140, 145–7

cartographic 17–18, 22–3, 31–5, 37–8, 40, 42–3, 47, 50, 163
Chao, A. 27, 137, 139
city 59, 85, 106, 136, 141, 158; *see also* city-state and global city

city-state 12–13, 93–5, 117, 147, 162
CMEL (Chinese, middle-class, English-speaking, liberal) 109–11, 119, 168
colonise 25, 37, 39–40, 45–6, 49, 66, 108, 163–4, 169
continuum 28–31, 34–5
cosmopolitan 1, 13–15, 59, 104, 126, 162, 171; Queer cosmopolitanism 13; working-class cosmopolitans 13
counter 9, 16–17, 33, 35–7, 46, 79, 83, 103, 120
counter-weight 7
counterproductive 90
critical regionalities 7–8
critical feminist 17, 19, 89, 171; see also feminist sexuality

decolonise 37; *see also* provincialise
developmentalist 4, 17–18, 29–31, 33–6, 38, 40, 42–3, 50, 121, 141, 146, 163
dichotomous thinking 42, 169; *see also* binary
diversity 27–8, 32, 58, 74–5, 93, 96, 105, 110–12, 171

edifice 16, 61, 122
ethnocartographic 32
elites 14, 19, 49, 51–7, 62, 71, 80, 84, 88, 91, 97, 101, 105, 129, 166
essentialist 164, 169
Eurocentric 7, 10, 33, 36, 39, 46, 51, 163, 169, 171, 172
evolution 3, 14, 28–30, 37, 111, 140

family 1, 15, 20, 61, 64–6, 69–70, 83, 104, 106–7, 114–15, 119–21, 125, 128, 132, 134, 138–9, 147–9, 152–60, 166–7

Facebook 20, 109–11, 159
feminist 18, 137, 140–2, 146, 177

Feminist Mentor 86
feminist sexuality 5, 16–19, 23, 47, 54–5, 77–8, 89, 166, 169, 171; *see also* critical feminist
femme 11, 126, 131, 135, 138–47
foundational 12, 21, 24, 34, 66, 129, 140, 148, 163
fundamental 9, 14, 16–17, 30, 32–3, 43, 128, 147, 163, 169

gender sameness 126: androgynous sameness 145
gendered 12, 21, 30, 63, 135, 137–9, 141, 143, 145, 150, 152–3, 155–7, 171n5, 181
genealogy 22–3, 26, 52
global city 59, 62, 82, 84; *see also* city and city-state
global gayness 16, 24–5, 32, 45, 99, 105, 111, 168
global/local 16–17, 43: local/global 34, 36, 47, 163
global gay domain 9–10, 14–16, 22–8, 30, 32–5, 38, 40, 45, 50, 163, 165, 176
global sexual melange 31, 33

Hall, S. 39–42, 67, 171, 178
heteronormative 20, 53, 66–7, 76, 105, 107, 141, 147, 149, 158–60
historical 6, 10, 12, 13, 15, 19, 23, 26, 27, 29, 36, 38–42, 46–7, 50n1, 51, 53, 56–60, 63, 75, 142, 164, 171, 175–6
homonationalism 118
human rights 63–4, 82–4, 95, 99, 114–15, 117–18, 172
hybridisation 17–18, 23, 42–7, 50, 92, 105, 163, 168

ideals 81, 137, 140
ideal-type 29–31
idealise 2, 22, 52, 55, 108, 152
imperialism 14, 24, 37, 68, 173–4
indigenise 11, 37
indigenous 12–14, 17, 24, 32–3, 36–8, 42, 57, 113, 169
International Gay and Lesbian Human Rights Convention (IGLHRC) 114
intersectional 112, 115, 118

lesbian feminist 2, 117–18, 137, 144, 165; *see also* queer feminist 23, 125, 143–6
legitimate 21, 29, 42, 96, 129, 157, 165, 168–9

linear 24–5, 29, 34, 36, 42, 46–7, 50, 100, 116, 121, 149

Jackson, P. 8, 12, 14, 36–7, 43, 131

Manalansan, M. 4–6
Martin, F. 7–8, 11, 25, 27, 43
material 8, 12, 19, 23, 40–1, 48–52, 58–60, 62, 77, 91–2, 147–8, 163–4, 170, 174–6
masculinity 2, 26, 28, 125, 133, 137, 140, 143, 145–6
McLelland, M. 8, 24
metropolitan 13, 39, 158, 169
mimic 16–17, 34, 38, 173
mimicry 2, 38, 41, 46, 104–6, 140, 146–7, 164
modernity 5–6, 9–10, 12–13, 15, 26, 29, 30, 34, 39, 53, 56, 58, 61, 66, 78, 82, 84, 118, 121, 137, 147, 171
modern/tradition 43: tradition/modern 1, 29, 31, 34, 36, 43, 45, 47, 121–2
monolithic 19, 54, 56, 77, 85, 89–90, 166
mutual 133, 143
mutually-constituting 21, 45, 108, 125, 128, 164, 169

nationalism 5, 19, 39–40, 51–6, 62, 76–7, 83–4, 88, 91–2, 99, 168
non-oppositional 21, 169
non-static 61, 108

'originary' model 2
Oogachaga 114, 134
Orientalism 37
Orientalist 7, 13, 98; *see also* self-Orientalising
origin 10, 16, 21, 25, 30, 33, 36–7, 39, 42, 129, 130, 145, 172, 176
original 10, 17, 26, 29, 35, 44–5, 51, 86, 106–7, 163, 165, 168–9

paradigm 10, 29–30, 34, 82, 108, 112, 165
paradigmatic 5, 21n2, 31, 35
pathway 2, 6, 18, 29–30, 33–4, 37, 46, 121, 157
People Like Us (PLU) 94–5, 101–2, 112, 122n5
Pelangi Pride Centre 113
Pink Dot 20, 102–14, 123n6, 123n9, 123n10, 123n11, 159, 164, 166–7
Plummer, K. 4–6, 28, 31–4, 43
pluralism 81, 93

postcolonialism 17, 39, 41–2, 44, 51
postmodern 4, 31–2
provincialise 10, 46
puristic gayness 168

queer Asia 7–10, 16–18, 38, 42–4, 149
queer feminist 23, 125, 143–6; *see also* lesbian feminist

RedQuEEn 113
relationality 9, 21, 108, 129, 169

Sa'at, A. 72–4, 109–11
SAMBAL 113
sameness and difference 16, 26–7, 32, 40–1, 44–5, 48
Sayoni 64, 69, 75n5, 76, 114–17, 130–1
Section 377A 19, 53, 62–5, 71, 74, 78–85, 87, 90, 99, 109–10, 166–7
self-Orientalising 9, 61, 121; *see also* Orientalist
sexual citizenship 24, 66, 101, 115–16, 179
sexual nationalism 97
sexual politics 5, 25, 27, 53, 80, 88, 97, 106, 112, 129
sexual selfhood 12, 15, 116, 122, 129, 148–9, 157, 160, 165, 167–8, 170, 177

Shohat, Ella 9
Sinnott, M. 7, 10–11, 14, 18, 43, 131, 137, 139, 173
spatial 18, 33–4, 41, 43, 163, 169, 171
static 17, 21, 33–8, 42–3, 46, 163, 169
Stonewall 3–4, 25, 168, 172

teleological 22, 28–31, 35, 37, 42, 46–7, 50, 163, 168
teleology 35, 45, 165, 168
temporal 12, 18, 23, 31, 33, 34, 39, 41, 43, 163, 169, 171
'transnational turn' 47
transnational sexualities 17–18, 21, 23, 42–4, 47–50, 120, 122
transgressive 12, 33, 108, 173

Women who love women 1–3, 13–14, 21, 112, 126, 131, 135, 137, 162, 172
'world city' 15

uni-directional 20, 26, 33
unilinear 25, 34, 42, 47, 55, 77
universalisation 3, 9, 12

Yue, A. 8, 92, 95, 98, 100, 136, 141, 160, 161n7